Meditation

AN OUTLINE FOR PRACTICAL STUDY

BY

MOUNI SADHU

D1176532

1974 EDITION

Published by

WILSHIRE BOOK COMPANY
12015 Sherman Road
No. Hollywood, California 91605
Telephone: (213) 875-1711

I believe, that even in the
present period of a general loss of
moral and spiritual values, there are
still living, souls intelligent and
inspired enough not to be drowned in
the prevailing trend of frustration.
It is for them that I write.

CONTENTS

CONTENTS

PART III

REGULAR MEDITATION

PART IV

ADVANCED MEDITATION

PART V

INTRODUCTION TO CONTEMPLATION

FOREWORD

During the twentieth century the term 'meditation' has become a very popular one among philosophically and occult minded intellectuals. The reason is clearly the now overwhelming interest in Eastern mysticism and occultism beginning at the turn of the century. At first, mysticism and occultism attracted only small numbers of intellectuals, but after World Wars I and II, the movement became popularized and reached other sections of Western society, at the same time as an unprecedented increase in all kinds of occult associations and groups, which were not calculated for the 'chosen', but for all and sundry.

Before long, every member of every such organization began to consider himself qualified to understand and judge all occult matters, which he could find in the ever-growing number of books, dealing with the so-called 'popularization of occultism'.

The results of this can be seen around us today, and there is no need to point out details to a discerning reader. Merely observe, and you will soon find the truth for yourself.

In this book I will deal with the term *meditation*, as it is so misused and misunderstood, when indeed it should take its honoured place among the loftiest and most inspired efforts of man—to find the real Truth of himself and to take his due place in the *conscious* life, free from the limitations of gross matter as is his temporary and mortal sheath, in which no Reality or Truth can ever be found.

But meditation is a science, an art, requiring solid preparation and study as does every branch of human knowledge, with the difference that the average intellectual may cope well with his official 'degrees', but the same cannot be said about acquiring the ability to meditate. Where lies the cause of this? Official science operates with the past experiences of men, and so a professor teaches his students what he himself has been able to learn and discover in his own particular field of study. The students then try to assimilate, memorize, and use such achieved knowledge, according to their needs, sometimes developing it further if they feel an attraction to it. Undoubtedly, their studies develop their brains and fill them with a lot of memorized facts, formulas, theories, laws, and so on.

11

But we should not lose sight of the fact, that all the examinations that we may be subjected to for our degrees are rather standard requirements, imposed and fixed by those who know more in the particular field. Are they interested in the real ABILITIES of the students, beyond their satisfactory answers and solutions of test problems?

Memory, concentration, the ability of orientation, and so on, are supposed to grow automatically during the years of study, and yet they are still measured by the degree of domination of a particular branch of human knowledge. They are not the main aim, or consideration. That is why we have good, and not so good scientists, doctors, engineers, and so on. All are products of the same universities, all have received their degrees, but there are enormous differences between them. This is the proof that there is something in man, beyond the capacity of merely accepting the average load of knowledge, offered to him during his years of learning.

But things are quite different as regards the science of meditation. It is the ABILITY to rule one's mind under all circumstances that alone counts, and not just the accumulation of memorized and used subjects, which belong to the lower manifestation of our mind's powers. These never rise to the higher degree of development of the human consciousness, that functions above and beyond that mind, although embracing its realm, in the same way as a man who, while standing on a hill and seeing the vast horizon, can, nevertheless, also see objects close to himself.

This relationship should be well understood during your further study of the subject, so that you will be able to discriminate between the knowledge accommodated in your brain, and the ABILITY to use that mind-brain in any direction you need, and not just in that which you were taught in school, and so on.

What does MEDITATION actually mean? It is the dynamic retention of our awareness on a chosen theme or subject. Of course, this is only a very elementary definition, but at this stage we will not enlarge on it, for we must realize what condition is necessary for the mental practice we call meditation. It is the ABILITY TO UNSWERVINGLY MAINTAIN YOUR AWARENESS ON A CHOSEN THEME FOR AS LONG AS YOU DECIDE TO CONTINUE WITH THE SAME. I believe that I do not need to explain further, as everyone will find the true name of this ability: it is the power of CONCENTRATION. Without it, the attempted meditation will be nothing more than a rudderless floating on one's own waves of thoughts, which come from an unknown source and defy efforts to put them in order according to a preconceived plan.

How often have I heard from incompetent and self-deluded persons, how they 'meditate', comfortably seated in a soft chair and often blowing smoke rings from their cigarettes, while passively thinking about whatever subject they like. As is to be expected, the results are only frustration, none of the anticipated enlightenment, and finally, scepticism regarding everything connected with the higher development of man.

That is why I am compelled to make the following statement: Before you embark on a practical study of this book, you must invariably become acquainted with:

(a) The theory of concentration and
(b) Through exercises, develop in yourself a certain degree of domination of your thinking principle. Such work will correspond to at least two well-performed series of exercises.

All of this belongs to my basic work *Concentration*, first published in 1959. Also, the companion volume—*Samadhi*, especially Part III, can be recommended for a special extension of knowledge on themes for *meditation*.

From this point of view, the present work is like a continuation of the two just mentioned, and I am writing it on *the assumption, that its two forerunners are well known to you*. It would be impossible to repeat in *Meditation* the material previously expounded in the other books.

Naturally, there have been several books published on the subject of meditation, and a few of them may fairly well elucidate certain aspects of this important art. My aim is to close all the existing gaps and so give the student a manual, from which he may be able to obtain reasonable theoretical knowledge of the subject, plus a systematic guide for the development of practical abilities in himself.

You must clearly realize, that the popular (but how fallacious!) idea, propagated by certain pseudo-occult and pseudo-philosophic organizations: *'Anyone can meditate!'* is sheer nonsense.

13

MEDITATION

Can you swim the English Channel without the ability to swim? Can you use a car, even after reading dozens of manuals about motor construction and driving, without spending several hours on practical lessons with an experienced tutor?

At the present time the terms 'occultism', 'occult psychology', 'initiations', and so on, are fairly well known to most intellectuals. But there is a lot of chaff among what is supposed to be occult wheat. I wrote at length about this sad fact in Chapter XLIV of my *Ways to Self-Realization*. But for firm discrimination, even a brief rule will suffice: seek for COMMON SENSE throughout a book, and if you cannot find it reject the work, as then it is of no value to you or anyone else.

There exists an unfortunate disproportion between materialistic knowledge and that of *practical psychology*, which latter is simply another name for true occultism.

Every savant would agree that there are absolute laws ruling the physical manifestations of life, as we know from our official science, and nobody would dare to question them without being considered (quite justly, of course) to be an *ignoramus*. But only a few guess, and still fewer *positively know*, that the invisible manifestations of life, like, say, the *processes of feeling and thinking* are also subject to exactly similar, definite laws, which control and rule these hidden processes, as well as many others, lying beyond the powers of the concrete mind.

Those who, during the course of their lives have learned to cognize these laws and make practical use of them—as a chemist or physicist does within his own profession—will know the meaning of the simile I have just given. Faced with the problem of the science of *meditation*, I put it to myself to explain the related laws and indicate the necessary techniques for their practice.

Consequently, this work will not be an easy and entertaining discourse, and that has not been my aim. Any earnest student will discover it for himself. My hope here is founded on the fact of having received innumerable earnest inquiries from my readers from almost every corner of the English-speaking world, besides from those who use the translations of my books. These prove that, fortunately, there are still many people who take their inner life seriously and desire to know and control it positively. Therefore, I am dedicating the present study to them.

14

Part I deals with the elementary theory of meditation, with which every aspirant must be familiar. The techniques and convenient texts of the first, simplest forms of meditation are included in Part II. As a further development, the full use of mental power is covered by Parts III and IV. Finally, the highest form of directed awareness, beyond the verbal forms of the previous chapters, is presented in Part V as *contemplation*, in which the consciousness operates beyond the realm of the thinking mind, and every movement in it ceases, being swallowed up by the contemplated idea. In other words, the aim of true meditation is achieved in this its final stage:

THE SUBJECT AND THE OBJECT BECOME—ONE.

Conclusions are arrived at in the Epilogue, linking the achieved *contemplation* with the so-called 'MUTE PRAYER' as practised by some eminent saints, and introducing the student into the 'mysterious world' of the Spirit and the ultimate Reality dwelling in it.

I have intentionally limited the Bibliography to only a few chosen books which contain material in common with the present work. This has been done in order not to dissipate the student's attention by directing it to works and systems which would be of little help and devoid of a practical character, or useless in another way.

The subject is hard enough as it is, and human time and forces are limited. Hence, the economizing of them is at once, assistance and the emphasizing of the cardinal factor of *concentration* on the main, chosen task.

Before starting this book, you are entitled to ask me an important question and obtain an answer to it.

'UNDER WHAT CONDITIONS CAN I HAVE ALL REASONABLE HOPE OF GETTING FULL PROFIT FROM THIS BOOK, AND CAN YOU GUARANTEE ME SUCCESS?'

The chief condition will be for you to treat this course in *just the same way as you did the compulsory studies* you have passed through for your bread-winning certificates, and so on. This means that you have to perform all that is prescribed without omitting, or abandoning anything because of the difficulties encountered. After all, if you abandoned certain parts of, say, *algebra*, simply *because they were tedious for you*, you know that you would not be able to sit for the examinations ahead.

Under such circumstances, that is, *if you continue to the end of the course*, your guarantee will be the writer's own achievement in this field, as well as many of those, who worked similarly and got their reward, which they would not exchange for anything in the world.

From the foregoing, you will see that this book is not for 'halfwits', but for intelligent men and women of common sense. An *'initiate'*, or a man who is able to become an initiate STUDIES AND REALIZES, while a 'layman', unable to do so, only READS AND TALKS. In this lies the whole of the difference between men. Hence, a scientist, who is well versed in his own particular branch of knowledge, is initiated into it whereas an ignorant person merely guesses. Such is our point of view.

PART I
THEORETICAL PRELIMINARIES

CHAPTER I

Definition of Meditation

THE highest instrument for the present average human being is his mind, with its physical organ—the brain. This fact is easy to prove. When Descartes propounded his once famous 'Cogito ergo sum' ('I think therefore I am'), he expressed this idea quite categorically. And for the majority of present-day humanity it seems to be right.

It is quite common to hear people say: 'I have a head full of thoughts', for they really feel as if their consciousness is located in their brains. This conviction is double-sided since: (A) *it is true in one sense* and (B) *wrong in another*. So, let us look closer at this.

When our thinking processes are closely connected with the physical world and its affairs, we are using the lowest part of our mind, and then operate in the well-known realm of almost automatic reactions to the happenings around us. For example, someone tells us that we can sell some of our possessions profitably, or acquire valuable objects cheaply. So, without entering into any further deliberations, our mind-brain will produce what we believe to be the 'natural' decision, that is, to explore the possibility and to act accordingly. Someone asks us to pay a debt, which we believe we have already paid, and so we start to seek for proof such as receipts, witnesses, and so on.

All these and myriads of similar activities of our lower mind, which we encounter daily in our lives, are derived from the purely technical skill which our mind-brain receives during the years of its maturing.

The wider our experience, the more our lower mind is ready and quick to react in this traditional way. And in so doing, we may really feel that it is 'our head' (actually, its 'contents'), which is working out the reactions and solutions to similar problems. If you are interested in knowing, it is just this level of our brain-consciousness, which is mainly involved in our average dreams, often so senseless and evidently just a kind of automatic repetition—with many imperfections—of our daily activities, or memories. If we think intently about a certain problem during the day-time, and especially continue this process just before falling asleep, the mind will apparently work subconsciously during the night, and sometimes we awake with a ready solution, which we could not arrive at the previous evening.

For those who are curious about this strange fact I can say, that the explanation lies in the finding of the *cliché of the solution* in a subconscious way, for our intense and prolonged desire to do so is like a magnet, which attracts the related clichés from the invisible world, which we can traditionally call the astro-mental plane. A full explanation of the very important term 'CLICHÉ' will be given a special place in the next chapters.

Here I am limiting myself to an exposition of the connection that a certain part of our human mentality has with the physical organ, which is responsible for its transmission into action in matter, that is, case A at the beginning of this chapter, and the considerations supporting it.

But, on the *other side* of the same coin, the contrary statement B will tell us something different. The cause lies in the fact that our thinking processes are by no means limited to cases like A. And then B is valid for this other aspect of them. The human mind can have ideas which are not connected solely with man's everyday needs and desires, but also with an infinite number of abstruse thoughts, free from all material attachment, often not even suitable to be included in the usual process of verbalization. Can you not have ideas about, say, beauty, loyalty, love, impatience, depression, and so on, without forming any material image or link with objects and feelings? The majority of more developed consciousnesses are perfectly well able to cope with such higher mental processes, and they do not at all feel that these are bound to and lodged in their skulls. A strange, but real awareness of freedom from material bonds develops of itself in those who persist in operating in this particular kind of mental activity.

So, in this case, statement B is true, but not A. In the introductory chapters of the present work I will try to explain the basic trend of psychology, which is necessary for an understanding of the methods and aims of true meditation, in the simplest way possible, as perhaps you have already noticed. This is because the subject is not easy even with this assistance and the giving of complicated theories and quotations from other authors, who have written on related (but not identical) matters, would only distract the student from his true aim. To finish this brief analysis, I will point out, that *meditation* is related to and operates only with the B kind of mental process. In other words, the aspirant who is meditating, or trying to meditate does not need to go back to the rather primitive way of thinking described in A.

His true realm will be rather those thinking processes which are not attached to the brain. By this I mean the type of processes belonging to category A.

You may immediately see for yourselves, that this statement implies the following logical and natural consequence. Not *everyone can meditate*, but only those who find themselves happy with the B way of thinking. This refers, of course, only to those periods of their day, which are FREE FROM THE COMPULSION OF BREAD-WINNING AND SIMILAR PROBLEMS THAT HAVE TO BE SOLVED. Do not forget this, for you cannot, and will not be able to dedicate (at least, for a very extended period in your existences in bodily form) ALL YOUR TIME to meditation, no matter how devoted you may consider yourself to be in this regard.

And it is not at all required for the harmonious development of an evolutionary human being. Let us be as clear as possible and practical, for practice means REALIZATION, while theoretical deliberations only lead to frustration.

The eternal words: 'RENDER THEREFORE TO CAESAR THE THINGS THAT ARE CAESAR'S, AND TO GOD THE THINGS THAT ARE GOD'S', are here the corner-stone of your future inner temple. All of us—except those who long ago transcended the level of humanity, but who still return here in order to assist true and sincere aspirants of Truth—have to work amidst continuous and persistent *binaries* such as: Spirit and matter, inspiration and dejection, happiness and suffering, light and darkness, peace and anxiety, and so on. You may add a host of other dilemmas, according to your own experience, once you realize the general meaning of those just enumerated.

But do apply the solutions immediately to your own life, for, without this your efforts in meditation may be frustrated. The basic philosophy, your own philosophy, which you *live* is the foundation of your success. To this add the *law of wave-like periodicity*, well known to all true occultists, and of which human incarnations invariably consist. This is graphically represented by the sine curve in Fig. 1. With all of this you will be well armed against the initial and ensuing difficulties and misunderstandings.

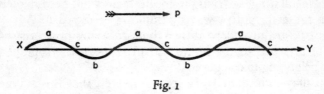

Fig. 1

The central straight line 'X–Y' represents an unalterable, steady movement or level; the highest point 'a' of the arcs indicate the peaks of exaltation (positive elation), while point 'b' shows the corresponding depressions, or fallacies. You can fit all the events of your life to this diagram; those of expansion and elation (or simply, the happy ones) and also those of depression and dejection (or the unhappy ones). The philosophy derived from it will be the understanding that life follows this wave-like pattern, that is, up's and down's. But do not forget that there is a *middle line*, 'X–Y' with points 'c' on it, which mean *absolute balance* and steadiness, or *full peace*, the ideal of spiritual Achievement, being the eternal heritage of the Perfect Ones.

Some day, after aeons of struggle and progress, you will find that Kingdom of God, that Nirvana, or final Realization and then there will be no fluctuation of the sine curve any more.

How suitable this pattern is for meditation! But we are still at the beginning of the work, so let us leave it to later chapters, when we will be better endowed and armed for the task. I am giving it here only as a useful idea for a happy beginning.

Now we can approach closer to the aim of this chapter, so as to obtain the first instructions as to what *meditation* is in comparison with its twin sister called 'concentration'. As has been mentioned, the aspirant for meditation must have as a preliminary condition (and a definite one too), the passage through the first THREE series of the book *Concentration*, that is, Chapters XV to XVIII. But Chapters I to XVII should also be read attentively several times, and fully understood. The exercises themselves are featured in the Third Part of the book, from which you should take Chapters XV to XVIII as a practical guide and manual to be followed.

So now, I will speak in the presumption that this preliminary work has been duly performed, and therefore the *alphabet of meditation has been studied with success.*

Do not hurry, for it may frustrate even the best of intentions. Realize beyond any doubt, that by working along the prescribed lines, you are working not only for one incarnation, but for eternity. You are winning *abilities* which will go with you for-ever, and not merely filling your mind-brain with mortal know-ledge, which may be suitable for only this incarnation of yours and for the conditions on this planet. On reaching another world you will again have to learn similar conditional knowledge. I hope that you are able to understand, even by following the simple mathematical calculations, arising from the fact, known even to official astronomy, that there are billions of suns and their planets in the innumerable galaxies of the Cosmos. I will not occupy your attention with quotations, and so on, merely adding that in any popular book about modern astronomy, you can find that the existence of habitable planets, providing support for intelli-gent beings, is beyond any reasonable doubt. It is simply a result of the combination of the numbers of galaxies and their solar systems and the deriving through the calculus of probability of the necessity for the existence of such planets.

The full understanding of our role in the universe and the variety of the conditions of our existence gives a wonderful exten-sion to our mental horizon, close to ecstasy. This is because the aroma of immortality is then felt in a subtle, but irrefutable way. We may begin to realize the greatest of all Truths acces-sible to the sons of Man: that we are immortal, in that we really are IN CONSCIOUSNESS, which is eternal and synonymous with the term 'Spirit'. But we are not our perishable bodies, no matter what substances form their components.

In using the term 'realization' I mean, of course, not just a mental conception, or theory, which may come and go, but exactly 'knowledge being a part of ourselves', in other words, being in us and beyond us.

It is hard to extend this explanation, which belongs to the awareness transcending the terms of a language, and which is something accepted, known and experienced by all. When you speak about, say, a table, the overwhelming majority of men will readily understand you. When you speak about Pascal's Curve, or a hyperboloid, and so on, only certain people, that is, mathematicians, will understand and accept the proofs of the existence of both.

But 'Realization' in the sense just used, is not an experience of many men and can neither be enclosed in a combination of logical elements, known and expressed through the mind's language, nor unfolded into similar components and, in that way, finally made accessible to the outer mind.

So, whether we like it or not, this is the fact of the matter and nothing can change it. Nevertheless, a kind of consolation does exist. Those who have experienced Realization will always recognize this among themselves, although they will be unable to express it in speech.

In the French language, so admirably suited to the finest kind of philosophical thought, there is a beautiful expression: 'l'odeur de sainteté', that is, 'the perfume of saintliness'. Using the same idiom, we may say 'the perfume of Realization', thereby attempting to define the indefinable.

Through deep meditation a man can arrive at that Realization, but only under certain conditions. I can do no better than to quote the Maharshi, that Spiritual Master of our own day, who departed not so long ago, when he answered numerous questions concerning the obstacles that prevented his devotees from attaining Realization. 'IT IS YOUR WANDERING MIND AND PERVERTED WAYS', said the Sage, evidently meaning 'ways of life'. I cannot find anything even approximately as exact and brief as this saying. Both obstacles must, of course, be removed before we can meditate as intended. The 'wandering mind' has been dealt with in Concentration, but what about those 'perverted ways of life'? For the initiated person there is no question, or doubt about it, for he knows for himself, what line he should follow on his Path.

Even so, in every man there is a criterion to which he can always appeal when needed: it is his own conscience. We definitely know what is right and what is wrong, if only we are willing to approach our innermost criterion with full and unconditional *sincerity*.

Unfortunately, experience and observation shows that this cardinal virtue of *inner sincerity* is not a 'popular' one among men and women of this century. Rather it is something quite the opposite: deceptions and lies seem to dominate the moral and intellectual horizons of humanity in this unhappy and troubled epoch. So what can I say in the face of such circumstances?

If perversion has dominated a man's consciousness so deeply that he cannot even discriminate between good and evil, it is premature to speak to him about meditation, for the condition of the mind as in A, at the beginning of this chapter, excludes it.

But, if there is still a little light in him then great words may be of assistance. Let him read and think about, say, the TEN COMMANDMENTS, THE SERMON ON THE MOUNT, THE GOLDEN VERSES OF PYTHAGORAS, the Lives of Saints, the Enneads of Plotinus and all other writings recognized as truly spiritual ones. Here I have given only a few titles as examples of different approaches to the same inner Truth. Develop this as you feel fit. No one else can make the choice instead of you.

Among the obstacles, mostly of a physical nature, which are obvious to everyone, there are: immorality, dishonesty, anger, untruthfulness, passions, bad habits, weak will-power[1] and lack of steadiness and endurance. By working with those given here, you will probably be able to complete the 'list' for yourselves.

Finally, we have reached the end of this chapter and now require a positive definition of the term 'MEDITATION'.

It is the ACTIVE, UNSWERVING DIRECTION OF YOUR AWARENESS UPON A CHOSEN THEME, WITHOUT ANY DEVIATIONS OR FORGETTING OF IT, HOLDING IT BEFORE YOUR MIND'S EYE FOR THE REQUIRED TIME.

[1] See end of Chapter XV of *Concentration*, 2nd impression, 1964.

CHAPTER II

The Science of Clichés

You will no doubt quite logically agree with me, that in order to start the study of meditation, aspirants must know certain related laws and their application before they begin to practice. Otherwise, an unprepared mind will most certainly lead them astray. During this course you will encounter many proofs to support this statement, but the laws must be known in advance.

There are different laws ruling the physical and mental life of man, and certain of them concern meditation. It is with these that we will deal in Part I of this book. In this chapter we will learn about one of the main laws, that is, that of CLICHÉS.

Usually, every intellectual knows about the forces operating in his consciousness. From the fore-runner to this work, which is *Concentration*, you already know about the foremost forces, that can be found in human awareness. They are—*feelings* and *thoughts*. So, let us occupy ourselves with them again, for meditation requires an exact knowledge of both, as it is these which will be confronted during the present course.

You know enough from reading *Concentration*, as to how these forces work. But *meditation* transcends purely factual knowledge, for its real field of activity is much wider than the domination of mind and feelings during the exercises proper. In other words, we have to be able to *explain* the laws we use. This means that we have to go into the depths of the matter, and then several problems arise, which must be known and solved. Otherwise our ship will have no helm.

The questions posed by these problems are:

(a) From where come our feelings and thoughts?
(b) What is their origin, action and final destiny?
(c) What connections exist between the happenings in this visible world and the invisible ones?

(d) Is there a factor, independent of our three-dimensional time, with its three sub-divisions (past, present and future) in which they find their source and final reason for existence?

(e) Can the ability to see into the past and future be logically explained, giving us a clear insight into the techniques, which operate during the manifestation of clairvoyance, clair-audience and similar transcendental faculties that exist in us?

(f) Has the drama of the manifested universe been explained? If not in the deepest recesses of its 'beginning', which may transcend even the most advanced human powers, then at least in the methods and active factors, which are like the executors of the immense *Primary Will*, so inconceivable for the mind.

Certain sublime human spirits, which have come on to this planet, have been occupied with similar problems, and have found workable solutions for them, and through the infinite *Chain of Initiates* these solutions have been made accessible to men of good will, who live even in this deplorable epoch of general deep diving into reckless materialism, that tends to deny everything which cannot be seen and touched.

IT IS THE GREAT SCIENCE OF CLICHÉS, WHICH BRINGS THE ANSWER TO THE PROBLEMS MENTIONED IN (a) to (f), APART FROM MANY OTHERS WHICH ARE BEYOND THIS COURSE ON MEDITA-TION.

Here I am giving only that which is really necessary for the present study. In the Western world, knowledge of Cosmic and all other derived clichés was released to a limited circle of Initiates just at the turn of the last century.

As you probably know from my former works, the Occult Tradition tells us that, *'there are few things known to the Western Initiation, which have not their counterparts in the Eastern Occult Tradition', and vice versa.* Let me add, that these 'few' things are without any basic importance and refer, if I am allowed to express myself in this way, not to 'strategy' but only to 'tactics'. In other words, the lines of approach always coincide, but details may have a different colouring. So, the factor corresponding to our CLICHÉS is the Vedantic AKASHA, or 'Akashic clichés', as they are often called.

What are the main differences between the two Traditions? The Eastern adepts, believing that knowledge of the Akasha is not so very essential for the human masses, taught only about the general lines of those clichés, in their ashrams. This happened because Eastern *meditations* used innumerable ready-made themes, available from the voluminous, scriptural archives of the Aryans, like the Hindu *Vedas* and *Upanishads*, and the Buddhist literature with its famous *Dhammapada* as the principal work.

Hence they were able to relinquish the creation of new themes since they had access to the ample available treasure of their age-old Tradition.

However, things were slightly different with the Western Tradition. The *Gospels* with their inexhaustible wisdom, as well as some pearls from the Old Testament, were as if monopolized by the Churches, which arose around the words of the Teacher, Who alone was able to say : 'Heaven and earth will pass, but My words will not pass.' So, many true occultists, although fully aware of this tremendous Truth, but who did not want any head-on collisions with the somewhat arbitrary and intolerable attitude of certain great Churches in past centuries, found some different texts for outward use. Moreover, we should not forget that in the main Christian Tradition there was very little known, or printed about the practical methods of elevation of the consciousness (meditation).

Of course, St Ignace Loyola introduced quite formidable techniques into his manual of meditation, and if we compare them with the age-old ones of the Indian Raja Yoga, we may find some striking similarity in method, despite the different ideology. There are also amazingly practical teachings about religious meditation in the Scriptures, left us by certain Saints of the Orthodox (Greek and Russian) Churches, but, for several centuries, they were less accessible to those who did not belong to the closed monastic orders, than were Loyola's 'Spiritual Exercises'.

Finally, it takes an exceptionally shrewd and deep-searching mind, in order to discover in the Christian Churches (Catholic and Orthodox alike) the hidden sense in the few texts, which can be traced to the Initiation into the *knowledge of clichés*. If you want proof, look attentively at the writings of certain

Prophets in the Bible, then, of course, at the four Gospels, and finally at the Revelation of St John.

But, our course on *meditation* belongs to the present day and it is better for us to operate without additional difficulties, which will invariably arise, if you start to seek a solution in the veiled texts, the deciphering of which is not accessible to all and sundry. That is why here, we have to have a ready exposition of the *science of clichés*.

The term CLICHÉS is a very wide one, just as widespread as are the manifestations of all Life. Therefore we cannot avoid speaking about the different applications of the LAWS OF CLICHÉS, instead of one universal (but impossible!) definition. *Such a definition does not exist.* But at least, we are aware *why* this is so.

CLICHÉS embrace the *whole of Creation* for, without them nothing ever was, is, or will be manifested. Now, do you know everything about Life? That is *why* only those kinds of clichés, which are connected with the KNOWN manifestations can be cognized. It seems clear to me, but if you have any doubt ask yourself: 'What forms of life may exist on the other planets belonging to our own galaxy, to say nothing of all the millions of others?'

But, just as *everything* here has its own cliché, so do the far distant forms of existence, which are unknown to us. Without knowing them you cannot know their clichés.

Quite definitely, everything we can, or cannot perceive has its own cliché, in the same way as everything we build has its own plan or draft. No machine or piece of apparatus can be produced without a previously created plan. This is the closest possible analogy to the idea of *clichés*. But, of course, it is only an approximation.

Clichés are incarnate in all forms, no matter whether we choose to call them 'living' or 'dead'. Actually, it would be better if you abandoned the untrue idea about 'dead things'. They do not exist for us, as everything has a certain gradation of life, and it is our limtations alone which do not always allow us to *see* the Unique Life everywhere. I say 'TO SEE' and not to imagine and guess about it. There is an enormous difference between *theoretical supposition* and *direct knowledge*. Just as a primitive native of Central Africa or New Guinea, who, on seeing gadgets and machines brought by the Whites, can un-doubtedly guess about their use and construction more or less wrongly. But those who know how to build and use such things have direct knowledge. Therefore, we can proceed with the explanation of clichés.

We are unable to give any direct and all-embracing definition of CLICHÉS. This is because, in our everyday world, we have nothing that corresponds exactly with this conception. Never-theless, a number of approximations and examples will suffice to explain to us the fulcrum and functions of clichés.

Firstly, clichés are similar to a plan, a draft of every object, action, happening, feeling, thought, in brief, of everything which exists, has existed, or will exist in the future. Clichés are in a *superior world*, beyond our time and space, neither of which limit, nor even influence the purpose and activities of clichés. This, of course, does not prevent clichés from working in all the lower worlds, that is, in the mental, astral and physical ones, just as we ourselves, who belong to the so-called 'three dimen-sional world', can still realize the one and two dimensional conceptions, and even use them in our mathematics, and so on.

Normally, we become aware of clichés belonging to the *present*. This is quite understandable, for we consider ourselves to be living in the *present*. Hence another sub-division of time (artificial of course), that is, the *past* affects us less, but still more than does the third one—the *future*. We have no real control over either of these, at least as ordinary men.

Consequently, all of our being is a kind of materialization of a mysterious cliché, about whose past and future we do not know. At this point, as you may guess, I am temporarily rejecting all theories and imagination referring to the subject.

Clichés are not unknowable factors, and when our limitations regarding present time will be removed, in other words, when we will enter into our unquestionable inheritance of Spirit-Life, clichés will become an open book for us. So says Tradition, and the existence of highly advanced beings, who could read and even operate clichés, provides a hopeful truth for every deeply thinking son of man on this earth.

Secondly, clichés are the foundation of every manifestation of life—objects, actions, happiness, disaster, and so on; but, never forget that clichés are beyond our sub-divisions of time, which our limitations show to us as past, present and future. How can this be? Well, imagine a many-sided geometrical body like a pyramid, for example. You cannot see all of its triangular sides at the same time when standing in front of it. And it is the same with our conception of time, which can be compared to the different sides of a geometrical solid. From any one position we are able to perceive only a part of that solid. In order to see another, we must change our position.

So, if we wish to see the other manifestations of clichés, we must change the range of our consciousness. Is this possible? Yes, if a man is able to enlarge his consciousness beyond the limitations of the three elementary sub-divisions of time. As an example, we can use the state of spiritual ecstasy which we may call 'Samadhi', because this term is already accepted in occultism and it allows us to shorten our terminology, thus avoiding whole sentences and replacing them by a single word.[1]

In Samadhi there is no such thing as 'time', that is, the sequence of events. There, all is ONE, at the same moment, if we can say so. No past, no future, only the glorious eternal PRESENT, extending into infinity.

In the lower kinds of Samadhi, that is, when the adept still experiences mental visions, the clichés are more perceivable, without any veiling of the past and future. This is the explanation of true clairvoyance, but we will deal with this in another chapter.

Here we make an amazing discovery. Correctly speaking, if we realize what clichés are, we may concede that actually the whole of Cosmic Manifestation is beyond time, for its great cliché exists apart from time. In brief, it is eternal. The fact that, at this moment, we can see only certain sides of it does not change the situation. We cannot see the 'other' side of the moon in our telescopes, but we are sure that it exists.

Thirdly, this is the moment at which to give an example of a cliché's action, and this will probably be most enlightening for the student.

The cliché of your incarnation started (on the visible plane, of course), with the union of your parents. Gradually, the process of materialization of your cliché will lead you through its sub-

[1] See my Samadhi, in which this state of consciousness has been analysed and explained in full.

31

divisions, through your childhood, youth, adult period and old age, ending with the cliché of your death. Do not forget that it is from our limited and time-bound point of view that everything happens in a sequence we call time. In reality, all of it exists in the cliché indefinitely, and embraces the whole infinity of what you could call the 'future'.

The same thing refers to every manifestation of life and existence. A cliché then, is like an exact picture, reflecting every event and fact. Therefore, in our efforts to give an indirect explanation and some similies of clichés, we can make the comment that there exist clichés of your relations with other human beings, animals, ideas, places, of your studies, interests, feelings, thoughts, the single days of your lifetime, periods in your life, state of health, property, and so on.

It would seem that the *knowledge of clichés* (and it may be just a theory for you until you have had positive experiences in the matter, as others have had) circumscribes human life, something like inexorable destiny, which deprives us of our dear free will. In essence it is NOT so, but it would be similar, if we could see the complete pictures of our clichés at once. But we do not, and this leaves us a sufficient amount of that illusory 'free will'. I deliberately say 'illusory'.

For, of WHAT, or of WHOM would you like your will to be independent? If you are able to foresee certain activities under given circumstances, performed by a being less developed than you are now, say, your own infant, *does the fact, that you know what that child will do in given circumstances, limit its free will?* Also, if someone much wiser than you, who can foretell your attitude under certain conditions, writes this down so as to give you unmistakable proof of his knowledge, and shows it to you after you have acted, will you feel that you were not acting 'of your own free will', merely because someone could foresee your behaviour in advance?

Simple sentences, as you can see for yourself, but think deeper about their meaning, and you may reach amazingly enlightening conclusions.

I would like to believe that you already see, WHO is the ONE who knows all clichés in their full extent, and not just from one side at a time, as we do. Perhaps you may also see, that HE might be the sole creator of all the innumerable clichés of the universe.

Then many otherwise insoluble and disappointing problems will be removed from your mind, and you may realize, that the age-old inquiry, inborn in the mortal mind, 'WHY are things as they are?', begins to lose its poisonous sting.

The sower, throwing grains of wheat on to the soil, will be the cliché of birth for the future ears of wheat, and the sickle or scythe during the harvesting will be their death-clichés.

So is the wood-cutter for a tree he fells; the hurricane destroying a town and killing its inhabitants is a manifestation of the death-cliché for them; the negotiations between the governments of some nations, which lead to a declaration of war, are the first traces of the clichés of death and suffering for the citizens of the affected countries; your love for another human being or an animal may be their cliché of happiness.

Think about these examples and add scores of your own to them, for in the future development of your study, you will have to learn to use clichés as the principal themes for your *meditation*.

And that is why I have spoken about them in this chapter. For, he who intends to study the *art of meditation* must know a lot beforehand, and his conception of life and of the world around him must also be established before, albeit in theory, of course.

Meditation will open new vistas for him, more real and closer to the *Truth*, which nevertheless will forever remain inexpressible. The famous Sage of India, Sri Ramana Maharshi (1879–1950) taught, that the only language able to express the wholeness of TRUTH is the SILENCE.

Successful meditation invariably leads to the establishment of that *Silence* in the aspirant.

CHAPTER III

Adaptations of the Laws of Clichés

A. *Clairvoyance and Clairaudience*

THE irrefutable fact that human beings, under certain conditions, may be able to perceive things and events beyond the limits of the present time, has its justification in the Laws governing clichés. After what has already been said about them, only a short step ahead is necessary to give us a full explanation of these so-called '*psychic powers*' in man. As the clichés of every thing and action exist beyond our three sub-divisions of time, the only thing necessary for us to perceive these clichés in their '*past*' and '*future*' forms, is our ability to read them. This ability can be inborn, or developed during one's lifetime. Either way there has to be a common basis, the faculty (conscious or even unconscious) of being able to temporarily still the unceasing vibrations of the mind, that is, to eliminate all thoughts, except what we want to remain. Then comes the most important factor, the ability of *completely stilling* the mind, that is, the cessation of every mental process. Yes, nothing less than that! *You cannot see an image clearly in the troubled waters of a pool, but only when the surface has become mirror-like.* You can read hundreds of occult and similar books, perform the most complicated physical and breathing exercises and fasts, and so on, but unless you are able to separate from your ever-moving mind, you will never be able to perceive any clichés.

This is the passive part of the faculty. The active and no less essential one is to be able *to direct a mute request* (without verbalization) to see or hear a cliché.

In practice, both abilities are used almost simultaneously and the operator does not think: 'Well, first I will clean my mind. Then I will create an active desire of my will-power to attract the cliché closer to me.' Perhaps some very green beginners might, but even so, only temporarily, until they really get the necessary powers.

Those who know and are in a position to operate with clichés think very little in words, or not at all. This is the true secret of attainment. It seems to be simple, but just in this simplicity lies the main obstacle to success. When asked why so few people are successful in Self-Realization and the Attainment of Spiritual Consciousness, and what sort of obstacles prevent them from the achievement of their aims, the *Sage Ramana Maharshi* said simply: 'YOUR WANDERING MIND AND PERVERTED WAYS OF LIFE'. Now take stock of yourself and be your own judge. How are things with you? Your own judgement will be the most important and true one.

Permit me an illustration taken from my own experience. I knew about *clichés* and their role in all manifestations of life long before I started to write my books. But theoretical knowledge was of no avail as is always the case. When in 1949, at the feet of my Spiritual Master, I at last became able to separate myself from my mind, with all the consequences resulting from that fact,[1] I also became aware of *clichés* as real things, which till then had been only *theoretical*. A little later I was able to use the practical knowledge thus gained, gradually more and more each year. Finally, all my books were produced in this way: suddenly an idea (if you prefer this term to the more 'mysterious' one of cliché) would persistently face me, at any moment. And, because I was able to leave the mind's activities, connected with the problems of everyday life, I saw the necessity to put in writing, certain thoughts and experiences information and methods.

B. How do Clichés work?

There is a definite Law, which rules our relations with clichés. If we face a cliché for the first time, but do not accept it, or start to realize its meaning and aim, it goes away for a short time, may be for days or even weeks. It is as if we forget all about it. Then it returns for the second time, and the man and the cliché again face one another. If it is accepted, both remain together for some time, and the mind of the man is continually occupied with the contents of the cliché confronting him. Days

[1] See my *In Days of Great Peace.*

and weeks may pass in such mutual contemplation. If the cliché is accepted during its *first visit*, the assimilation will be almost spontaneous and quick. But on the second visit it usually takes more time and the realization is more difficult. If the rejection happens for the *second time*, the cliché goes for a long period, and then returns for the *third* and last time. In such a case, assimilation takes longer and is much more painful and full of apparent obstacles, than for the first and even second time. If it is again rejected then 'finita la comedia', as our Italian brothers like to say, and the man will never again have an opportunity to use that cliché.

In practice it is seldom that one, who knows all these laws, will proceed like a 'text-book case'. Seldom will he say to himself: 'Well, this is the first time that it has come to me. I will wait and let it come again!' There are hidden forces in us which will direct our activities in this or another way. 'Also a cliché?' you may ask. Perhaps, but solve it for yourself. Any induced or suggested idea will not be your own and therefore it will not have any realizable power.

Returning to my own case, and taking the latest example, that is, this very book, it happened in this way. After finishing *Theurgy* and having seen its copies in the bookshops, I was 'free' for a few weeks. As has been usual for many years, I awake for a short time some two or three hours after midnight, face some thoughts, dismiss them and then continue my 'astral life', that is, allow the body to go back to sleep again.

But when a cliché comes things are different: one feels that one should not and cannot treat it like an ordinary thought, the creation of one's own mind, or its reflection. The encounter lasts longer night after night. Streams of ideas come like unrolling films and one is as if enchanted with their freshness and clarity.

Then one day the title of a new work is conceived, the contents already having been 'seen' in one's mind more than once. The typewriter is set in its usual place, a ream of paper is bought, the foreword and chapters follow, and as a result, you now read these lines. No plan is established in advance, nor are the titles of the chapters. The 'contents page' always placed first in a book before the text, in this case, appears when the book has been finished. And so it is!

C. How to attract a cliché

If such an idea appears in your mind, you might say that it may be just the same cliché introducing itself to you. You may well believe so, and there is nothing wrong in that. Wrongness starts when we begin to deliberate from a lower mental point of view, as to how we have, or have not to accept new ideas, give them form and an 'incarnation', and so on. What would you say if, in a restaurant, you saw a hungry man, who went there to satisfy his hunger with a hearty meal and, although in that he is logical and reasonable, he then looks first at the waiter and asks his name, the number of cooks in the kitchen, its size, where they get the produce from for use in the meals, and so on. Next, looking at the menu, he starts to calculate the probable number of calories in each course, then the percentage of vitamins and their qualities, and so on.

In the meantime, the waiter has probably gone off to serve other customers, and the man's worries about his prospective meal have spoiled his appetite and thereby adversely influenced the flow of his stomach juices, thus inviting indigestion to his table. The simple activity of feeding the physical body was transformed into unnecessary and nonsensical deliberations about things which were not needed at all.

The Sage, the Great Rishi Maharshi, who has already been mentioned, once explained the nature of mind:

'Mind is only a bundle of thoughts; remove them, stop thinking and show me then where is the mind. When many thoughts appear simultaneously in a man's mind, they are all extremely weak and ineffective. But let a man concentrate on a few or even one thought and then it will become a power with a far reaching range.'

If you wish to grow and progress, you may find real and positive instruction in these words, as to how to deal with your thinking apparatus.

Meditation together with its twin sister—*prayer*, is the right means to put yourself into relations with the desired clichés. That is why here I am giving material connected with both.

As you already know from earlier pages in this book, *meditation* is a very scientifically controlled process in our consciousness, in other words, in ourselves. Therefore, no nonsense should have any access to our meditation, or it will be thwarted and we ourselves frustrated. Imagine (and this is the truth) that your present or future attempts at meditation, their success or failure are also clichés. Now, with which of them would you like to associate yourself? For remember: 'ALWAYS MAKE THE RIGHT CHOICE: YOUR CHOICE IS BRIEF. IT IS LIKE A MOMENT, BUT IT IS ALSO ETERNITY.'

We have the right to choose. We also have free will, limited by certain factors and very often, by circumstances, but we do have it. The more lofty and progressive are our intentions, the more free will we will be able to put into them. But if our intentions and desires are trivial, we will find a lot of obstacles and delaying factors in our lives, which work against our will. But speaking practically, we may then not be in a position to realize such a will at all.

By 'meditation' about, say, our digestive processes, and so on, we may harm our body, for certain animal activities of our physical organs are at their best when we leave them entirely alone from our mental interference. I do not deny, that if our physical organs are not working satisfactorily, that is, we are sick and not healthy, the control exercised by mental or pranic action from our side may be useful in certain cases. But let us have common sense and ask ourselves how many people know how to conduct and realize the fruits of such an action? Do we belong to those few specially trained and taught people? For any bungling by the operator with unknown and not fully dominated forces only brings the contrary results, a worsening of whatever we wanted to improve.

Do you know what happens to those seduced by all the occult practices, advised by the ignorant and performed by similarly ignorant folk, who have tried to develop all those 'kundalinis' and other nonsense which are unsuited to our conditions and ways of life? Well, I have scores of letters begging for help, when the harm has already been done and is impossible to make good. For there is one realm in which bungling, or acting from sheer curiosity (and there cannot be any other motive in such cases) is most severely punished and scarcely redeemed. And that is the occult realm: for in it a man contacts (if he has been able to) the forces which he does not properly know, and with which association is illegal for him. Some try to justify themselves, saying that they would like to have more powers *'in order to help others'*. You will no doubt agree that this is a complete *untruth*. Those who really want to be helpful will be no matter how seemingly limited their means might be, while those who are unable to assist with their present abilities, will not even think about it, once they gain some 'supernatural' powers. They will do just about the same as they do now : think only about their own egos. '

Therefore, for us, the term *'meditation'* means the higher and better use of the enormous power which lies hidden in us, in everyone of us. It is the spiritual force of man's true Self-Spirit. In this sub-division of the present chapter we have to obtain information on *how to attract proper and positive clichés*.

Most probably, after reading the foregoing paragraphs you already know the answer for yourselves. It is done by meditation on suitable themes and also prayer, directed to the SOURCE OF ALL CLICHÉS, to their Creator.

When, in due course, we come to later chapters in which you will find actual instructions and advice about the techniques of meditation, you may reach the conclusion, that *only elated and inspired meditation is worthy of the name and effort*.

The more dense the realm in which we use our will-power, the more limited will be the results. It is very difficult—but possible under certain conditions—to produce physical changes by sheer effort of will-power. On the other hand, in those less material worlds in which we also live and operate, that is, of feelings (astral) and thoughts (mental), will-power produces infinitely greater results. By purposefully creating *feelings* and *thoughts* we are able to influence the same realms in our surroundings. And because the *physical world of facts* has its origin in the worlds of *emotions and thoughts*, its manifestations can be affected by the powers used in those worlds. The whole of the Kabbalah, true magic and Hermetic philosophy are based on just the right application of these simple laws. It is that 'mysterious' creation and sending of 'vortexes' which is spoken of in the Traditional Tarot. You may find this subject fully discussed in my *The Tarot: a Contemporary Course of the Quintessence of Hermetic Occultism*.

CHAPTER IV

Some Basic Questions Answered

IN Chapter II you found six vital questions, but so far, no direct answer to them. It will be only after reading and realizing the meaning of the following pages, as well as the whole of Chapter III that some kind of satisfactory solution will be found by an earnest student. Therefore, I presume that I will only have to give formal expression to the answers you already have in your mind.

(a) Our feelings and thoughts come from clichés, which approach us, are accepted and then sent into space—not just the physical one of course—by the living power of our thinking consciousness.

(b) The question as to what is the origin and action of our feelings and thoughts finds its answer in (a). But we may add, that certain *physical* conditions can also produce certain kinds of feelings and sometimes even thoughts. I am speaking about physical pleasures and suffering. We may feel happy or miserable according to these conditions, if we are only average people, not in possession of full power over our lower manifestations in matter.

But the last part of this problem, that of 'final destiny', transcends the language of the mind. And I will not present you with any theories in that regard. But, as a man speaking to my fellow men I ought to express my own attitude: *the final destiny of* ALL *is the attainment of Harmony and Peace.*

I found it in the depths of my innermost being during my 'mute', wordless meditations. That is why I wrote this book, for you, so that you may try (and succeed) in achieving the only thing which ever counts—*true personal experience.*

(c) The connection between happenings in the visible and invisible worlds arises because of the fact that clichés are multiplane beings. They manifest themselves on every level of consciousness and matter, in just the same way as you live in the physical as well as in the astral and mental realms.

(d) As we read before, the factor, independent of our three-dimensional time (past, present and future) exists, just as a human being exists beyond its senses, feelings and thoughts. There are several terms to describe this state beyond everything man knows in his everyday consciousness. In the East, in Vedanta, for example, it is called the 'Fourth State', for numerically it is the next beyond the first three just mentioned. Buddhism calls it 'Nirvana', the final Achievement beyond any change. In Western occultism it is known as the 'Spirit', the all-penetrating, but immovable in its perfection, Consciousness, being the Cause of everything, the Alpha and Omega of Hermetists, the Beginning and the End of the Ancient Greek philosophers, and so on.

Religions, I mean those in the great Christian Tradition, call It the Kingdom of God, the Holy Trinity, Paradise. And in the true Rosicrucian Tradition (long since extinct as a body), it may be the Infinite Eternal Lord Himself.

While at the feet of Sri Maharshi, the last Great Indian Rishi (1879–1950), who has already been mentioned, I learnt yet another idea, that of the Central Self, the True Self, equal to what we call 'God'. Sri Maharshi once said: 'The Supreme Self is God, for if it were otherwise, God would be Self-less, which is absurd.' Here self-lessness means 'lack of Self or Consciousness', and that is why the Sage asserts that God is Consciousness itself.

(e) The perception of the past and the hidden present and future find their perfect explanation in the teachings concerning clichés. As clichés operate in all the sub-divisions of time, those people who are able to 'see' and 'hear' them may, by this fact alone, participate in knowledge of these sub-divisions. One of the chief factors for the development of such abilities is a well-understood and well-conducted study of meditation, which finally teaches us to operate our consciousness beyond the limits of the physical mind-brain. These faculties already potentially exist in us, and may be 'unveiled' under certain conditions and by definite study.

(f) As the drama of the manifested universe operates, apart from the planes conceivable for us and also beyond them, it cannot be translated into words. Theories, being children of the same limited mind, are not conclusive. In the higher state of consciousness—called Samadhi in the East and the State of Grace in the West—this problem is solved individually, but cannot be communicated by words and thoughts. The Primary Will can neither be explained nor conceived in the limited terms of the thinking brain. Once again theories are inconclusive and therefore useless. It is much wiser to look truth in the face and not strive after what cannot be achieved. And it is not even necessary : we can be happy and good without that knowledge. The *Central Cliché* of the universe is beyond any form of time, for our time, which, as we say, is 'three-dimensional', is not the only one that exists. In the plane closest to this physical one, that is, the astral, time is different, just as space is different. The same applies to the next, or mental plane.

Along with the innumerable clichés of lesser meaning, which are close to the human race, there exists another factor which has not yet been mentioned as regards the encounter of a man with a cliché. Where we have the case of a man and a cliché 'contemplating' one another, and when the man accepts that cliché, not only does his attitude become changed, but the cliché itself is influenced by the man's consciousness. It departs slightly altered, although it retains its primary character. When a writer realizes a cliché and puts it into a written work, he gets new ideas and progresses. And it is the same with the cliché : it leaves the mutual contemplation 'magnetized' and perhaps intensified in comparison with what it was before their meeting.

How do we explain that some people are apparently more influenced by clichés of a special type than are others. Why, for example, was Edison able to read certain clichés, which were inaccessible to other people and as a result, we have his inventions, which changed much in human life. Let us first use a kind of simile, as it will help us to arrive at the right idea.

There are radio receivers which are more or less sensitive and with a greater or lesser range. There are radio amateurs more and less skilled, and all of them get some reception on their wirelesses. But a refined and powerful radio receiver will catch more and quite distant stations, inaccessible to cheaper sets, while the skilled amateur will probably have a better instrument than an unqualified listener of popular local stations. And it is the same with clichés. Some men possess the ability to receive certain complicated clichés and, as a rule, clichés are attracted to better brains equipped with previous experience of the same type as that represented by the cliché.

When Pasteur discovered vaccination, the idea found him suitably receptive, for he was probably more qualified to catch the cliché, than any other person alive at that time, when the cliché had to be materialized through Pasteur's discovery. That is why important findings in different fields of science are usually made by the savants who have a corresponding education. No shoemaker ever discovered an effective drug, and no clergyman has developed the atom-bomb.

Now you will realize the meaning and value of preparation in the form of education or special study (the occult included) for contacting desirable clichés. The latter still remains in the realm of occult studies, for 'official' knowledge does not know and apparently does not want to know about clichés. This cannot change the fact that the same unrecognized clichés do their prescribed job and reveal to humans what it is timely for them to know, no matter whether they like it or not.

As we may see, many difficult questions can be answered through the use of the knowledge of clichés, although we cannot say that we can embrace their essence in full.

But, after all, how much does an ordinary man know about himself, and what explanation can he offer about his own nature? Yet, still he *lives* and *acts*, without knowing what Power permits him to do both.

Here I do not mean those people who belong to certain initiatory religions, which possess powerful Egregors, and who believe according to their faith. Such people have much less to be worried about as regards the difficult questions of life, and the after-life, since for them God is their ultimate hope and refuge. Are they wrong? By no means, for: 'IN MY FATHER'S HOUSE THERE ARE MANY MANSIONS', and there is surely a suitable cliché of higher rank, which looks after them.

*　　*　　*

It seems that in this epoch, many people are interested in certain higher manifestations of human consciousness rather than just the well-known ones, used by men and women in their everyday lives. Let us briefly enumerate the faculties we already possess.

43

(1) We are conscious of our life in our *physical bodies*, which we usually identify with ourselves. We perceive the same kind of life around us in the so-called human, animal, plant and mineral forms. There is no need to be convinced of these facts by any factor outside ourselves, as we do not doubt them. They are like axioms for us and in their own realm of relativity they are true and workable conceptions. They become wrong only when we *try to make them the sole true and real conceptions which they are not.*

(2) We are conscious of our *feelings*, although our knowledge about their origin and mechanism is not so definite as it is with physical forms. No doubt they are often connected with our purely physical impressions like pain, well-being, tiredness, influx of energy, and so on. In this aspect of feelings (the astral region in occultism) they can be classified and traced to the past, present and even to the future. For we may know how we will feel and react (astrally, so to speak) following on certain physical events and circumstances. A headache or toothache often provokes a general depression in our world of emotions. Sexual activities may bring some elation and a feeling of expansion of the life in us. When the sun shines on us after a period of cloud and rain, almost every human being feels a pleasant reaction, while a heavy storm accompanied by darkness, rain and cold, and so on, will rather depress us, to a degree according to our receptivity and emotionality. However, there are men who can bar all outer influences from the side of the surrounding physical world.

So, to a certain degree, we can evaluate our astral world and its manifestations in all three sub-divisions of time. We remember our feelings in the past, we know them in the present and, to a certain extent, we can foresee them in the future, if the conditions are to be forecast by our mind.

The following are examples:

(a) When we remember a serious sickness of ours from the past, we may relive our feelings of anxiety and perhaps fear, at the time of the dramatic moment when we heard our physician's diagnosis, telling us of possible complications and disablement, if not worse.

If we recall our joy when some good news came to us, when we had success in what we call 'love', or, say, the winning of a large amount of money, or the making of a profitable business deal, we may like to relive those feelings again and again, and in fact, many of us would do so quite often. These are only a few simple examples, and you are free to multiply them as much as you wish. The fact to note is that, IF THE ASTRAL RECOLLECTIONS ARE BASED ON OUR PERSONAL OR THEORETICAL EXPERIENCES, THEY CAN BE RE-CREATED AND LIVED IN THE PAST AS WELL AS IF WE WERE LIVING THEM IN THE PRESENT. But this applies *only when they have their origin in our experiences, not in completely unknown conditions and possibilities.*

This means that we are able, in general, to review the personal (sometimes even wider) sort of clichés at will. This is clear enough for a logically thinking mind. It is not any clairvoyance, only ordinary operations in consciousness.

(b) As an example, the projection of our feelings into the so-called future may serve us for the preconceiving of pleasure or pain connected with imminent happenings, similar to ones we have had before in the past. A foretaste of a pleasant meeting of persons, or profitable activities, and so on, will create attractive feelings and a desire to repeat them again. The visit to a doctor for a periodical test of say, our stomach, connected with the pumping of its contents, or the swallowing of special, far from tasty liquids, the drilling or extraction of a tooth, an interview with a person, who can tell us unpleasant things, or endanger our material or other status, will bring a painful foretaste into the stream of our emotions. Once again, in such cases we are projecting our astral activities into the future, even before they actually happen; but only when we have had some previous experience of them, even in our imagination. This is neither clairvoyance, nor the reading of clichés belonging to the future sub-division of time.

I am giving these primitive, easily understood examples merely in order to assist you, and when you will pass on to the practice of true meditation, you will not be misled by certain problems arising in your mind, the same mind, which will try, at any price, to prevent you from obtaining unconditional command over it by the *excellent means of meditation.* What may actually happen?

Imagine that, after having duly studied the material expounded in this book, you will attempt to take your first steps in the realm of meditation. It is vital that these first steps are right and not misguided, for in starting wrongly, one will proceed wrongly. And the inevitable way back, before making a fresh start, is rather discouraging and tedious. So let us avoid what can be avoided, and do not allow frustration to poison our best aspirations, for it really is the most deadly poison that one can imagine in all the realms and planes of life. The *mind* will try to instil in you, the conviction that easy thinking about the chosen theme of meditation, with numerous deviations, interruptions, and so on, are a kind of meditation, when in truth, all these errors simply lead us far from our real aim. Therefore, you must be aware of this kind of deception and deal with it in a suitable way: by the *destruction of the false suggestions of the mind*. Something like the destruction of cancerous cells during the processes of radiotherapy, which leave the healthy cells undamaged, or only very slightly and certainly not seriously affected, while acting on the malignant ones.

Meditation, as you may see, needs an attitude that is deeply reasonable and full of common sense. Do you want to have it summarized in a few words? Then accept the truth, that you and your mind are not one and the same thing, that your mind can lead you well astray, and that it is not interested either in the development of your self-knowledge, or your abilities to dominate it. Know, that if you can stop its activities for even a short time, or direct them according to your own will, it is a proof that YOU ARE NOT YOUR MIND, just as the car you drive is not identical with the driver himself. This, if you like this term, is one of the MOST IMPORTANT INITIATIONS MAN CAN PASS THROUGH DURING HIS FIRST STEPS TO THE ETERNAL LIFE IN PURE CONSCIOUSNESS. After this initiation the mind will be no unknown quantity for you. I cannot explain what your inner attitude will be like after you have passed this *basic meditation*, for it is beyond the realm of the same mind, and words are the very children of mind. But, I presume you have followed my advice in the early part of this work, and that the book *Concentration* has been successfully and practically studied by you. If so, you know what this 'Initiation' is and by that fact alone you are already 'initiated'.

DELIBERATE AND PROLONGED STILLNESS OF THE THINKING PRINCIPLE IMPOSED AT THE DESIRED TIME BY YOUR OWN WILL GIVES THIS INITIATION, AND NOTHING ELSE CAN SUBSTITUTE IT.

It is the first essential quality you will need for starting your study of meditation.

(3) With the *three-dimensional, so to speak, operation of your thoughts*, with which we will now deal, it will be much easier and more comprehensive when item (2) has been carefully studied. The similarity between feelings (astral) and thoughts (mental) allows us many enlightening analogies and comparisons. Hence we can be brief when explaining the work of the mind in our *present*.

(a) There is no need to emphasize the everyday functions of our mind in the *Present* sub-division of time. Everyone knows. We think and are conscious of this fact. When you read these lines you are supposedly in the *Present*, just as was the case with actual feelings. In other words, you are conscious in your *mental world*, with the necessary reservation, that impressions of that world are being filtered through the apparatus of your brain. From this statement we may draw conclusions of first class importance. As our brains differ, with certain limitations, of course, to the impressions just mentioned also differ, to a certain degree. Not one of us sees and thinks in exactly the same way as another person. Official science may recognize that even physical colours are not one hundred percent identically perceived by different individuals, because their retinas are not and cannot be mathematically equal. But naturally, these differences are not so great, that one mind will believe that two times two are four and another that it is five. In the last case we would simply call it a mental aberration, with the full right to do so. Similarly, only Daltonism can make a man see blue instead of red, and so on. But, in general, the mental Present is very similar for all men. Actual mental impulses find their immediate reactions, and so the mental character of thinking in the *Present* is largely retained.

(b) Let us look into the *Past* and how we can operate in it. This is very similar to the past activities in our world of feelings (astral), with the difference that this 'look' may be devoid of the emotional elements of the *Astral*. I can re-create the mental picture of myself typing this work yesterday, and even remember the contents of the previously written chapters. A stronger effort will allow me to re-write (in my mind) the pages belonging to the past. Likewise you can re-evoke in your mind pictures as seen in bygone days or even years. And you will call them 'mental clichés of the past', which is perfectly right. But will this make it a process of perceiving *clichés of the past* not previously seen and which same constitute *clairvoyance in the Past?* The answer will be firmly in the negative. This discrimination should always be used during the practice of *meditation.* You should be conscious and knowledgeable about the differences between the process of *remembering,* that is, re-using your own mental clichés, and the *reading of real clichés,* which occur during meditation, and to which meditation is the real key. This lack of discrimination is usually the main cause of so much erring and unsuccessful attempts to meditate on the part of people, who have never studied any comprehensive manual on the subject.

(c) The *projection of our mind into the future* now becomes clear. We simply know from past experience what happened during certain mental experiences, which we presume will be repeated again. We then make the mental picture, or, if you wish, create our *personal cliché* of the future, based on our past. I have to mention here, that ALL CLICHÉS ARTIFICIALLY CREATED BY MEN WITHOUT ANY KNOWLEDGE ABOUT THEM IN THEORY AND WITHOUT USING THE POWER OF THE SPECIAL ART OF CONCENTRATION, ARE OF SHORT DURATION AND HAVE VERY LITTLE MEANING FOR THE GENERAL PICTURE IN THE MENTAL PLANE.

Briefly, it means that our remembering and guessing processes are of little importance and are short-lived. The reason? Easy to see: the *Energy* which created the basic clichés, materialized in the picture of the universe, cannot even be compared with the spark of will, which evokes the images of our past or (limited) future in our own minds. After all, can we create anything? Even the most advanced branches of our science are based on existing laws and *matter,* using the former and sometimes transforming the latter, but *never creating anything* from 'nothing'.

Those of you who are acquainted with the great tradition of Hermetic philosophy and its initiation, will readily add: it is only another proof that the Emerald Tablets of Hermes are always right: 'As below, so above and as above, so below' (the Law of Analogy). Others will also add: yes, physical science can now see, that the basic laws for the construction of matter are always the same, differing only in size, as it seems to us. The *atom* is a *miniature solar system*, and the *latter* is like an immensely enlarged *replica of the former*. A similar relationship may exist between the solar systems and galaxies.

All of the foregoing has been given in order to assist you in the inevitable troubles at the start of meditation, and to help you to deal properly with such difficulties by not permitting mental whimsies to make you deviate from the right path.

These are things which every meditating person should know, and our predecessors, who followed the Path, found these laws through their own incredible toil and effort. And they have left their findings to us in that which we now impersonally call 'THE TRADITION'.

Nevertheless, let us be grateful to those who showed us the way and whose mortal dust disappeared hundreds and thousands of years ago from our planet's face. But their Spirit is still enlightening the Paths for those who are able to evoke and attract the Ancient Clichés of Attainment.

CHAPTER V

Achievements Made Possible by Regular Meditation

NO energy spent ever perishes and even if it seems to be so, it is only an illusion of our imperfect perception, which is unable to see the eternal process of transformation, which rules the universe.

Actually, no sane mind would ever doubt the incessant working of that *Law of Transformation of matter and energy*. Everyone of us can see it every day and at every moment even through our mortal eyes, which are able to perceive only an infinitesimal fraction of the activities that fill the infinite field of Creation. No day is exactly similar to another and nothing remains without any change even for the smallest period of time. Look at your garden. How many of its plants have changed during last night? Some of them have faded away, others have developed and are reaching maturity. Seeds have germinated, old leaves have fallen, fruit have ripened, old buds disappeared, the grass has grown higher, and so on.

In your own body processes are also under way without cessation: tissues are growing and are then replaced by new ones and in general you are becoming older with every second, heading for the common end as a physical being. Mountains are slowly eroding; granite is becoming fertile soil; the soil is being used by plants, and at the end becomes sterile until new processes on the surface of the planet change the whole picture. Your feelings and thoughts of today are vastly different from those of a few years ago. The ancient Greeks expressed this briefly, but exactly in the famous 'Panta rei', or 'Everything is flowing'. We can add, that the *Great River of Time* takes everything with it, and nothing in this world remains unchanged or stabilized.

Such is the picture as may be seen in the three manifested worlds known to us: those of physical matter, feelings and thoughts. Your meditation will be subject to the same *Law of*

Fluency, but not forever, as you will know from the final chapters of this book.

The principal task for the beginner in meditation, after he has finished disciplining his mind, as prescribed in *Concentration*, is to transform his incoherent flow of thoughts into a steadily moving stream, the direction of which belongs to the aspirant himself. During your course of concentration you learned to stabilize your mind, to compel it to be directed towards one simple object, without any deviation or interruption. It was a fixation of your attention on immovable targets. Later you also learned to exercise your concentration on imaginary moving pictures, simple ones, but sharply defined. Then came the passive phase, when the mind was completely immobilized, and no outer or inner impression was able to disturb this crystal-like state.

Finally, as the crowning point of your toil, you were instructed on how to expand your consciousness—already balanced through the submission of the formerly unruly and anxious mind—into THAT which abides beyond the realm of mind, of that subtlest manifestation of matter ever known.

Meditation starts where concentration ends. In it, the ability to retain the purity of consciousness unstained by fluctuations and changes in the mental is pushed further forward. Remember this definition, it will be useful for you when you start practical study, in subsequent chapters of this work.

The purified awareness is then directed *solely to the theme of meditation*, which, of course, cannot be long, but as brief as possible, initially expressed in a few words and then melted into ONE idea beyond any words. But you know that you *cannot create* anything in the world of true clichés, and ideas belong to such a world. How can this be and then what happens? This process needs an exact explanation.

Firstly, the term 'purified awareness' should be clarified. What is it by comparison with 'ordinary' consciousness? Once more an old, but valuable example can be used. In an unclean pool with a rippled surface you will never see a clear image. The purified awareness means that a man is able, when he needs and wants to do so, to still his mind and emotions, to set them at peace and thereby clear the field for that part of awareness, which lies beyond the muddy sea of occasional thoughts and

51

feelings, coming as if 'from nowhere' and leaving in an unknown direction.

As you may see, concentration again comes to light. Without it one cannot transcend the frontiers and fences of the average uncontrolled mind and emotions, which make our pool muddy and irregular of surface, and therefore unable to serve as a mirror.

A man who has passed successfully through the course of concentration, possesses quite a different mentality and awareness to the untrained person. Meditation comes easily to him, for he is acquainted with the ruling of his thoughts and their elimination when he so desires.

What then does the acquired habit of regular meditation bring? Possessing the filter of our consciousness, which is the ability to accept and exclude every astral and mental impression from outer space, or the astro-mental world surrounding us, we can attempt to become aware of ONLY a *certain current* among *clichés*, which we need or want to develop. The mind starts to work.

We choose the mental frame in the form of a deep thought, axiom, text or prayer, being aware that to each of such currents there corresponds a definite *cliché*, which expands far more in time and space than the chosen theme. Therefore, starting with little and sailing first on a rivulet, we come to something greater and a large river for our consciousness to navigate. I hope that my readers will forgive my simple examples and similies, but I still think that they are best. It is easy to compile complicated sentences behind which one can hide one's lack of personal experience. I know of many (too many, unfortunately!) writers of spiritual and occult books, who start and finish their works with a 'conscientious research'. Let us take a look at what such 'research' is like. A gentleman goes into libraries both large and small, finds suitable titles of books and then examines them to see what their authors thought about such and such a matter. He notes the opinions he likes, provides an enumeration of their sources and uses them as a framework for the main chapters of his future book. The *role of cement* will be given to his own guesswork and interpretation of the '*sources*'. And, at the end the *work* looks very '*scholarly*', but, unfortunately, very *useless* for anything except reading alone: it cannot provide a basis for practical study for an earnest student. Science keenly notes

the character of the predominating occult and initiatory ('in spe')
works, and quite logically, and with full reason, decries both as
unscientific and too problematical. Because of this, well-developed
minds will also look on them as on something desultory and consequently, disdain any kind of literature about occultism and
spiritual wisdom. Add still the innumerable quacks, who prey
on naive seekers of the 'miraculous' and thus you may have the
picture almost completed.

So, we too have to learn to distinguish the wheat from the
chaff, which is by no means an easy task. There is much more
chance of encountering falsity and ignorance, often dressed in
quite splendid outer trappings, than a simple, earnest and truly
practical source of higher cognition (see my *Ways to Self-
Realization*).

But the 'Great River' on which we want to sail during our
meditation still exists, despite all the thick jungle covering its
banks. And to find it is our true aim.

The example, which I mentioned before, is that of the *seed*
and the *crop*. When starting to meditate, it is as if we placed a
few grains in the soil (of our consciousness, in this case) and
finally got full ears of wheat in exchange. Now you know why
occultists meditate and advise aspirants to do the same: they
become *rich* from the initially small capital paid in, by comparison with the final Achievement. The incoming clichés are
the crop.

I trust that the theoretical part of the application of meditation
is now basically clear to the student. Subsequent chapters will be
allotted to its practice.

When I started to practise meditation, my inner knowledge
of the basic laws and their realization in the spiritual realm was
like a large collection of guesses, more or less logical, but having
no experienced life in them. I read a lot, knew most of the relevant authors in several languages, and I could lecture, using
them as guides and quoting profusely from them, to produce
what audiences considered to be *'very scholarly expositions'*.
That is just what the majority of popular lecturers on transcendental themes do even at the present time. Go, say, to a Theo-
sophical lecture, or meeting, and you will have your first-hand
proof of this. They will smoothly 'explain' to you how many
incarnations you still have to live through before you become

an Arhat or Bodhisattva; who the 'master' is for your special 'ray' of development; what you should do in order to secure riches in the next incarnation, if they notice that you look a little on the 'mammon' side of this miserable life; how you can help humanity during your sleep (it is much easier than to act on the physical plane, of course), and so on. In certain cases, in other organizations, you may be regularly charged member's fees for receiving periodical 'initiatory' booklets, or 'monographs', sealed and secret and 'only for your personal use', but composed from scraps taken from the old second-class and doubtful pseudo-occult literature, no longer subject to the laws of copyright. You will be lucky if you are able to discover, that these 'personal and unique' scriptures were 'prefabricated' and stored in scores of thousands many years before you were 'initiated enough' to get them for a sound fee.

But there are few people, who do not believe in any 'mysterious' rubbish, simply because it lies outside, or is opposed to the existing 'narrow', religious teachings. In my own case, when testing all these widely-advertised 'initiations', I left them as soon as I saw through them, without any grief or disappoint-ment (as unfortunately, many have been compelled to do). I never took any *outer thing* to heart and had an intuitional feel-ing, that REAL THINGS are simple, pure and come from a Source which one cannot but recognize as supreme in its sanctity and Truth.

Why am I writing all of this? Simply because every man has to pass through much deceit and many frustrations along his path in life, but he can reduce their unholy numbers by reason-able use of the great *Law of Discrimination*: 'ALWAYS CHOOSE THE RIGHT THING, FOR BRIEF IS YOUR CHOICE. IT IS LIKE A MOMENT, BUT IT IS ALSO ETERNITY.'

I had known this pearl of inner control since my youth, but the full extent of its realization came, naturally enough, only in maturity. It too was the result of *systematic meditation*, of hours spent in silence and separation from the noise of the outer world, when others were merged in it with pleasure and passion.

Meditation if practised with knowledge and common sense, gives us the invaluable ability of intuitional cognition of truth, or falseness. Moreover, you will recognize the people you encounter on your path in life: whether they KNOW, or only guess and so deceive themselves and others. In this way you will 'debunk' many formerly admired 'initiates' and writers, as well as ordinary people. This may cause the number of your 'friends' to dwindle and the barbs of criticism may be directed against you. What then?

Once more, I would like merely to quote a sentence, once said by someone much wiser than you and me:

'WHOEVER WAS ONCE ABLE TO PERCEIVE AND FEEL THE SPIRIT OF THE HIGHEST CAN NEITHER FORGET IT, CONFOUND IT, NOR DENY IT. O WORLD, IF THOU WOULDST DENY ITS EXISTENCE EVEN WITH A UNANIMOUS VOICE, I WOULD ABANDON THEE AND STILL PRESERVE MY FAITH!'

Let this be a fitting conclusion to the title of this chapter, dealing, as it does, with the achievements made possible by the regular practice of *meditation*.

CHAPTER VI

Obstacles to Meditation

IF there would be no obstacles to meditation for all those who attempt it, the world would be changed, for the numbers of people who direct their lives according to the highest standards, achieved by the reasonable use of the art of meditation, would grow very considerably. As the world, (that is, the human population of this planet), consists, in its ultimate evaluation of single units, of men, the value and qualities of these components are decisive for the whole.

Unfortunately, only a very small percentage of all those who attempt to study *meditation* are successful. There must be some definite reasons for this fact, and in this chapter we will occupy ourselves with the finding of the causes, which prevent most aspirants from achieving their aims.

For the sake of better understanding, we can divide the obstacles into *two main groups*: those arising from physical obstructions and those from the inner qualities of men.

Both kinds of opposing factors are pretty similar to those which prevent our success in practical *concentration*. This is clear because, as we already know, *meditation and concentration* are really twin sisters, and furthermore, something like the famous Siamese twins, who could not be separated, as they would have died from any surgical attempt in that direction.

Common sense tells us not to minimize the physical circumstances of an aspirant. A strange statement perhaps, coming from a writer who believes more in the invisible and transcendental than in dense matter. Not at all! A moment of deliberation will show why.

If we say that the spiritual realm is *more real and therefore more important than the purely physical one*, we must bear in mind, the inherent conditions, which support and explain our statement.

(1) FOR WHOM? Perhaps for all and sundry? CERTAINLY NOT! (2) And does the superiority of the spiritual over the material reveal itself independently of any conditions? Once more—NOT SO!

The answers to both questions lie in your own wisdom. In the case of the *first* one the answer is that, for the majority of men material conditions and events are of the utmost importance, since these are on the first plane of their awareness. So, can they ignore any physical obstacles, which arise when they start to practise meditation? For example, how do they react when they have a violent toothache; when digestive troubles make them miserable and disturb their efforts, and when they suffer from lack of necessary rest and sleep, so that every attempt to sit quietly and recollect themselves leads only to falling asleep? No more examples are necessary, for you have already solved the problem.

One should not attempt an elementary study of meditation when one is not in normal physical health. I want to emphasize that this refers to the *beginning* of the study, for later, when a man has definite experience in super-physical activities, he will be able to transfer his consciousness into the higher regions even when his body is suffering an agony of pain and discomfort. Ramana Maharshi (1879–1950) suffered from an extremely painful *sarcoma*, which finally killed his body, yet he never complained, nor lost his usual composure and serenity right up to the end. But, usually in such cases, ordinary mortals are under constant and very heavy sedation, to prevent them from becoming violent because of the excess of suffering, which is beyond their ability to bear.

The answer to the *second question* is similar and, that is, that those who have achieved the basic and undisputed supremacy of the spiritual over the earthly qualities in themselves, can dispense with any conditions. They meditate not only in the quietness of their rooms, or in specially arranged, secluded places, but even when walking, in trains, briefly almost without any difference in outer conditions. This also applies even during their physical sleep, but this belongs to later chapters.

So now we know something about how we should arrange our circumstances and surroundings during our earliest stages of meditation. PUT YOURSELF INTO THE MOST FAVOURABLE

POSITION while you are still a beginner and weak. Some may say, that this is impossible for them, and that they cannot afford to be alone and at peace during their everyday life. Unfortunately, this cannot change the rule. I still believe, judging from my own experience, that if the decision to start a study of meditation is strong enough, a man can always afford to arrange things to suit himself. If not, this may be the sign that this path is not for him. Then the *Theurgic* way, which is that of sincere and intensive prayer may be open to him, and it is by no means inferior (in fact, from certain points of view, it is superior), to that of evolution through the art of meditation. Remember, that *true prayer* always has its answer, for 'the Supreme responds when approached' (see my *Theurgy: the Art of Effective Worship*).

Now we come to the next kind of obstacles, those of an *astral* and *mental* character, that is, those based on our feelings and thoughts. Can we start meditation while being in a state of real emotional or mental unbalance, in other words, in trouble? I think NOT. Just as a beginner in athletics is unable, during his first lessons, to lift the heavy barbells, which are set as his target at the end of his course. If we are in grief, depression, uncertainty of mind, or full of anxiety about our next hours or days, and so on, it is better to delay starting, for there is a danger of becoming a prey to that deadly enemy—disappointment, or even frustration, which is able to destroy the tiny seedlings of the study of meditation within us.

Always be in accordance with our best friend—*common sense* and do not make any decision at the wrong time and under the wrong conditions. If the cliché of your Attainment in this way is real, you will not miss anything if you delay the work for a few hours or days. If this cliché does not exist for your present period of life, this fact alone will not let you conduct the study successfully through to the end. How can we guess what really is the case with those clichés? Turn to Chapters II and III for a detailed explanation. Put your attention on the fact that if a cliché confronts you, *it will not leave you so easily*, and you will not be able to forget about it immediately after the idea has entered your mind. But if it so happens that you do forget, be courageous enough to accept the due consequences and continue the search in another direction.

I am trying to explain these questions about the obstacles in this rather detailed way, simply because of experience with my readers during the last decade. In my *Concentration* and *Samadhi* certain directives were given as regards how we should deal with the problem of the *all-important start*. But letters showed that prospective students still had many initial difficulties and sometimes became lost among the obstacles and unfriendly environment. I hope that now they will be sufficiently well informed to cover all circumstances.

However, let us be more optimistic. If the matter was absolutely unsuited to you then even the problem of it would not arise in your mind for a considerable length of time. Sri Aurobindo Ghose of Pondicherry went even further when he said: 'The apparent impossibility of doing something now, is only a proof that it will be done in the future.'

After all, obstacles arise for us in order to be conquered. Without them, achievement would merely be like a motorless gliding through the air, while relying upon certain currents and thermal conditions in the atmosphere, and making the reaching of the aim little dependent upon our own will and effort. But, the presence of an engine makes us feel sure that we can fly even against the wind and in any temperature of the air, without being concerned about its ascending currents, and so on. Then we simply break through the obstacles and achieve our aim.

Now, about the 'motor' which, of course, is your WILL-POWER. You will find a complete explanation and advice for building and using this 'motor' in Chapter XV of the second impression of my *Concentration*, so it would be superfluous to repeat it all again in this 'sister work'.

Finally, all that has been said here about obstacles and their conquest concerns only those, who have an earnest intention to follow this path. Those who know nothing about it, or who are not interested in it, are, naturally enough, bound by other ways, and there is no need to convince them, or try to attract them to something which does no lie in their nature.

Two of the most dangerous obstacles are self-pity and self-indulgence, which must be abandoned before true meditation can start. When we forgive in ourselves what we condemn in others, we very efficiently bar our way. But, by judging ourselves severely we gain a thousand times more, and attain inner peace and justice. Do not forget, or permit yourself what you know to be bad when it is done to you. Laziness, inefficiency, insincerity, an impure mind and feelings, so repulsive when seen in others, must be still more repulsive if they are in you.

REGULARITY IN MEDITATION is a factor which has deciding power in it. Without it nothing can be done, for 'occasional' attempts are only a useless waste of time. Therefore, the exact hour should be chosen, which is the most suitable and disturbance free, and it must be rigidly adhered to, unless an extraordinary occurrence makes it absolutely impossible. Early morning and evening are the best, but if you can arrange some other regular time, use it. In my *Concentration* you may find a detailed explanation of the 'magnetism of time', which rules the law of regularity in meditation.

CHAPTER VII

Assistance on the Path of Meditation

JUST as there are obstacles, so there must also be certain assisting factors for our *meditation*, and it is essential that we know about them as well.

The chief one is, at the same time, the simplest:

(1) A MAN MUST BE RIPE ENOUGH TO DISCRIMINATE AS TO WHERE LIES HIS TRUE INHERITANCE (SPIRITUAL) AND WHERE THERE ARE ONLY THE MAYAVIC VEILS OF THE MATERIAL CURTAIN, WHICH HIDE THE WIDER HORIZONS FROM HIS EYES.

This is the cardinal difference which makes some people able to dominate their mental apparatus, while others do not even see the very possibility of concentration of life in the higher region of consciousness. Intelligence has little to do with this, for alone it cannot give any guarantee of spirituality; on the other hand, the intelligence of people perceiving spiritual vistas is far beyond that of those who are blind to these problems.

How can these apparent incompatibilities be reconciled? The best answer will be to quote a portion of a conversation held between the Master *Andréas* and his pupil, as given by P. Sédir in his famous book—*Initiations*.

Sédir: 'What truth is there in the popular belief, that the coming of a comet (at that time, 1910, the well-known Halley's comet was seen in the sky) means war on the earth?'

Andréas: 'Wars do not come simply because a comet appears in the sky, just as when rain is imminent, snails appear; but the rain doesn't fall because they emerge.'

We always have to hold the true sequence and inter-dependence of events before our mind's eye, in order not to confuse them in their causality and chronology.

(2) Often it is as if life itself pushes us towards certain decisions, in this case, to transfer the fulcrum of our consciousness on to a higher plane. Some people have stated, that losses and troubles

in life have gradually created in them the conviction of the existence of different values, not so fragile, impermanent, and as conditioned as are the things in the purely materialistic life. Usually they then come into contact with some serious books dealing with the higher aspects of life, or they even encounter men, who have been actively engaged in higher pursuits. But these are circumstances which arise from invisible causes, rather than causes in themselves. Speaking in the language of clichés, which allows us to shorten definitions and to operate with brief descriptions, we might well say that, when a certain cliché starts to confront us and to present a new pattern of life before us, it may create inspiration if accepted, and in further development may lead this life along different paths.

The appearance of such an inspiring cliché may be the result of a man's former search, or a benevolent act of an advanced human being, supervising those who are ripe enough to enter on to a path of special development, as is undoubtedly the case with a practical study of meditation : in both cases the man's karma plays the deciding role.

One's attitude and ways of life can also be changed by one's own will, and this then accelerates the contacts, which lead to the new path. Let us now look at what we can do in order to attract such assistance by our own efforts.

Meditation is the evolutionary factor, therefore it belongs to the *good*, or so-called WHITE OCCULTISM. Properly speaking, meditation, on evil, that is, egoistic themes, or those harmful for others, does not exist. The technical cause is that the higher mental vibrations are beyond the reach of the lower impulses in man, and have no expression for them in their realm. How then do the retarded souls, the so-called BLACK OCCULTISTS operate? They do not meditate properly, but they create evil, harmful and egoistic currents by *concentration* on such themes. If such a debased person wants to harm a man, from whom he does not expect sufficient resistance, he creates intense feelings of fear, hatred, impurity, empty curiosity, revolt against the Deity, and so on, and concentrates on them and intensifies them until the moment of the 'launching' comes, that is, when he believes the force is large enough to be thrown against the prospective victim. In any case, the black occultist must have a *material contact* with the body which it is intended to harm, in the form of a part of it

62

such as hair, fingernails, blood, and so on, or even a photograph. In the latter case complicated formalities will be needed in order to establish a real contact between the image on the paper and the body of the victim. All these activities cannot be compared with meditation. Moreover, when you really meditate, no harm can be done to you by any evil people in an occult way. The same, and still more, applies to prayer and selfless activities. It sometimes happens, than an unwise *black magician*, as these evil and debased men are often called, tries to attack a *white occultist*, or even a *man of really saintly* life, who *knows* about the impending attack. But the latter have a terrible weapon at their disposal, quite apart from meditation, prayer, useful activities, and not leaving room at any moment for a *passive attitude of mind and heart*, and it is—FORGIVENESS, which is eventually connected with a sincere prayer to the Almighty. This destroys all the traps and snares of the Enemy, usually together with his own life, or at least his health. I am not speaking here about the *astral* consequences of such a defeat, which are still more far-reaching.

To forgive one's enemies and to pray for them needs an *especially high spiritual development in a man*, and it necessarily also results in a *powerful spiritual force* in such a man.

I think the above information may be useful for students to elucidate certain problems, which sometimes appear for aspirants of the path of meditation. The more you know and the more questions you are able to answer, the more peace you will have during your concentration and less anxiety will arise in the curious mind. That is why I am giving all these explanations at this point.

At the present time, when so many things belonging to the occult realm (that is, to practical psychology, which is true occultism) are being unveiled in innumerable books and also in other ways, 'new' means are being introduced into the art of meditation, in order to facilitate the advance and remove the obstacles, as far as it lies within the power of the aspirant. And I have been glad to find that prominent exponents (few as they unfortunately are) give great importance to their advice to *use the power of prayer* (that is, theurgic practices), before starting any advanced degrees of meditation.

I would like to add, that this will bring the best possible

results even for elementary efforts and perhaps even more so. This has a firm foundation in the fact, so far seldom mentioned by writers on the subject that: TRUE, MUTE MEDITATION, WHEN THE CONSCIOUSNESS LEAVES THE PHYSICAL BODY AND IS DIRECTED INTO THE HIGHER MENTAL LEVEL, AND THEN INTO THE FOURTH STATE (Initial Kevala Nirvikalpa Samadhi), BECOMES IDENTICAL WITH WHAT IS SO WELL KNOWN AMONG THE SAINTS AND IS CALLED—MUTE PRAYER. But we will dedicate more time to this important problem in the final chapters of this work.

Great assistance on this Path comes from the self-imposed *discipline of reading*. What actually are the majority of books? They are crystallized thoughts of other men, related to the varying realms of human life. I will not enumerate them here, as you can do this for yourself, if you wish to spend time on it. The major parts of these thoughts in print have no actual meaning for an intelligent reader, who discriminates between his mind's moods and desires. Here I am not including all manuals and books, which give direct knowledge in any branch of human science. The authors of such works do not give merely what they think (rightly or wrongly) about this, or another matter, but simply expound the achieved knowledge of Nature's laws, and so on. But fictional literature confines us to the writer's mind, what he thinks about this or that, and what he invents by means of the same mind. This literature can flourish only because of the passivity of the minds, encountered in the mass of men and women. They like the *very process of reading*, that is, the following of the stream of fiction created by another mind.

From our point of view, and in relation to concentration and meditation, all such reading is unnecessary and only weakens an aspirant's concentration and attention, the powers he so badly needs for a successful study of meditation. We learn to use ONE idea for the development of the essential process of inner cognition of the perennial values and abilities present in our consciousness. So, of what use for us are the deliberations and fiction created by other minds, not engaged in any similar, basic search?

In meditation we learn to direct our mind to selected aims, but not merely to review the lower functions of other minds.

Are we eternal on this earth, where we create the causes, the results of which we will 'feed' to, or live through ourselves when we leave these bodies? Every second, minute and hour cuts shorter and shorter the path before us, until the last, when the inexorable and unavoidable moment of leaving everything comes. It seems so clear and so true, but look around. What are men doing in their short-lived existences in matter on this planet? They are incessantly squandering precious time, that limited time, which never comes back.

The student of meditation must know about the foregoing and pronounce his own, uncompromising verdict, and then live according to it. This is the only way to avoid the final frustration, that 'hellish fire', as described in Chapter XLVIII of *Ways to Self-Realization*.

The conclusion then arises, that the limiting of our reading to a few books which really matter and the complete exclusion of the unnecessary products of fictional minds is of *great assistance on the Path*.

There are things, which are independent of the will of men and their means, and yet they are still worried by events, which they cannot prevent, exclude, or change. Is this a right attitude for a man who expects to obtain more wisdom by meditation? If a man is affected by the sayings of others, their opinions, relations, and so on, how will he destroy *anxiety* in himself when he starts to meditate?

It is a well-known law of mental economy, that anxiety brings enormous losses of time and energy, which otherwise would serve for much loftier purposes.

Perhaps someone will put to me the question : 'Doesn't such a controlled life become infinitely boring and commonplace?' The answer, which comes from experience and practice of what has been previously told is : 'Just the opposite !' The feeling of inner freedom and certainty, unknown before the conquest of mind, is incomparably more precious and satisfying—apart from its practical value—for the man, who has taken the helm of his boat of life in his own hands, and is able to steer it to the chosen port. Never a thought of regret about the lost 'mental pleasures', just 'condemned', even enters the man's conciousness. And the so-called '*future*', now seen from quite a different point of view, does not (and cannot) bring anything unreasonable and frustrating. The mastership of the '*present*' rules the 'future'.

Meditation is then approached as a joy and a source of happiness, and not as an unpleasant duty, as so often happens in the beginning. You should know this as it will help you to overcome the *resistance of the mind*, together with all its whimsies, which sometimes can be quite deceptive and very clever. Here the main assistance for you will be the firm realization—at first only in theory, and later in deed—that YOU AND YOUR MIND, TOGETHER WITH ALL ITS THINKING PROCESSES ARE TWO, BUT NEVER ONE!

In this or another way you must reach this conviction, as without it, there cannot be any achievement or happiness.

You will readily agree that there is *no bliss in slavery*. So then, also agree, that slavery to mind and feelings may be the main cause of human misery. The Great Ones say so.

And many years ago, I had the privilege of hearing the same from the mouth of one of Them, when I sat at his feet, in a secluded place, deep in tropical India. To reach that place and be able to live there, required much effort, which someone else might even call 'sacrifice'. But it certainly was not, if compared with the values obtained instead! I found this truth at the same time.

You can now hear the same words without making similar efforts and travelling long distances. Do they therefore become less valuable and useful? Retreat into your deepest recesses and ask for the answer there. It will be the right one.

Great assistance will come to you if you start a *gradual* detachment from the perishable and evanescent in life. The mind, devoid of its passions, becomes like a well-tamed animal, obedient, useful, more productive and more exact. What, before its conquest, needed three days of intense work, can afterwards be done in a fraction, in less than one third of the time. Perform your duties exactly and according to the best of your knowledge, but *be apart from them in your heart*, which thereby will become free and happy, since it will no longer be affected by the inevitable losses and even deceptions, which may occur during the initial steps along the Path. But you will deal with them through your meditation, then unaffected by the alternating sine curves of your life. Through meditation you will see, that after every plunge there always comes an ascent.

Finally, a constant attitude of *understanding* of every being you encounter on your path is also of great assistance for the purification and stabilization of your meditation. The old French saying: 'TOUT COMPRENDRE—C'EST TOUT PARDONNER' ('To *understand everything means to forgive everything*') has always had a charm for me. And involuntarily one must add: '*And forgive us our debts, as we forgive our debtors. . . .*'

Some day, when well advanced in this study, you will come to meditation on these eternal words of Truth, of Life, as were told to us about two thousand years ago. May you then discover what others have done, and your march to the Goal will be fast.

CHAPTER VIII

Further Questions Explained

ONE problem, which may be met with by some students of the art of meditation, touches on the concept of HYPNOTISM and its fundamentals. I will not give any special explanation of this power in these pages as the subject has been well described and analysed in so many books. But there is a certain side of *hypnotism*, which is connected with the teachings about clichés, given in previous chapters.

Hence I will comment only on those points which are common:

A. *Clairvoyance under Hypnosis*

Good operators can influence the hidden powers of human consciousness in different ways. One of them is the production of certain kinds of clairvoyance such as: *seeing into the past and the future*, as well as in the *present*, of course, that part of it which is inaccessible to our ordinary means of cognition and at a given time.

(1) By his suggestion, a hypnotist influences the abilities in the hypnotized person, for seeing the desired *clichés*, which now belong to our past. Innumerable cases have been known where the hypnotized person has been able to see and report on events, which occurred in the past, and which were unknown to any of the other people present. As you know, clichés embrace all three sub-divisions of our time, and extend far beyond them. And so, like all manifestations of hypnotism, such clairvoyance is nothing miraculous in itself.

An 'eye', so far unknown in the subject, has been opened for a short time through the skill and power of the hypnotist.

(2) This explanation also applies to the phenomena of seeing into the *future*, although it is not always possible to establish the veracity of it immediately after the session, but that is only

natural. People have to wait until the facts predicted by clair-voyance operating in a hypnotized person come to realization. *Clichés of the future* have been 'read' and translated into human language. The reach of such 'revelations' are dependent upon the intelligence and abilities of both the operator and the subject. This explains why, in the relevant books, we usually find descriptions of the most trivial and limited pictures from the past and future. This is because the *Great Cosmic Clichés* are not so readily opened to human curiosity and investigation.

(3) As regards hypnotically induced clairvoyance in the *present*, that is, related to events actually taking place, at the time of the hypnotic session, there can be two possibilities and conse-quently, two explanations. The first follows along the same lines as with (1) and (2). The subject sees the *present* sub-division of the required cliché, which is not one manifested in the environ-ment where the session is occurring. In other words, the operator does not ask his subject to say how many cups are on the table in the same room, or the names of the participants, and so on. It would be pointless to bother with things which are well known without the aid of clairvoyance. He sends the hypnotized person into a totally different environment, which could not be known, or seen by those assembled in the room. The inform-ation thus obtained, although belonging to the *present time*, possesses the character of being something beyond our 'normal' means and ways of cognition. That is why the character of these phenomena belongs to the same type as in (1) and (2).

* * *

But occultists know that there can be yet *another explanation* of (3). I mean the so-called 'exteriorization of the astrosome' of man, or, of his usually invisible, subtle body, also called the 'astral body', or phantom. Under the orders of a hypnotist, the subject performs his 'astral exit', leaving his body in a state of trance, while he himself, in his conscious astral vehicle, travels to the required place, notes the information and brings it back into the physical world.

A striking and authentic story about such astral travelling, witnessed by men who had nothing in common with occultism, and so on, and who used the results of the action for official purposes, can be found in Chapter V, pp. 126–9 of my *Tarot*.

In this case, the operator ordering the exteriorization and the subject performing the phenomenon was one and the same person, a powerful magician and hypnotist of our own period.

B. Warning

We know, that a person who submits himself to hypnotic experiments and allows himself to accept suggestion, inevitably loses his former, full freedom, and become susceptible to the action of a foreign will. We presume that most hypnotizers are honest and reputable men, especially as now they are often doctors and have diplomas, allowing them to practise hypnotism for therapeutical purposes. So we can believe that from this side there is little danger of misuse or abuse threatening us. But the hard fact still remains that, once hypnotized, a man remains susceptible to this intimate psychic influence, not only in relation to the first operator, who exercised his powers on him, but even to any other person who has the ability to hypnotize and who has no diplomas or knowledge.

In this chapter I have mentioned the possibility of contact with the world of clichés, so that the student can realize for himself the *difference* between the reading of clichés under the influence of another person's will, and that of acquiring the *same* ability through his own active study of meditation and by his own efforts. Such a way is much better and of greater quality. Often a hypnotized person does not even know what sort of information he, or she brings back from the astro-mental world. But not so with a meditating occultist. He operates for himself and obtains his knowledge from first-hand, fully conscious operations, made possible by his own development, brought about by the successful study of meditation.

Consequently, it but remains for me to give you some final advice. It is this:

NEVER ALLOW ANYBODY TO HYPNOTIZE YOU UNDER ANY CIRCUMSTANCES FOR, IN THE BEST POSSIBLE CASE, YOU MAY NOT OBTAIN ANY KNOWLEDGE, OR SUFFER ANY EVIDÉNT AND IMMEDIATE HARM, WHILE IN A NOT SO GOOD ONE YOU MAY LOSE YOUR FREE WILL AND GAIN NOTHING.

Even the active part of hypnotism, that is, operating on others, is not too sure and propitious for your Karma : you may harm, even without being aware of it, but the responsibility will still rest solely with you. The fact that *ignorance of laws* does not excuse those who break them, is fully operative in occultism.

As a study of meditation implies definite effort and mental strain, just as with any other study, the problem of participation and regulation of the brain's functions enters into the question. As we are living in physical matter, use it, and to a certain degree are dependent upon it, we have as a counterpart of our mind, its physical representative in the form of the complicated mechanism of the brain. I once heard someone say that 'the matter forming the brain is the finest and most evolved on this planet'. It is only logical, of course, for this matter makes it possible for the vibrations of the infinitely more subtle mental plane to be reflected in the physical realm. What else except the finest combination of molecules, and so on, could perform the infinitely complicated functions of the brain?

In my own mind I found a simple comparison, giving the idea in a clear and sensible way: why not imagine the mental counterpart of man, like himself, playing on, say, a violin? This violin, of course, will be the brain. The better the player, the better the instrument he would like to use. With a poor violin, even Paganini himself would be unable to fill a concert hall with his wonderful tones! But in our earthly lives we usually get what we deserve in the way of a physical body, its qualities included.

One who studies meditation plays some noble melodies, and he must give full consideration to his violin—the brain. If it is easy to damage a wooden musical instrument, how much more dangerous it is to abuse such a subtle thing as the human brain.

I would like you to recognize the difference between ordinary school and university studies that we pass through, and the study of *meditation*. From the beginning, with the former, we fill our memory with appropriate material and gradually extend our abilities of understanding, combining and judgement, all of which affect the brain's cells comparatively gently and indirectly. I say indirectly because memorizing the alphabet, and so on, touches only ONE side of the working brain, while leaving others at their ease. When we pass on to, say, mathematics, then another part is affected, and so on. Moreover, our brains are accustomed to working in this way, not only during our present childhood, but also because our mentality educated our former brains in the past, although we may not realize, or recognize this, but the fact remains.

However, when we commence meditation, it is no longer a passive swallowing of information, or standard activities. For then we begin to impose vibrations on the whole of our thinking apparatus, to compel it to work in a way that is new and unusual for it; to CREATE vibrations along a specially chosen line, under the strict control of awareness, while using the power of *concentration*. Then the cells have quite a different matter with which to deal. All of this produces tension in them, which parallels the same in your unconsciousness. So that is why we should be careful, and not overcharge our mental vehicle.

The exercises you will come to in later chapters are so calculated, that if you follow the instructions exactly as given, no harm whatsoever can arise for your brain and nervous system. This, of course, under the condition, that you will follow certain elementary rules of physical behaviour before and during the exercises.

(a) Never attempt to meditate:
  1 For at least one hour (better two) *after meals*. The drinking of water is excluded from this rule.
  2 For at least two hours after the *use of alcohol*, or *tobacco*, if you still have these unfortunate habits. Under the term 'use' I mean a glass of beer or wine for alcohol, and a cigarette for tobacco. When full of intoxicating liquor, or after chain-smoking, one must not attempt to meditate at all during the whole of that day.
  3 When you feel any fever, have a cold or pain. Let them pass before you start.
  4 With the body in an uncomfortable position. It would be best to read attentively the beginning of Chapter XV of my *Concentration*, which discusses the 'Westernized Asana', as this is the most suitable for meditation.
(b) A few *pranayamas* (see Chapter XV of *Concentration*) will do a lot for your mind. And also, do not subject your brain to additional strain by intensive reading during the time immediately preceding the exercises.

If you will follow this advice exactly and intelligently, you will be doing the best for the preparation and continuation of your study, without any danger whatsoever for your physical and mental health. For those who were advanced enough before undertaking this study to realize the *power of prayer*, I recommend that they do not omit a short, but sincere worship in the form which most corresponds to their inspiration at the moment. Otherwise, you will find a source of effective prayers in the book —*Theurgy*.

Before finishing with the problem of physical and mental hygiene, as recommended for meditation, it is still necessary to deal with another plague of this epoch: that of *excessive and unwarranted reading*. We educate our mind-brain during our lifetime, according to what use we are going to make of it. As with everything, it too is liable to form habits, which we often refer to as '*our attitude of mind*'.

Excessive and unplanned reading is something like the swallowing of food without chewing it, thereby compelling our stomach to perform the work our teeth missed doing.

There is no need to explain to you what will be the result of such a habit. Your doctor's bills will give you a better idea. It is similarly so with reading. Not all physical food is suitable for everyone and this applies to reading. The crystallized thoughts of others, that you find in books may sometimes be good, easily digested food, or just the opposite.

We can avoid the damage that comes from unintelligent and spontaneous reading, excessive and superficial alike, if we control it by common sense. Ask yourself, when you next intend to buy or borrow a book: 'Do I need to read it? Is it worth the time I will use? Will I be mentally richer after reading it? What useful instruction can I extract from it?'

You may still add several questions of your own choice, if you find them useful in preventing you from unhealthy mental food, the consumption of which you will pay for later in a regrettable way.

* * *

C. *Other problems*

The last problem, that of sexual relations, should be regulated according to item (a), section 2 of this chapter. The considerable loss of pranic and other energies, which follows such relations will lower your ability to control your mind for the given time, therefore it is wisest to await the return to normal balance.

One of the important aids we may obtain as our steps advance in meditation is the realization of the UNITY OF LIFE. It is a very popular belief in the twentieth century, at least, in theory, for it seldom means anything in practice. So, I am mentioning it here, while presuming that the student is not well-informed in this regard. But if he is, I congratulate him, as it will greatly facilitate his advancement, when the 'mute' meditation appears on his schedule. However, an intellectual acceptance will suffice for the moment.

If you look even at your physical body with due attention and draw logical conclusions from what you see, you will then reach the conviction that you are NOT something absolutely *separated* from surrounding matter. From a microscopic cell in the beginning, your stature has grown to its present billions of cells, all drawn and assimilated from the same material sources around you. And all these are not, properly speaking, *your* own! In due course you will give all of them back to the same earth, from which they came. In modern parlance, you are living on borrowed capital, which has to be repaid. If you put enough attention on this idea, you may come to the same *feeling of certainty*, which I myself have when writing these lines for you. You are dwelling in a house which is temporarily yours, but it is NOT YOURSELF. It is impossible to add something more to this in our human language, in order for you to have the same experience of truth about yourself and your outer appearance. But if you think deeply about it, you will reach the same conviction and experience, which will then give you a wonderful *feeling of freedom and joy*: for it is a ray of Truth in you.

If now you look at your feelings and thoughts, you must surely recognize that they are not something completely independent from the immense ocean of other feelings and thoughts, which affect your fellow men. The majority of your opinions and convictions are shared with others and that is why we can understand one another even without manifesting our emotions and mental states by outside gestures, and so on. Look at literature today with all its novels and stories. In all of them, the authors have not only coldly depicted the happenings they have concocted for their 'heroes' and other types, but they open certain sides of their minds and psyche to us.

This can happen only because they KNOW them from their own experience, and readers like chiefly to find out about something already known to them as a *small fragment of a whole*. Then the unfolding story attracts their attention and 'literary taste'. Here lies the reason why some 'light' novels run into millions of copies, although they do not reveal any great depth, or new ways of life. People in this second part of the twentieth century are often sexually minded, that is, they like to read of the similar experiences of others, even if, practically, they cannot afford to do the same in their own lives.

But earnest books, which present different non-trivial, inner experiences, require not merely a superficial reading, but rather co-operation with the writer and a working along the lines he indicates for us. As a result such books attract far less numbers of interested readers. And that is why, as an example, the number of printed copies of that which you now have before your eyes will be expressed in thousands, but *not* in hundreds of thousands (or even more) as with some other books.

Thinking along these lines we come to another impression: that our emotions and thoughts may well be common to many other human beings. So, in the end, *we really are not anything separate and exclusive*.

These mental deliberations are still quite far from the actual experience of UNITY. However, this *Initiation* is not expected to be reached at the beginning of the study of meditation, but only as the crowning success of your final Attainment.

You will find all of this knowledge very useful when you start the actual practice of meditation, and do you know *why*? Simply because it *anticipates* the mind's enquiries and anxieties, which usually precede the exercises, and sets you free from the toil of combating the interference of mental activities.

There is also another attitude which will facilitate success for you. Thousands of years ago it was expressed by the practical Romans as: '*Festina lente!*' It means *to make haste slowly*, and it looks like a paradox. But it is NOT! We cannot, while hurrying, pay the necessary attention to details, and how can we reach right meditation without being exact in our inner work?

When on the old Continent I knew another simple proverb:

'By travelling slowly you will go farther!' Of course, this was coined when the means of communication were limited to horse-drawn vehicles. In those days, when the roads were not our present smooth highways, but full of potholes and other pleasures for lovers of fast riding, a broken wheel or axle meant serious delay and trouble for the travellers.

But in *meditation* haste means only inner imbalance and lack of control. Remember from previous chapters, that good meditation is like a clear river, flowing majestically in the direction of the ocean, without cascading waterfalls, sharp bends and other irregularities. Such should be your attitude from now on and it will be one of those factors which give most assistance in your work.

As you know, the book *Concentration* is the twin sister of this manual of *meditation*, and I presume that you always have it at hand beside this work.

Then, look as often as you can at its parts I, II and IV, because it will be another useful aid for you at the present stage.

CHAPTER IX

Different Types of Meditation

ARISING from our definition that MEDITATION IS MOVING CONCENTRATION ON A CERTAIN THEME, we find that there must be quite a few types of it, according to different aspects of the basic themes which are used. So here we will analyse the main direction and channels in which our consciousness can operate.

Accordingly, we will consider these channels, in separate chapters, starting from *elementary meditation*, based on physical activities, and finishing with *contemplation*, or meditation beyond words, feelings and thoughts.

It is important that you realize and accept as a fact, that meditation is A STATE OF CONSCIOUSNESS IN WHICH THE HIGHEST (that is, SPIRITUAL) ELEMENT IN MAN'S COMPLICATED STRUCTURE TAKES THE LEAD AND ACTS. Unfortunately, this enlightened LEAD happens rather as an exception in twentieth century man's life. This statement implies that more often than not, other elements rule man, and now we are obliged to prove it.

1. *When does the physical, that is, bodily conciousness prevail and rule?* Fortunately, the cases of purely physical awareness are almost as rare as those of true meditation. In order to be 'only his body' man needs to be merged in his physical senses alone, without mixing them with his astral and mental counterparts.

When we do not think, or have any emotions and are only aware of the pulsation of the living body, of some of its senses, that is, experiencing sensations like touching, cold, warmth, hunger, the feeling of physical satisfaction (after a good meal, for example), pain (without thinking about its possible causes and having no fear of serious disease), then such a state is close to purely physical awareness.

77

But, because this is very rare, I am mentioning and describing it only because it is a logical duty to see that it does not remain unexplained, no matter how impractical it may be. It seems that our younger brothers, the animals, and especially the higher kinds among them, the so-called domesticated ones, who live with us and contact us throughout their lives, can sometimes be used as an example of temporary, purely physical consciousness. When a well-fed and beloved family cat, which has no worries or fears finds delight on a soft cushion in a warm room and lies with eyes closed, *but not asleep*, it is probably living only in its physical consciousness, having excluded the outer world from it.

This well-being can be noticed, or rather felt by us, as it is expressed in one of those 'charming' postures, which the little animal is able to display for our admiration.

Now, what happens when the 'astral' consciousness, that is, the realm of emotions takes over the lead in us? You probably know the answer.

2. *When are we overwhelmed by emotions?* I presume, of course, that no infinitesimal addition from the physical and mental realms are associated with us in such moments.

Examples:
(a) When we are so happy, after getting some good news, or other positive impressions, that the feeling of 'bliss' rules supreme. For a short time we do not even think instinctively feeling that it would interfere with our present state.
(b) When anger is so strong that we are unable to dominate it and think about the possible unpleasant outcome. This again represents a form of purely emotional domination in us.
(c) In all these and similar cases, the mental element seems to be absent and the mind is as if devoid of its usual verbalization.

There is no need to multiply actual examples, for everyone is perfectly well able to provide more of them.

Also, as with the theoretical *'purely physical consciousness'* we cannot persist for any length of time, while being absolutely merged in an emotion: the physical and mental factors will soon slip through and start to exercise their own properties.

3. *When do we live purely in the mental realm?* Apparently, when we think, without any emotional or physical addition. Again, this too is neither easy, nor does it happen so often. But in theory it does and should exist. Try to perform certain considerable mental effort, which will so occupy your awareness that you will temporarily forget about your body and feelings. You will not need them for your mental task. It is quite possible, especially for those who possess certain control over their mind. Let us imagine a three-figure number, like 999. Then start diminishing it, that is, subtracting one unit (1) from it, in your mind, getting 998. If this is too easy for you, that is, it does NOT ABSORB all your awareness, make it harder, by subtracting two, three or even more units. But remember, the process must completely absorb your mind, and there should be NO ROOM for anything else. If you succeed, you may then claim, with justice, that for a certain time you have been living only in your mind-brain.

Incidentally, it can be mentioned here, that such exercises are often used during a course of concentration, and with good results. Many years ago I found them to be very useful and capable of adding a lot to one's self-assertion in the mind's realm, for, in every kind of concentration there is an element of power present, which can even influence the matter of the surrounding, outer world. There is a book, a highly interesting and intelligently written one, in which many examples of this influence can be found. If you read Chapter 10 ('Tibetan Buddhism') from *Exploring the Occult* by Douglas Hunt (Pan Books Ltd., London), you will learn about the phenomena obtainable through special concentration of the mind.

* * *

We know that man is not limited to these three sub-divisions in his conciousness, which have just been mentioned. There is *something* which can use and rule all three. Necessarily, IT cannot be any one of the factors ruled. It is simply impossible.

The purpose of true meditation is to FIND OUT this unknown, but essential SOMETHING, without which all the other manifestations of life in man become non-existent.

Naturally, the great *'leap'* will be performed from the highest known platform in our consciousness—the *mental plane*.

When mention is made of meditation, it usually means just mental meditation, and the two lower levels (physical and emotional, or astral) are usually omitted as if they do not exist. Of course, this is a fallacy, for the student should know everything which works in his awareness, otherwise he will be lost in the higher degrees of study, not having any firm foundation in the lower ones. So, logical as it is, this is too often forgotten, and that is why there are so many failures even for men of integrity, who have sufficient will-power. They simply do not know certain essential things, which inevitably occur during their work.

In the previously mentioned book—*Exploring the Occult*, there is a very reasonable statement, which is well placed and emphasized, although it is not new. Its gist is that, because man is a conglomeration of physical, emotional and mental properties, plus the *spiritual peak* towering over them, the good health of all of the first three is necessary for the development of conscious spirituality in man. It is completely true and that is why, in all occult manuals, magic included, the operator is warned *to be in good health when acting*. Similarly, in a former chapter I said that no attempt to meditate should be made if the student does not feel well physically and in other ways.

In brief, *when you fight, you should be in your best form!* True yogis also look carefully after their health and good conditions on all three planes, although their aims are much higher. The now much popularized Hatha Yoga is a necessary preparation for those who do not yet possess excellent health and no spiritual (the only real!) Attainment. Fakirism, that is, the mutilation of the body in order to show one's superiority, or domination over it is a cruel fallacy. There are better opportunities to do the same, such as *mastering* a healthy body rather than a weak and disfigured one, which cannot even offer any resistance, either for good or evil. And we should know this.

But how to explain, for example, when we may see a truly spiritual being, a Master—as happened to me—whose body is weak (in old age) and suffers from a terrible disease? Here discrimination, common sense and intuition must help us to solve this riddle, so seemingly incompatible with the former statements about bodily health in the advanced sons of man.

The solution is this: when fighting a battle, one must be in top form for victory. When it has been achieved, the victor always remains the victor and his enemies remain slain.

When a Master reaches *spiritual initiation*, it means that he has simultaneously won all the battles and left them behind him. He cannot again become an ignorant weakling. Attainment is FOR EVER, it cannot be lost either in this, or in any other possible life. Never forget this! So, the Spiritual Master, that I had the undeserved privilege of encountering in Ramana Maharshi (see my *In Days of Great Peace* a diary from his Ashram) could be sick and suffering physically in his last days on this earth, but that did not affect his Attainment in the slightest. As his suffering was his offering, his redemptory action for us, who so badly need all assistance, it only sublimated his greatness. No sign of spiritual eclipse or any weakness was even perceptible, rather just the opposite: the *spiritual Light was made still brighter, when It shone through the declining physical body.* And for such a man, death itself is something quite different to that for an average human being, so we cannot compare ourselves with FULL ATTAINMENT.

Although it is right for a Master to allow his body to become anything he agrees with, it is *not so for us.* Once Attainment is achieved, it does not matter what happens to the perishable sheath, the body, actually abandoned long ago, as consciousness remains for ever in the realm of ONENESS WITH THE WHOLE, or, if you prefer—WITH GOD!

The cruel sickness, cruel because of its painfulness, of the Maharshi did not affect his conciousness, merged as it was for ever in HIM, any more than a sore finger affects us at the present time. And we should always have this before our mind.

Look at a baby: how much care and tenderness that little, weak body needs in order to survive! But wait for a few years and you will see a rugged man, or strong woman, exercising their bodies without any of the former frailties of their infancy and childhood.

For our meditation we will still need some special conditions, suitable surroundings and avoidance of distractions and interruptions. This may be right for us now. But a Master is in *eternal meditation*, even when answering our not too wise—from his point of view—questions and while being surrounded by the feverishly anxious and restless world.

Far off in the past he too started, as you do now. Some day, on some Earth, you will have, like him, that eternal smile of Wisdom and Peace, which are the reward of Achievement, for returning into the FATHER'S HOUSE, in which there are many mansions, awaiting everyone of us.

CHAPTER X

Subconsciousness or Hyperconsciousness

IN modern psychology one often hears terms such as, *'unconscious'* or *'subconscious'*. Are these words exact, and have their
users any experience with both, or do they merely depend upon
the recorded experiences of others, with which they then try
to evaluate cases, according to their own theories and conviction?
In meditation you will enter into another world, full of new
experiences. So you may rightly expect me to give you some
advance information about what you may encounter and how
you should attune yourself to such experiences.

Men like Dr C. Jung, who have dedicated their lives to
scientific research in the realm of human psychology and consciousness, although not in the experimental (personally, of
course!) way, have coined the terms given in italics at the
beginning of this chapter. But we need more, we need to find
the corresponding values, or factors in ourselves. Only then may
we mean what we say.

Some years ago, when preparing my breakfast, I dropped a
couple of thin porcelain cups on the hard floor of my kitchen.
They duly broke into several pieces, and there was nothing excep-
tional in this small occurrence, everything went according to the
Laws of Nature.

Then one morning, some time later, a cup again slipped from
my hand and started on its way to destruction on the floor. But
this time it was different. In that infinitesimal fraction of a
second between the moment when the cup slipped from my grasp
and that of hitting the floor, something happened in my consciousness, far beyond any thought or desire, and there lies the
whole difficulty in trying to convey this to you. A strange, mute,
inner conviction, coupled perhaps with the intention that the
cup would break, arose in me, and at the same moment I knew
that in this lies the power which can defy physical laws and

83

perform the impossible. Also, it was not at all any thought, or perception as such in words, for there were no words present in my consciousness, only deep silence and separation from all thoughts.

Before the cup fell, I 'knew' that this time it would not be broken. And it was not. It lay on the same hard floor without any visible damage, and it is still in use to this day.

In due time I started to meditate about this *small miracle*, as I called this event in my own mind. I tried to remember the state of my consciousness at the very moment that the cup fell. I tried to relive it, but in vain. The subtle feeling of that strange depth in me, which could act upon 'dead matter' and produce results, impossible from any logical point of view, could be recalled, but that was all. Nevertheless, I found a link with similar happenings.

The earliest was in my childhood, when I was about six years old. I went to play in a garden, constructed on the steep slope of a very rocky hill, while my parents and their friends were in the latter's house, a hundred yards distant. Something tempted me to climb to the very edge of the garden and then I looked down, as if into an abyss, lost my balance and started to roll downhill. According to physical laws, there was little chance of remaining alive, and none of avoiding injury. But I KNEW that no harm would happen to me, as I rolled down for about a hundred yards, between the sharp rocks and crevasses. It was just as if something took hold of my body and preserved it from any hard contact with the surrounding material world.

When my parents finally found me at the bottom of the garden, beside the high, stony fence, they first looked for broken bones and bruises; but there were none.

On another occasion, only a few years ago, I was involved in a serious accident, because of thoughtless road authorities, who had poured tons of gravel along the edge of a steep and narrow mountain road, leading to the summit some 3,000 feet high. On the left was a very steep drop of about 2,000 feet deep and at its bottom the plain. The slopes were covered with some shrubs and widely separated trees, which apparently offered no possibility of holding anything which rolled down.

I was not aware that at least two feet of the gravel rested loosely on vegetation, and did not indicate the true edge. So, when a large car came recklessly rushing down towards me, to what looked like being a head-on collision, I drove a foot or so to the left, thereby avoiding the worst, as I thought.

What happened next? There was a bang and I found myself head down, then upright, then down again, I do not remember how many times. I knew that death was waiting at the bottom of the mountain. Then the strange certainty of not reaching the fatal depths so far below arose in me. It was so quick that it seemed to be beyond any measure of time. At the same moment I felt the rolling stop and the car stood quietly on its four wheels, facing back towards the road high above. No broken glass, no great damage, and no blood on me or the passengers. On checking, to see if the car was only at momentary rest, or whether it would roll if I tried to open the door, I found that an enormous, half-rotted log was behind the rear wheels. The car was resting so firmly against it, that it seemed as if movement could not upset its position.

What happened later was of no importance to me. By repeatedly using the horn, we finally attracted the attention of cars passing high above us. And after a long rope was found, we climbed up and waited until the alerted tow-truck came and hauled the car back on to the road.

The important thing was just that sudden change in consciousness, when all thinking disappeared and a new state arose, momentary but powerful, silent but efficient, and intuitively I knew that IT was infinitely greater than my everyday awareness.

Just before starting to write this book, I tried to evaluate and analyse the consciousness, which has been occasionally opened to me in my life. Jung and others of his school would call it 'subconscious power', or the 'tapping of the all-embracing, unconcious Source', perhaps suggesting the conception of the Supreme Being, or God.

What I *know* is different, although similar in appearance.

IT IS NEITHER SUBCONCIOUS NOR UNCONCIOUS. IT IS ABOVE AND BEYOND ALL KINDS OF KNOWN CONCIOUSNESS, AND PERHAPS ONLY THE TERM 'HYPERCONSCIOUSNESS' COULD ALONE DESCRIBE THE INFINITE POWER, MANIFESTING IN SUCH A WAY IN LIVING AWARENESS.

When I started to analyse it I found, that when this state was later repeated, not necessarily arising as a result of definite effort, but rather by evading all control of the mind, it always happened *after a specially successful meditation*, followed by a prolonged silence of the mind. That is why I am mentioning all of this here, as the student may also be confronted by this HYPER-CONSCIOUSNESS, and while knowing in advance about its greatness, will greet the Rising Sun in himself, with confidence and joy.

Further conclusions can be drawn from the foregoing. If the infinitesimal manifestation of the Hyperconsciousness (as we may call that mysterious power in pure awareness) is able to defy known physical laws, or rather to rule over them, what happens when the SOURCE ITSELF ACTS, or, in other words, when IT manifests ITSELF in ITS full power, that is, in the creation of the universe?

Then *everything is explained* by the simple fact of annihilation of the conception of *impossibility*. Let us focus all of our attention on this problem! When we say '*impossible*' we consciously, or unconciously measure the '*possible*', according to our own meagre scale of activities, to which we try to reduce everything else, even when beyond any comparison with those activities. It is, from a purely philosophical point of view, a great fallacy. We are NOT in the position to judge about and decide on the 'POSSIBLE and IMPOSSIBLE', once we transcend the limited frontiers of the material world, or, rather, of that portion of it which we believe we know.

It is worth remembering the famous saying in the Scriptures: 'Nothing is impossible for God', or for the HYPERCONCIOUSNESS, which must possess all the attributes we usually ascribe to Divinity.

If in us there is a spark of that *something* which, while in no way being matter, still possesses the ability to rule that matter, then the WHOLENESS of this Power must be beyond any laws of *possibility* and *impossibility*, or *cause and effect*, and both conceptions then become unreal and non-existent. Then the enigma of the universe ceases to remain an enigma. I am aware that it is extremely difficult to try to explain, in words, something which lies far above and beyond any word or thought, and therefore I know that realization of the ideas expounded in this chapter will set an unconquerable obstacle for many of you. Moreover, I believe, that without a flash of intuition, they will most certainly remain without any answer in the awareness of the student. But I have no ambition to write of these deepest matters for all and sundry, it would simply be illogical, if not ridiculous. But SOME will recognize the fulcrum.

And then will happen what is perhaps the greatest miracle: all the problems and questions will immediately cease to exist, being once and for all solved in the moment of supreme lucidity of the flash of the *Hyperconsciousness*. For example, how could you explain the mysterious words of the Great Teacher—Christ: 'AND GREATER WORKS THAN MINE WILL YOU DO'?

In the following paragraphs you will find a unique explanation of Christ's miracles, and of the superhuman wisdom in the teachings contained in the sayings of the Sage Maharshi, as quoted here, when he ascribes all of them to the peculiar state of consciousness of the Teacher, being UNITED WITH THE FATHER, that is, with the WHOLENESS OF ALL CONSCIOUSNESS.

The cause then, lies in the possession of this *Hyperconsciousness*. Deep and intense meditation will be needed in order to realize this short and apparently simple statement. I hope you will try it with success and because of it I would say: if in any form of life this consciousness is awakened, the *'miracles'* cease to be miracles. For we call 'miracles' something which transcends the laws of Nature, which we know, or believe we know and also things which we never saw and never believed to exist. But, as you will certainly recognize, the conception of a 'miracle' belongs exclusively to our mind, and does not exist apart from it. Nature, for example, does not recognize, nor produce any miracles.

All of the aforesaid does not in any way diminish, or debunk the wonderful actions and deeds of the GREAT ONES. We have to establish a criterion firmly in us, which will help us to discriminate about and compare our own powers and abilities with those of the Beings who infinitely transcend us.

From this is born the cardinal virtue of every advanced occultist and spiritually-minded man: it is *his humility*. This virtue must have great power in itself, for the famous *Monsieur Philippe*, the great Theurgist and miracle-worker of the end of the nineteenth century told those, who asked him about the

87

source of his powers that : '*It is because I am so very small, quite a small one. And you are big. . . . But God helps only those who are small and weak.*' Thus spoke the man, who could cure any sickness, and who knew the past and the future, in the same way as we believe we know the present.

The kind of superconciousness we know as *Samadhi* does not possess the power of the Hyperconsciousness about which I am speaking in this chapter. At least, its lower forms do not. We do not know what happens with the highest one, simply because we have not experienced it, for the *Sahaja Samadhi* is the exclusive privilege of a spiritual Master.

Let me forestall the eventual inquiries in this matter and at the same time issue a warning to every earnest and sincere student. The 'DIVE' into the HYPERCONSCIOUSNESS does not depend even in the slightest degree upon our mental, or any other attitude, which could induce IT. In other words, we are unable to experience this STATE deliberately at any desired time. I reached this conclusion by way of much toil and many experiments. There always exists a powerful but unknown BRAKE, which prevents any abuse or premature '*diving*'. What is it? Although it is impossible to give any true description, it is similar to an absolute *forgetting* of the 'way', and even of the very possibility of experiencing THAT. I had a striking example of something acting beyond our mind and in spite of all our efforts, when I came to the end of my stay at the feet of the Great Rishi Ramana (the Maharshi) in his Ashram, in South India. I was very close to him spiritually after those months spent with him, without much talking, only the merging into the depths he was able to reveal to me. So, on that last evening before my departure, when, according to custom, I had to ask his permission to leave and his blessing for my further life, I got the idea of obtaining his autograph on a large photograph of him, that always stood on my desk. I knew that he never signed anything. but my feeling of spiritual intimacy with the Maharshi was so strong, that I was unable to resist the idea. So I put the picture on the table in my room, along with a pencil and board on which to sign, and started to dress myself in the Indian style 'evening attire' accepted in the Ashram, consisting of a loose white shirt and similar trousers, instead of the usual shorts. I looked at the beloved face of the Master, anticipating his gracious signature, which would be a symbol of his perpetual Grace. I knew that his days were numbered and only a few remained. Finally I stood before him, and then happened that which I described in Chapter XVIII—'Farewell' of my *In Days of Great Peace*. But when I returned to my cell, I saw the picture lying on my table, left just as it had been prepared for signing. But some power had erased even the slightest memory of it from my mind during our last talk. It seemed to me to be absolutely impossible for I had been thinking about it for so long. It would have been easier for me to forget my own name, rather than to forget to take the photograph to the Maharshi! Yet still it was a fact, unbelievable as it was, but quite real.

It was impossible to go back to the Master and ask him for anything: the final farewell had been said, and one could not treat the Great Rishi as an average man. Later I understood the cause, and it dissipated all my apparent grief about not having the desired autograph. I realized that if I had taken the picture for signing, two possibilities would have arisen. *Firstly* the Rishi never signed anything and in doing so for me, he would be immediately inundated by similar requests from the thousands of other people around him. This he most certainly would not have allowed. Also, it would not even have been good for me. Who knows if I would have been able to show the signature to the outer world without experiencing the poison of mute pride because of that sign of Grace, which was refused to all others?

Secondly, if he refused, I could be wounded in my deepest recesses before I arrived at the understanding I have just described. It is clear to me now, that all reason was opposed to my wish, and I will be happy with this to my last days on this earth.

So, there are 'limits' and 'brakes' in our consciousness, about which only a few know and with which still fewer agree.

While we can be reasonably sure of merging into a lower kind of Samadhi ('Kevala Nirvikalpa') after fulfilling all the necessary training (see my *Samadhi: the Superconciousness of the Future*), we cannot do the same with any certainty (in our minds, of course) in order to assure ourselves of the HYPERCONCIOUSNESS. Inner insight, extensive and true meditation and a pure and devoted life are evidently the unavoidable forerunners of IT, but still—IT is free! Like space, it is absolutely free, and does not come at any '*command*', even if such a silly conception could

89

arise in the realm of that old deceiver—the mind. The omni-potent greatness of the HYPERCONSCIOUSNESS is beyond all com-pulsion or even laws. We can only sincerely fulfil the supposed pre-conditions and—wait.

Even so, I am the last man to tell you, that the task is hope-less. Just the opposite! So seek, knock, and you may find that then it will be opened for you. In this sad epoch, humanity (the majority, in any case) tries to PULL DOWN everything it desires, instead of raising itself to the level required for attain-ment; instead of raising and developing the *awareness* to the realm above and beyond the mortal mind, to the peaks we want to achieve!

Even in this materialistic and cruel world, so full of material cravings, as can be clearly seen in the present global politics, this pernicious trend of corruption is quite visible. For example, certain large, but undeveloped nations, on seeing the prosperity of other races, which was certainly not achieved 'for nothing', but by enormous toil and the labours of several generations, would simply like to plunder those prosperous nations of their riches, instead of trying to learn how to produce such wealth in a similar way for themselves. They are unable to see, that even if such aims were realized, it would only result in poverty over-whelming the whole of humanity in a very short time, instead of being on a fifty-fifty basis as it is now.

I once heard an old and interesting story, which comes from the Eastern legends. It is said, that a king who ruled a certain country, became dissatisfied with the apparent inequality among his subjects. Some were rich, but the majority were rather poor and jealous of the wealthy classes. Finally, he ordered that all property be collected and divided equally among everyone of his citizens, so that no one could complain of any injustice being done to him.

Unfortunately, a few years later, when he took part in a procession beyond his vast palace grounds, he again saw some beggars on the streets, and some apparently well-dressed and well-fed people.

With the course of the years the differences had grown greater, until the old order had almost restored itself.

Those who had wasted and squandered their part, which they had obtained without any effort or work, returned to their former beggar's state, but in the majority of cases, efficient and able people had regained their position as of old.

Not one of the Great Teachers of humanity have ever cared about wealth, as history unfailingly shows us. Who is right, are we, or are They?

Sometimes I have tried to draw a parallel between this 'Hyper-consciousness' and Samadhi, but I have found that they *do not cover one another*. At least, this is so judging by what we can know from the practical experience of Samadhi. They are both different states of the extended consciousness, beyond the narrow limits of the human mind. Consequently, it seems that it would be useful to explain and describe here some aspects of Samadhi. This term, coined by our Eastern brothers (originally the Vedantic Hindus) is very useful and replaces long explanatory sentences. Hence it is better to explain it at ONCE, and then use just the word itself. Of course, those who have studied my *Concentration* and *Samadhi* will find little that is new in the following lines.

(A) There are *two* main sub-divisions of Samadhi, the one con-cerned with certain *visions* in the mind, is called 'VIKALPA SAMADHI', or that WITH FORMS. However, some of the leading spirits of Indian philosophy, as was Ramana Maharshi (1879–1950) refuse even to call this type of superconsciousness Samadhi, merely limiting it to the definition of *'ecstasy'*, a state far lower than true Samadhi. Because of the usefulness of this analysis and the following definition, I agree in full with the Master Maharshi. But, because many writers (including those in the East) still continue to use this term (*Vikalpa Samadhi*) to describe mental ecstasies, it is being mentioned here as (A). From our point of view, this state has a direct connection with visualization of certain kinds of clichés from the outer world, as well as from 'inside' the human mind. The Revelation of St John, the prophe-cies of Nostradamus, and so on, are classic examples of the well-developed system of cosmic clichés, as perceived by inspired visionaries.

As we know, some more restricted and not so ancient clichés are strikingly strong and, apart from the visual, may even extend to sound impressions, which can be perceived as visions with sound, even by untrained occultists. The famous examples of the battles of Edgehill, Naseby and Waterloo, with their life-like changing scenes and thunder of battle, can be seen by sensitive people every anniversary of these historic happenings and are too well known to be described here again. Even the realistic cries of the wounded and dying combatants can be heard.

(B) Now we come to the second category of Samadhi—that of the FORMLESS one, or NIRVIKALPA in Sanskrit. In it there are no visions at all, as this state of Superconciousness is beyond the mind, and belongs to what, in Vedanta, is called the FOURTH STATE (physical consciousness being the FIRST, astral the SECOND, and mental the THIRD). In our terminology it will simply be called the SPIRITUAL SUPERCONCIOUSNESS.

Then there are TWO different forms of Nirvikalpa Samadhi, with very essential differences.

(1) *Kevala Nirvikalpa Samadhi*, or *temporary one*, which can be of long or short duration, but after which a man inevitably returns back to his 'normal' awareness in the physical world. This state of temporary Samadhi is connected with catalepsy of the body, which is then merged in a motionless state, with stiffness, or other similar symptoms. Upon returning, a man usually has a period of mental ecstasy, which is connected with happiness, joy and often tears, as the aftermath of the basic experience. This then is what a man, whether saint, yogi, or advanced occultist can expect to live through, until his development brings him to the threshold of mastership, to the conclusion of the lessons of living as an incarnate being in matter.

Kevala Nirvikalpa Samadhi may well be accompanied by certain psychic powers called Siddhis by Hindu occultists, such as clairvoyance, clairaudience, magnetic forces which can be used for the cure of certain diseases, and so on.

But we should never confuse it with the *last, and the highest* form of Superconsciousness which, at least, is known in theory. It is:

(2) SAHAJA NIRVIKALPA SAMADHI, when the word 'Sahaja' is used instead of 'Kevala'. Sahaja means the *'perennial'* or *eternal* state of spiritual Superconsciousness, accessible only to those who have finished their earthly evolution and learned all its lessons and hence have nothing more to know.

This mysterious (only for us, of course) state of Sahaja does not call for any limitations of the bodily functions, as is the case in the Kevala form. Man can then live in this world as does every average human being and can move, work and sleep, in brief, can act in any way he chooses and still NEVER LOSE HIS SPIRITUAL CONSCIOUSNESS, which has become uninterrupted and eternal in him. That is all we know, from the mouths of those who have experienced this peak of achievement, and the Maharshi's testimony about it is the most direct and authoritative. He was gracious enough to tell us everything that could be expressed in human language about that mystery, he being the only man in our epoch, who has risen to that final *Peak*.

We can only guess that unlimited spiritual powers are associated with Sahaja, judging by Maharshi's own, although he did not like to show them in any way. But these manifested themselves as knowing all the three sub-divisions of time; being able to read the innermost depths of human consciousness; being visible in different places at once; assisting decisively in the spiritual advancement and enlightenment of those who truly turned to him, as to their Master and guide; promoting the hidden faculties in his devotees, and leading them to Samadhi in an unobtrusive and sure way; purifying their minds and turning them towards spirituality, instead of the illusions of the visible, earthly existence, and supervising their spiritual growth even after leaving his physical body, according to his own promise 'not to abandon us' after death. Involuntarily the great words of Christ come to mind: 'I will not leave you orphans, I will come to you.'

This is not the place to delve deeper into this fascinating realm, especially so as it has been treated in full in another book —*Samadhi: the Superconsciousness of the Future*. . . .

But, in the words of the Spiritual Master for our own period, we can find an amazing statement, of incalculable value for our investigation of the *Hyperconsciousness* and its properties. In speaking about Jesus Christ, the Great Rishi Maharshi said: 'Jesus, the man, was utterly unconscious of his separate being when He worked His miracles and spoke His wonderful words. It was the WHITE LIGHT, the LIFE, which is the cause and effect, acting in perfect concert. "MY FATHER AND I ARE ONE".'

By analysing these words of the Sage, who certainly knew more about Christ than any other among the sons of man, we may

93

perceive a tremendous Truth. And it is, that the state which allows the most incredible miracles to be performed is just the Hyperconsciousness, which was mentioned in a few examples at the beginning of this chapter. Only then it is EXTENDED INTO INFINITY AND PERFECTION (instead of infinitesimal fragments, only accessible to us in certain very rare cases, noticed by still fewer numbers of men), which is the *Oneness with the Father* ('My Father and I are ONE') and which is the ALLNESS and WHOLENESS of Life.

There is neither purpose nor need here to delve into the *Unfathomable*, '. . . . *Who asks doth err, who answers, errs.* . . .' Therefore, let us be still and try to find the inexpressible answer.

*   *   *

Even so, we may be able to analyse and guess about the pre-conditions, making the experience of the Hyperconsciousness closer and more possible. But in such deeply-rooted problems one can only speak for oneself. It is for you either to accept this testimony, or to seek another for yourself.

It seems, that the *ability* (sometimes innate, sometimes acquired by life-long toil and striving) of *voluntarily stilling the mind*, of *separating* ourselves from the mental functions, of flattening the ripples on the surface of that symbolical pool, which represents the mind, is the ESSENTIAL pre-condition. There may be others of which we do not yet know, but this is one of the most important. Why? Simply because the flashes of the Hyperconsciousness invariably include elimination of the mind's functions. Also, training in well-directed meditation seems to dispel the clouds around the pure spiritual awareness, which I am defining as the 'Hyperconsciousness'.

I believe that, in starting a course in the practical art of meditation, you are entitled to know as much as possible about all that I have expounded in the chapters of the First Part of this book, so that the exercises will not catch you unprepared, and your mind, which will invariably try to place every obstacle on your path, will be better known to you. *This mind is*, as you will undoubtedly agree if you have ever tried to perform some initial exercises in concentration and meditation, *definitely inimical to such an undertaking*. The statement that: 'The Mind is the great Slayer of the Real. Let the Disciple slay the Slayer.'

94

(taken from *The Voice of the Silence*), is and always will be the ultimate Truth.

Hyperconsciousness is also beyond intuition, which can be defined as the ability of cognition without thinking, and which is infinitely higher than the mind's power. For in IT there is nothing more to know since everything is known. Eminent psychologists like Dr C. Jung knew about the powers of the *Hyperconsciousness*, which they called the 'subconscious' realm of mind, because the 'normal' mind was not present in operations of the 'subconsciousness'. We can only guess why they did not realize that the term is unsuitable, since powers manifested in this state are far superior to the mind's usual ones.

It could be because, for many psychologists, thinking is the highest manifestation of human consciousness. So, if they find something *apart* from and *independent* of the mind's functions they place it *below*, what according to their theory, is their highest level.

This attitude prevents them from making greater discoveries, for which the transcending and domination of the mind is a prerequisite. In my *Concentration*, which is, as you already know, a necessary introduction to *Meditation*, I emphasized that the awareness of a man who has been able to separate from his thinking processes, to rule them according to his own will and *to stop all mental functions*—which brings the most far-reaching results—is very different from that in an ordinary person. Such people of the latter type do not know from where thoughts come and how to handle them. As you can guess, the first man has the ability to discriminate and select clichés, while the other takes almost everything as it comes to him from the mysterious 'space' in which clichés operate.

Meditation, if studied earnestly, may put you into that superior category of men, but it must be preceded by a study of practical concentration, quite apart from introductory information you find in Part I of the present course.

As with my former works, my advice remains the same : *read every chapter at least seven times*, to gain the best results from the study. Scores of letters from my readers, confirming that excellent results can come from this method, are the best proof of its soundness. 'Reading' alone is of little if any value.

This chapter would not completely cover the subject of its

title, if the very important idea of Realization of the true Self in man were omitted, and unless it analysed this last approach to the problem of Hyperconsciousness. Self-Realization, or the entering into the realm of the *Central Consciousness*, the all-embracing Great SELF (or God, if you prefer this term) although very rare among our contemporary fellow men, is not as un-known as *Sahaja Samadhi*, the *Hyperconsciousness*, or the true power of *Faith*. There were and still are living people, who have experienced this Realization in their loftiest moments on this earth. It is true that they do not speak very much (if at all) about it, for they know that speech is powerless to express the experiences beyond the language of the mind.

I believe, that when the state of *Realization* is no longer sporadic, but permanent, It might even merge with the *Hyper-consciousness*, being one and the same state. Maharshi called the *Supreme Self*—God. From the first paragraphs of this chapter it can be seen that the *Hyperconsciousness* most evidently possesses the attributes which we ascribe to the Almighty.

Finally, we have these strange and mysterious words of Christ: . . . 'if you have faith as a grain of mustard-seed, you shall say to this mountain: Remove from hence hither, and it shall remove. . . .' This fits in perfectly with the idea, expressed previously, that if even an infinitesimal flash of *Hyperconscious-ness* in us raises us beyond all known physical and other laws, then more extended periods of it must bring greater results. The term 'FAITH' still remains mysterious for the overwhelming majority of people, who mostly confuse it with quite a different one, that of 'belief' or 'believing', which has little in common with real *Faith*. Those interested in this cardinal problem will find more about it in Chapter IV of my *Theurgy*.

In concluding this chapter, I am inviting you to make the final findings about the *Hyperconsciousness* and other higher states of consciousness like *Samadhi, Self-Realization* and *Faith* for yourselves, by your own efforts. It will be a very useful exercise, before passing on to Part II of this book and will thereby finalize your 'theoretical preparation' for MEDITATION.

PART II

TECHNIQUES OF MEDITATION

CHAPTER XI

The Main Difficulties for Beginners

I gave the sub-title of this book as *An Outline for Practical Study* and I wish to retain this character throughout the whole work. This means, that I will be obliged to give an earnest student everything he may need in order to successfully start and continue the art of *meditation* through to its actual domination. Such a book can be written only when based on real and practical experience by one, who has tried and passed along this path in his own life and obtained the desired results. That is why I will give a lot of details, which usually raise questions and problems for beginners. My method will be the same as in my *Trilogy*: to anticipate and explain such problems. Those of you who think that they have solved them before should be patient in relation to others, who still need all my explanation directed to beginners. Especially so as I know that the great majority of prospective students of meditation belong just to the beginner class.

As mentioned in a former chapter, the main and basic difficulties are very similar to those, which the student of concentration encounters, and these are:

HARDSHIP IN UNSWERVINGLY RETAINING ONE'S ATTENTION ON THE THEME OF MEDITATION, AND DIFFICULTIES IN FIGHTING THE ONSLAUGHT OF FOREIGN THOUGHTS WHICH, INSTEAD OF ALLOWING MEDITATION TO BE A HARMONIOUS LINE, EXTENDING ITSELF IN THE DIRECTION OF THE CHOSEN OBJECT, DISRUPT CONCENTRATION AND MAKE IT RATHER LIKE A RISING AND FALLING CURVE. THIS SAPS THE FORCES OF THE ASPIRANT, SPOILS HIS EFFORTS AND ROBS HIM OF TIME, ALL OF WHICH USUALLY BRINGS DISAPPOINTMENT AND FINALLY— FRUSTRATION.

That is why there are so few people who are successful in meditation. Here, of course, I am not referring to those who only imagine that they 'meditate', when, in reality, they are merely floating on the lazy waves of their own mentality, which is only too happy to deceive them in such a treacherous way. Often such misguided people will not even believe when told the truth, still imagining that they are performing meditation, about which they actually know nothing.

I do not wish to try to convince them. In spiritual matters there is no such thing as 'mental conviction': ONE EITHER KNOWS, OR DOES NOT KNOW. It is INTUITION which tells you that this Path is true. And *Intuition* does not come from just anywhere, or without precedent. If you have it, it is the result of your former efforts, about which your mind, in this present incarnation, cannot know anything, for it was utterly destroyed during your '*Second Death*', and only the previously earned *abilities* were transferred into the next manifestation in matter.

When you sit and start to direct your mind according to your chosen aim, you may well feel that, after a very short period—which may last from a few seconds to a minute of so—you lose the power to continue in an uninterrupted awareness of your theme. OTHER THOUGHTS COME TO OCCUPY YOUR MIND, LEAVING NO ROOM FOR MEDITATION. This is an axiom, and you may check it for yourself. Does this mean that you have to yield and resign? Never! Know that everyone, Spiritual Masters included, had exactly the same problems at certain periods of their lives, and they overcame them, rising as victors from their battle against the mind's tyranny and despotic behaviour.

Of course, after studying former chapters and knowing something about clichés, you may tell me that evidently different clichés came to you and took the place of what you planned to do. Well, that is so, but I am seeking to explain to you the cause of this regrettable happening, for without this KNOWLEDGE it is unlikely that a man will overcome this primordial obstacle.

To start with, I will give you two examples, letting you draw your own conclusions and then, will add my own explanation.

In olden times there was a king in India, who was interested in Yoga and honoured the wise men, who often visited his court, knowing that the good king would support them and listen to their teachings. On day, an old sage gave a long discourse before the king and his ministers, about the cardinal factor in Yoga, which is domination of one's thinking principle, or the ability of concentration of the mind. He explained, that most of the 'miracles' performed by certain yogis were based on just such a perfected power of concentration, that is, unswerving attention on a chosen object.

One of the younger ministers disagreed with the old yogi, and told him that he did not believe that the human mind could ever, be ruled and directed as a ship is by its helm. 'I do not think that even the greatest of yogis can so concentrate his attention, that he will not be distracted by any other thoughts or images,' said the sceptically minded man.

The king was evidently displeased and his eyes looked grim. After a moment of reflection he said: 'Bring the executioner here along with his sword and block for decapitating, and also fill one of the large golden bowls full of water.' When the orders had been fulfilled, the king turned to the doubting minister and said to him: 'Your opinion shows that you are a fool, and have only misused my confidence when serving me. The penalty for it is death, and that is why the executioner is waiting. But I will give you one chance to save your life. Take this dish full of water in your hands, and keep looking at it while you walk briskly around my palace and gardens, finally returning here to the same place. Seven guards will accompany you and if they see that even one drop of water is spilled, you will immediately go to the block.'

The luckless minister became pale, but there was no choice. He took the vessel full of water and started on his way. When, after half an hour, he returned exhausted, the guards confirmed that not one drop had been spilt.

'You are free,' said the king, 'but under the condition that you tell me what you saw during your march.' 'Oh! My sovereign,' said the minister, 'I neither saw nor heard anything, because I was so anxiously watching the water in the dish, in order not to let even a drop fall.'

The wise king's face became happy. 'You see, my son,' he told the man, 'concentration is perfectly possible, and you *can exclude all thoughts from your mind*, when you have a genuine desire to do so. When your life was at stake, you used all your powers so as not to be distracted, and thus escape the sword.'

Now, here is another example, of more recent origin. Furthermore, you might have had similar experiences during your own lifetime. I have often sat in my study, listening to favourite music on my record-player. On one occasion I recall that I had to read a very important section of a recently ordered book, which lay on the table before me. So opening it and finding the required reference, I started to read through it.

After a while, someone entered the room and told me that the record had stopped, and asked if I wanted to continue listening to the opera which had been playing for the last half hour. 'Thank you,' I answered. 'those records can be played again, as I was so busy reading I *don't remember hearing a thing.*'

There is nothing extraordinary in this story, as it has happened many times in my life, not only with records, but even when people present in the same room have been talking among themselves. At such times I was mentally merged in another way, and I believe that you too must also have had certain experiences of a similar kind. It doesn't matter for how long a time you happen to exclude your senses from your awareness, the fact alone remains and speaks for itself. There is SOMETHING in us which *can switch off the senses,* despite the fact that actually they are still physically influenced by outer things such as vision, and sound waves, as you may clearly perceive from the simple examples just quoted. So nobody can tell us, *that such concentration is not possible!* IT IS, and there can be no doubt, or opposition to this practically proved idea.

But these examples are not all, for we need to draw scientific and logical conclusions from them, which we will be able to use during our own study of meditation.

You see, perfect concentration IS POSSIBLE, but under one basic condition: that we are *interested in only one object of attention, which by far surpasses all curiosity and other interests in our mind.* This is the right and most useful conclusion.

The POWER which allows us to reach one-pointedness in our mind is called: ATTENTION, OR INTEREST IN A PARTICULAR SUBJECT.

Our difficulties in concentration and meditation come from the same unique source. When sitting at our exercises, we are still not free from our *mental curiosity and other interests as to what is happening and what might happen,* even if we swore to ourselves, that we will concentrate, or meditate ONLY ON A CHOSEN THEME. In practice, this 'oath' seems to be insufficient unless it is based on the knowledge of the deciding role of the

power of attention in concentration. One simply has to teach
oneself to be interested solely in the subject of one's concentration, at the same time creating in oneself an *absolute lack of
interest* in anything else. How can this be done? This technique
is like auto-suggestion. The mind is taught to believe in the fact
of non-interest in anything else. There is nothing wrong in such
a method, for it only eradicates the old, very old, mental habit
of dissipating attention, and therefore losing the power of concentration, the only one which is able to lead the student to a
successful conclusion to his work, be it concentration or meditation. Little wonder that we have to use counter-suggestion in
order to exterminate the old and wrong attitude of our mind.

Now, when I look back into the past and compare the difficulties I had to face under the same circumstances as those of a
beginner, with the present use of the same mind, the truth of
the overwhelming role of the law of 'attention' and 'interest'
becomes still more resplendent. How easy things are now, which
before (see my *In Days of Great Peace*, Chapter IX, 'My Path
to Maharshi'), that is, some eighteen years ago, presented apparently unconquerable obstacles.

What was possible for one human being, may be possible for
another. So let this statement assist you in your own efforts.

To summarize, the *first cardinal difficulty*, unification of your
interest and attention with the aim of your meditation has now
been explained, and you KNOW what you have to do, when you
start your first exercise with elementary meditation. Therefore,
I will not repeat this law any more. But in any case, start to use
it immediately after the *first obstacle* faces you, so that the
elementary exercises will be performed as required. If they are
NOT, the following, more complicated and serious ones *will not
be feasible*, and the end result will be the creation of confusion
and disappointment.

The *second difficulty* will arise from another habit of the
human mind—ITS RESTLESSNESS, EXPRESSED IN THE ATTITUDE
OF CONSTANT EXPECTANCY. And what is it? To a certain degree
this enemy is related to the vice of CURIOSITY, as described earlier
in this chapter. In brief, we are usually EXPECTING something
in time and space. This law will not apply to everyone, because
there are some disillusioned and frustrated people, who have no
definite or even indefinite expectation of anything that may

happen to them. Fortunately, this extremely passive part of humanity is not too numerous, and to it belong mostly very old, or sick persons, who, in any case, have no chance or desire to try any psychological or occult studies. Therefore, let us leave them alone, and return to the living.

If we look deeply into that obstacle of the attitude of constant EXPECTANCY, not controlled or justified by any serious movements in our conciousness, we may discover something like a paradox.

The ROOTS OF EXPECTANCY lie in one of the chief virtues of every advanced human being, which is—HOPE! But our ability to discriminate must immediately put things into their true perspective. *Hope* is a *true cliché*, and association with it can only enhance and stimulate our progress and work. Uncontrolled mental expectancy is a *perverted cliché of Hope*, something like a golden sovereign, changed into farthings.

Do not forget, that there are TRUE, PRIMARY CLICHÉS, as well as distorted and perverted ones, which are like a caricature of the former. Involuntarily, we come to the great problem of GOOD and EVIL. Remember how, in the scriptures, the Lord of Evil, or the Devil, as some like to call him, is described as the FATHER OF LIES. According to what we know about the great Law of Clichés, we may also be able to use it successfully in this case.

The ARCHETYPE, the Perfect Cliché of the Universe, as it was conceived in the beginning of Time, has its counterpart, the disfigured and debased cliché of a deformed reflection in matter. This also explains the old axiom of Spiritual Masters of all periods, that Matter is Maya, or illusion, linked with Evil, while Spirit, being free and independent of that Maya, is eternally good and is the only true aim of Attainment. Something like two sides of the same coin, with the difference that the right side is real and the left one is illusion. I think that the true face of the *second enemy* has been sufficiently revealed to start seeking a remedy against it.

Once again it will be similar to the weapon we recommended against *curiosity of the mind*, which produces lack of attention towards the chosen subject. REALIZE, THAT THERE IS NOTHING TO EXPECT DURING THE TIME YOU DEDICATE TO YOUR EXERCISES IN MEDITATION. This must be firmly embedded in your mind, by same *process of auto-suggestion*. Here the great words of

Hahnemann (the founder of Homoeopathy): 'SIMILIA SIMILIBUS CURANTUR' (like cures like, that is, an ailment can be cured by similar means), have their full application. When a wedge you are using becomes caught in a thick piece of timber, or tree-trunk, you take another wedge to help in freeing the first one. Simple but effective.

I have known men, who, for many years, delighted in smoking, until they realized that this habit might well ruin their health and create an incurable disease. Hence they started to convince themselves, that tobacco is an abject thing, unclean and tarry, and that every inhalation of its smoke brings harm to their lungs and digestive system. As a result, they succeeded in overcoming smoking and never returned to it.

Suggestion worked properly in them.

Also, when I look back from the perspective of many years, as I did with the overcoming of the *curiosity of the mind*, it seems to me that now, in the few moments preceding the start of meditation, the attitude of expectancy is removed by a simple act of my will. Perhaps this is so, but I was able to use will-power only after practising the means, which have been recommended in this book. When the ability to deal with both of these obstacles (by the means explained previously) is born in man, he does not need to return to his 'infantile' tricks to overcome the difficulties every time he starts to meditate. Just as, when reading these words, we do not do primary school exercises with the alphabet before looking at every letter.

To resume:

(a) I AM NOT INTERESTED IN ANYTHING ELSE DURING MY MEDITATION.

(b) NOTHING WILL HAPPEN DURING MY MEDITATION.

These two formulas give the weapon against the two most embarrassing difficulties, which attack beginners in meditation.

* * *

When the student has a good grasp of the theoretical part of his defence against unwanted intruding thoughts, he can, for certain purposes, reduce these two formulas to ONLY ONE, and it will repel both kinds of difficulties: that of CURIOSITY of his mind, and also the spirit of EXPECTANCY.

(c) In fact, I have used this shortened formula (or, as some might prefer to call it, a kind of invisible, 'magic sword', or even exorcism)—'NOT INTERESTED!' with full success.

The thing is that the energy which intrudes into your mind without permission, or against your will is *limited*, that is, it can be both, strengthened and weakened, depending upon your behaviour and degree of knowledge. In this book you are told *everything* you should and must know, so the moment of ignorance is thereby annihilated. You cannot say that you do not know how to defend yourself! You may not wish to, but that is another matter. *Nobody can help one who does not wish to help himself.*

The Master Maharshi, when dealing with the same subject of mental obstacles to meditation, or *Self-Inquiry*, also called the VICHARA (Who am I?) gave us a simile: 'Imagine that you are besieging a fortress in order to conquer it. This fortress is your disobedient mind. Its defenders and dwellers, which are *thoughts*, try to escape from it. As they appear outside the fortress, slaughter them one after another with the *Vichara*. If you will kill every one of them the fortress will finally be yours, as there will be no defenders left in it.'

The Master was speaking about the weapon of *Self-Realization*, which is just the *Self-Inquiry*. In our case we can substitute it by the formula— 'NOT INTERESTED!' and obtain the desired results, the cessation of the mind's interference in our meditation.

If it would be possible to picture this method graphically it would appear as if you were turning your back on every thought, not wishing to have anything in common with it. In us lies the mysterious power, which is the spark of LIFE, the only true POWER which exists. It is our *consciousness*, our *attention*. That is why all those thoughts, clichés and even feelings try so desperately to suck from you this power, which is life-giving for them. If you refuse, they will be weakened and disappear; but if you allow them a place in your consciousness, that is, if you WILL OCCUPY YOURSELF WITH THEM, they will enslave you pitilessly and your dreams of becoming a strong independent and wise being, will be temporarily strangled.

Now you may understand, why the 'Voice of the Silence' tells you to 'slay the Slayer', which is your mind, and why the Master Maharshi similarly advises us *to kill the defenders of the mind's fortress.* This battle will be *fatal* for one of the fighting powers. So let it be that way *for the enemy, not for you!*

How many treacherous tricks this enemy will use! And all in order to be allowed to suck your blood, as vampires do, to weaken you and to gain a hold over you. Very pious thoughts, bright conceptions, inspiring ideas, everything will knock at the gate of your consciousness, asking for admission. And all of them will finally be useless in their apparent inspiration, but once admitted, they turn from 'angel-like' to blood-thirsty larvae which have no pity nor sympathy for the fool, who believed them and allowed them to spoil the temple of his supreme good and treasure—his *pure awareness.*

Every 'justification', which may appear in your mind during the 'battle' will be a spy, sent by the enemy in order to split your defences. You will have to listen to these *magnificent ideas, interesting thoughts, inspiring* (as they seem to be) *conceptions* almost all of your time, because the enemy wants you to surrender to him, even this meagre half an hour, which you want to dedicate to meditation! Should you have any consideration for such a voracious monster? The decision belongs to you, and with it—your destiny: to live according to your ideal, or to be cast on to the mind's waves like a boat without a helm.

In this chapter you found the ultimate *Initiation* into the art of meditation. Everything has been mentioned and explained, so that no questions, or doubts should arise in you. If they do, know that they do not come from a friend, and treat them accordingly. Then you will win.

CHAPTER XII

Introductory Exercises – Series I

Now that you know the theoretical part of this work, we can pass on to the first practical exercises.

Exercise A : Having arranged the time and taken up the position as recommended in the First Part of this book, while seated beside a table, you perform a few pranayamas (see *Concentration* Chapter XV) and close your eyes. Try to remember all the objects surrounding you, which you still have in your memory. You will be astonished at how few they are, in comparison with their real numbers.

Here is an important piece of advice. At first you should imagine yourself sitting, as you were in the beginning, seeing ONLY THAT WHICH YOU CAN SEE BEFORE YOU WITHOUT TURNING YOUR HEAD.

In other words, try to look almost exclusively ahead of you. You may see the table, then a picture on the wall opposite it, with perhaps, one or two books resting on the table, and so on. You should try to imagine them to be as real as possible, just as they actually are, when you look at them with open eyes.

When you consider that this is all that you can 'see' in your mind in this direction, TURN YOUR HEAD TO THE RIGHT IN YOUR IMAGINATION, AND PERCEIVE OTHER OBJECTS, VISIBLE FROM THIS NEW POSITION.

After this, turn about 90 degrees in the same direction, and AGAIN STUDY THE SCENE BEFORE YOU. In this way you will already have turned about 270 degrees.

For the last time, again turn and 'see' what you can. This concludes the first part of this initial exercise.

You thus turned *four* times in your mind, in order to 'see' the objects surrounding you on all sides. How long should you allow yourself to remain in each of the four positions? Do not be too quick in the beginning, but rather try to remember as many objects as you can, and visualize them exactly with sharp definition and not as if in a mist. Your former study of concentration should let you do this without much strain. It is an easy and interesting introduction to *elementary meditation*. You cannot start from advanced degrees, for they will be unsuccessful and inexact.

Now, open your eyes and look slowly and quietly around you, checking as to how many objects you missed or placed in the wrong position in your mind's eye. Do NOT VERBALIZE, but operate exclusively with your sight. Do not say mentally: 'Now I see that wall, which is yellow in colour, the picture on it representing a village street, while on the table before me there is the book *Concentration* in its pale-blue jacket, and so on.' IT IS WRONG. You must have only mental pictures, nothing more. You will still have a lot of trouble with the extermination of that *harmful habit of verbalization*, when you pass on to more complicated exercises.

Exercise B: Now do the same as you tried to do with your eyes closed in Exercise A, in the same FOUR STAGES, each of 90 degrees, but this time looking around you. Try to memorize thoroughly as many details as you can in your field of vision. Actually, you should memorize ALL of them, therefore it is recommended to start in a room where there are not too many objects.

Devote about two minutes to each 90 degree turn. If you feel this is too short, prolong it a little and if you think it is too much, shorten.

DO NOT FORGET TO NOTE ON THE MARGINS OF THIS BOOK THE TIME WHEN YOU STARTED AN EXERCISE AND WHEN YOU FINISHED IT AND WERE READY FOR THE NEXT ONE.

The pictures in your mind must be clear and exact. This is the purpose of the present group of exercises.

After finishing your observation, again close your eyes and repeat Exercise A, but, of course, more perfectly now, as you are better prepared for its technicalities. IMPORTANT NOTE: do ONLY WHAT IS REQUIRED, during every exercise: no other thoughts should dare to enter your mind. If you feel that they are closing your consciousness and are ready to occupy it, strike at them with your formulas from Chapter XI. From the practice of concentration you must already have the feeling of when thoughts and clichés are approaching, so do not allow them to take up residence in your mind. Chase them away pitilessly, for they will try to destroy your efforts and turn you to nothingness!

At first, these two exercises A and B should be done together, in sequence as indicated. Well-trained students who profited much from the study of the book *Concentration* will not need to spend long on Exercise A, giving more attention to B, or treating both equally. They will forget little from A, and will re-create pictures exactly without difficulty.

Exercise C: Repeat everything as in A and B, but in another room, where there are more objects. When I was concluding this series for myself, the exercises were done in a little church, during the hours when no services were in progress. This meant that there were many things to remember and re-create in one's mind, but I do not recommend such attempts before you are well established with exercises in your own rooms. The important point in the three exercises of the *First Series*, A, B and C, is to repeat in your mind, when the eyes are closed, everything you saw with them open, that is, when observing the objects which are to be recalled. This will include, foremostly, the *mental* turning of your head, when you face the 90 degree turns. In the beginning some people have found it easier to do by *physical turns* of the head and body, exactly as was done in the preparation, but, of course, with eyes closed. If you feel it may facilitate your work, do the same for a certain time, but later, when you are already able to perform the whole of Series I faultlessly, stop it and do the exercise again, with ONLY IMAGINARY turns. This first series still belongs to the so-called 'stationary' exercises, that is, without any actual change of position of your body, such as walking, but merely *sitting* or *standing*. After having finished with exercises A to C in a seated position, you MUST PERFORM THEM STANDING. This will also fit in better with the present period of your work, when you will actually turn your body and head with eyes closed.

UNDER NO CIRCUMSTANCES OPEN YOUR EYES BEFORE THE EXERCISE HAS BEEN FINISHED. If you feel your memory has become defective in certain moments and, for example, in performing the last turn (270 degrees), you see that you cannot re-create everything well from this position, it would be better to finish with a 'misty' visualization and later start the whole exercise again. But DO NOT OPEN your eyes even for a moment in order to see what actually lies before you. This would bring a lot of harm and only form a habit to repeat this erroneous method again and again. The exercise, when spoiled by such behaviour, will be valueless and your will-power will be additionally weakened. In brief, a full-scale defeat! This advice is being given from long practice and experience in the matter, so there is no way of changing things, especially for a beginner. To end this Series, I would like to add, that in general, it should present no great difficulty, and normally be performed in about three weeks, if the exercises are done daily and exactly as prescribed. The opposite may happen only if the student neglects the instructions in the foregoing chapters, especially if he has omitted passing through at least three series of exercises from *Concentration* (Part III), for then he is 'green' and cannot expect to be successful, just as an elementary school pupil cannot leap to matriculation without passing through the intermediary studies. One of the reasons why there are so few really successful occultists and students of meditation is, that the majority of prospective 'adepts' are not earnest enough, and believe that they are able to omit stages in their occult education, which they do not like, or consider to be 'tedious'. But you should realize that the results will be exactly similar to those which you may expect if you treat your 'official' studies in the same manner. It simply means that you will never get your degrees, and so on.

Now a few questions will be answered. I am taking them from the innumerable letters I have received during the past ten years from my readers, who tried to practise what is given in the three books, which form my *Trilogy*.

(1) *How often* should exercises be performed?

As often, as you can afford the time, but once a day is the minimum otherwise you will advance too slowly, and the period between exercises will be too long, so that what you gained today may be, in say, three days of inactivity, dissipated and half-forgotten.

(2) What if I *cannot manage to arrange the necessary conditions* for exercises (lack of suitable rooms, circumstances, and so on)?

As no one else is able to arrange such things for you, you may simply abandon the studies, as perhaps they do not fit in with your Karma.

(3) What if *my mind is still disobedient* and prevents me from a clear performance?

This means that it is still unripe and you have not followed my advice, first to establish firm ground for the study of meditation, by the study of concentration. In such a case you had better turn back to it. No one can acquire the basic ability of ruling the mind for your benefit, just as no one can eat your lunch instead of you yourself, so that you will be nourished by it.

(4) *Can I ask for help and from whom?*

Yes, you can. The best known means would be on a Theurgic way, that is, praying to the Lord, asking for His blessing on your efforts. In the book *Theurgy* you will find many suitable formulae and prayers. For the Lord responds when approached meekly and with full sincerity of heart.

(5) Can you advise any *special worship* suitable for acquiring domination of mind and overcoming its resistance?

There is a very effective one, but it needs a lot of insight and the basic element of *Faith* in the Omnipotent Supreme Power. I surrendered my mind to Him and asked Him to grant me a spark of His infinite Wisdom. 'O Lord, *take away this my mortal, imperfect mind, and be gracious enough to give me even the smallest ray of Thy Light.*'

If performed properly, the results may be close to a personal, but undisputed 'miracle'. In brief—IT WORKS!

(6) Should I continue with exercises when I am *excessively tired*?

I have already mentioned, that such a study must not be started without a comparatively well-balanced physical body. Too much passivity due to weak health, or old age will prevent achievement in this way, which requires considerable effort. If your circumstances are such, why not turn to another Path, which is no less effective, but not so complicated, offering a better outlook for immediate assistance 'from Above'? By this I mean Theurgy, the Path of Worship.

(7) *Should I tell my family*, and so on, about my endeavours with meditation?

Only if you are one hundred percent sure of their sympathetic understanding. I know of quite a number of cases where the efforts of a talkative aspirant were destroyed by stiff resistance from those around him. On the other hand, I also know of many examples where husband and wife, who were both interested in occultism and spirituality, have sincerely tried to assist one another. It is up to you to know just what applies to you personally. Otherwise, because such a study is a very intimate undertaking, it should be kept from the curiosity of this cruel world.

(8) Are there any *special rules regarding food*, and so on, during these studies?

Food should keep your body healthy, and obedient to your spirit. In general, a vegetarian diet is best, if reasonably chosen and not abused. It keeps the body more alert, active and pure. But exaggerated notions such as avoiding the most natural and strength-giving foods like milk, honey, eggs, beans, certain fruits, and so on are unreasonable and suitable only for rare cases, where people live like true hermits, without having any special physical or mental work, or lecturing, and so on. But drugs, narcotics and alcohol are definitely harmful for the nerves and brain, which play such an important role in the study of meditation. And always remember: 'The Sabbath was made for man, not man for the Sabbath.' Excess in anything is a hindrance.

(9) What *is the best time* for exercises?

It is accepted that early morning and evening are the most suitable from the point of view of natural influences, connected with day and night. But, if you can find a peaceful hour apart from these times, use it without a second thought. It will do just as well as any other.

(10) What about *sexual relations*?

If they do not interfere with your time-table or weaken you in any way the problem remains your own. Advanced degrees of meditation usually set men free from all their physical habits, sexual included. It is useless to anticipate, or forecast what comes only as a result of one's real inner progress. Such anticipation is also a weapon of the enemy—mind, which tries to occupy you with every problem, except that of its control and final submission. Do not forget this.

(11) *Are there any organizations*, which might be able to facilitate my advancement? There are so *many advertisements* about this in today's press.

All such organizations where you are supposed to get 'initiation', and so on, for fixed member's (or otherwise concealed) fees can, and do facilitate only the material well-being of their leaders, giving them money, luxurious homes and undue admiration from gullible people, who, unfortunately, still form the overwhelming majority of men and women of this century.

No wisdom ever comes from advertisements or payment of fees. Even the curiosity, excited by certain pseudo-occult organizations, is never satisfied in the end. No superman has ever yet been created by the people who claim to do so. All the 'awakening of Kundalini' and other nonsense, for average men, only leads to neurosis (in the best possible case), or to moral and physical ruin, if such an 'adept' has really been stubborn and unwise enough to perform the risky (and unnecessary) practices. We can find some of these supposed 'supermen' in mental hospitals, usually among the incurable patients.

(12) Can meditation be *used for magic practices*?

True magic is also a definite science, a very special one requiring a special type of man. Certain kinds of meditation are basic for the preparatory work of an acting magician. More about this will be found in my *Tarot*, but personally, I do not think that, in this epoch, magic has any great meaning or use for humanity, when *Theurgy* is sure and not dangerous.

(13) What about *Hermetic Philosophy*, including the Tarot?

If followed strictly in accordance with the true Tradition (which is not easy to distinguish among the many existing, incompetent and simply useless books) and under the tuition of an exponent, who is an experienced occultist, it may suit certain intellectual mentalities, who otherwise would not be convinced about overcoming the gross materialism of this era. Meditation is widely used in the *Tarot*. Like magic, the Tarot's practical philosophy is designed for a definite type of man, who is rare enough in our day. It calls for a strong, well-disciplined mind and intuitive *perception regarding the right and left paths of development*, if it is not to lead to deviations.

(14) Will meditation be useful *for yogic study*?

If you mean the true Yogas, and there are several, the answer will be in the affirmative. Jnana, Bhakti and Raja Yogas are not separable from certain methods of meditation. Actually, the present-day interest in meditation was created half a century ago just by yogic teachings, which were then penetrating the West from the Eastern countries, especially India. But the physical preparation called 'Hatha Yoga' has little in common with meditation. It is very useful for forming a healthy and well-controlled body, which may later fit well into the other serious yogas just mentioned. But used as an independent system, Hatha Yoga is little better than any other reputable system of gymnastics like the Swedish, and so on.

(15) What do you think about *pranayama*?

It is of great assistance in meditation, especially in the beginning. If rightly performed, it will many times over repay the effort and time devoted to it. But it is only a means, not an aim in itself.

(16) Is there something useful in *Spiritism* (wrongly called 'spiritualism' by ignorant followers)?

Nothing at all, except harm for both body and mind. Ninety percent of these experiments are frauds and the remaining ten percent belong to lower astral manisfestation, useless and sometimes dangerous for the sanity of the participants. No good power would be attracted by groups of haphazardly collected people, devoured by the vice of curiosity and basically ignorant of what they are doing. Moreover, spiritism is liable to bring some men to their downfall.

Nothing of value was ever gained from spiritist seances, and many intelligent people, who have investigated the 'revelations' allegedly given by the 'spirits', have found that all of the answers were in one or another way already hidden in their own minds. In other words, there was nothing new. Moreover, the innumerable books and reports written about spiritist activity are so contradictory, that to this day nobody has ever been able to concoct any definite doctrine about the 'conditions after death' and similar matters. Such reports simply differ according to the minds of the questioners and the supposed 'spirits'. It is a pity that such time and effort could not be used elsewhere with more profit.

(17) Do the so-called 'Secret Societies' really exist?

If they are really secret, you cannot know anything about them. Even if you and I are members of them we will never divulge it. Such organizations do not advertise themselves or try to augment their numbers of fee-paying members, accepting them without any dicrimination or insight.

Personally, the only thing I can say is, that proselytes are invited in a secret way, and only then, when it is known beyond any doubt, that the neophyte is ripe and suitable for the Society's purposes. How they know this fact remains their secret. The 'quasi-secret' societies are numerous, but, because it is very problematic that at the top there are any real masters, supermen, the gradation and other such things used in them are open to your own judgement. In my Tarot you will find more detailed information about such organizations, their origins and activities.

(18) In some religions I find books offering meditation on spiritual themes. Have they something in common with the present work?

Yes, they have! In Part III, which deals with advanced meditation you will find excerpts from certain religious books, Christian, as well as non-Christian. The art of meditation was not invented yesterday, it is a very ancient form of supreme spiritual effort in man, on his way towards the Highest. These books are far from being secret ones. Who searches will find them.

CHAPTER XIII

Introductory Exercises — Series II

AFTER you have satisfactorily finished Series I, you can pass on to the next exercises, involving *movement*.

Exercise D: For this you need to choose a day when there are clouds moving reasonably fast in the sky, so that you can easily follow them with your sight and without tension.

Of course, find some quiet place, in a park, or on the seashore, and so on, from which you can observe the sky without being disturbed by your surroundings. With a little goodwill you will easily arrange this.

Look at your watch and decide the time you are ready to devote to this exercise. At an appropriate moment start to observe the scudding clouds in that part of the sky directly in front of you. Try to memorize it for, say, some five minutes. This should be ample for the purpose. Then close your eyes and visualize the movement, as observed, in your imagination, trying to 'see' it with the utmost clarity and sharply defined edges of the clouds, just as you saw them before.

Do not have any thoughts apart from silently following the imaginary movement of the clouds before your mind's sight.

For the first time it will be done for five minutes. But, an important warning: I mean FIVE MINUTES OF REAL EXERCISE, that is, the picture in your mind must be uninterrupted and no other thoughts should dare to enter your mind. This condition actually means that you will use only ONE faculty of your imagination, that of SIGHT, and no words should accompany the visualization of the clouds.

If you fail to maintain a clear-cut visualization on say, the third minute, return and start again, and keep doing this until FIVE MINUTES are performed as required. Do not worry about these unavoidable 'relapses'. Every beginner has had to pass through them, the writer included, although many years ago in his case.

Technically speaking, you may take only one cloud and follow it slowly, for this will assist you in having a clear-cut image of it. There is no need to have the whole sky in your memory. It would be impossible for a beginner and even unnecessary for an advanced student. If you would like to analyse the gist of this exercise, you will find that the fulcrum of it is the RETAIN-ING OF YOUR UNSWERVING ATTENTION ON A MOVING SCENE. When you reach true meditation, this ability will be a 'sine qua non' for your performance. But, being of a practical turn of mind, we have to do everything gradually, one step after another, thereby ensuring success. This exercise must be done until you feel that you are able to keep following the mental image of the cloud for at least FIVE minutes, without any great stress, or failure. Then we will proceed.

Exercise E: Go back into your room as before, stand in the middle of it and look around, memorizing everything as you did in the exercises of the First Series. Now open the door and go into the next room or passage, which leads outside to your garden, or the street. Walk to the gate, looking both right and left with full concentration, in order to memorize everything around you. Do not take a long walk in the beginning. A few yards well done will be much better than a quarter of a mile with misty and inexact visualization. Always remember this.

When you think you are ready for the next phase of the exercise, return into the room from which you started and close your eyes, mentally trying to perform the same short journey, just as in the previous exercise. In order to 'see' better, you may mentally 'turn your head' on both sides as you proceed, and, without words, observe the picture you have just memorized.

Repeat this until you feel that it is going well and that the image of what you saw when walking with open eyes is close to that in your mind. This exercise must be performed in a stand-ing position, do not sit at all.

Develop the useful habit of noting every day what has been done, in a special notebook. Write date, day, length of exercise and number of 'repeats', when you were compelled to start again and again, because of faulty work. This book will be the mirror of your development, and under no circumstances treat it lightly. What is the difference between 'official' schooling as in colleges, universities, and so on, and the methods of occult training, if we may so call the manuals of concentration, meditation, and prayer? It is a very noticeable one. In the FIRST instance you are loading your mind with many facts, theories and technical matters, and acquiring certain abilities of the mind as an additional benefit. There is no question, that after passing through tertiary education one is more mentally developed (some call it more intelligent) than previously. But on *our* way, all weight is placed on development of ABILITY, and not only of mind, but equally of the supermental realm, inaccessible without this special training, no matter how many 'degrees' you may possess.

Similarly, a man working physically will probably strengthen his muscular power by comparison with what he was before; but an athlete who performs *special* exercises and training in order to develop his physique harmoniously and far beyond the powers of an ordinary man, will undoubtedly be much more powerful and 'record-breaking' minded than, say, a wharf labourer, occasionally handling heavy boxes.

A mathematician, for example, must necessarily possess some power of concentration gained during his studies and subsequent work, but not to the same degree and many sidedness, as one, who has done special study leading to domination of his mind by means of a manual of concentration.

Exercise F: After a successful performance of Exercise E, we have to pass on to the further development of this Series.

Your objective will now be a longer journey, the best being the one you probably do often, if not every day, by train, tram, or some other means of communication, EXCEPT FOR DRIVING A CAR PERSONALLY. This is because in that case you MUST be, at least, partially concentrating on your activities of driving, and then the attention is compulsorily divided, as you will be unable to register exactly in your mind the landscape you are passing on both sides of the road.

As you can see, such a position is against the basic rule of concentration and meditation, so it is unacceptable. If, despite this advice, you try it, you may neglect your duty as a driver and become involved in an accident.

Take a position close to a window in your compartment, and so on, and carefully observe what you see (from one side first). Next day, travel with eyes closed and instead of looking, build an image of the environment you passed through yesterday. It is possible that you will need several 'sittings' before your mental picture will satisfy you. But this is only natural and no cause for worry.

The spirit of haste and anxiety must be banished during your present study. Look at the world around you: millions are dedicating their lives exclusively to physical, materialistic achievements, which they will never be able to take with them on their further travels, beyond their graves. And still, some day they too will come to the 'Father's House', a shorter way to which is now before you. This understanding may ease your nervous tension, which often attacks us at the beginning of the Path.

Exercise G: This is the last of the present Series of elementary and preparatory exercises, which may apparently have little in common with the generally accepted concept of meditation. But this is not so, and the training which brings forth their exact performance will decide about further, more complicated developments.

This time, walk out from your home, when the streets are not too crowded, or go into a park, and in your mind, start to register everything around you as you pass by. Of course, disregard any people you may encounter, paying attention only to objects such as trees, houses, and details like doors, windows, ornamentation, and so on. Try to see the street or road as it would be seen by an artist, desiring to make a picture of what he sees.

The length of the walk rests with you. It should not be measured in miles, but rather in hundreds of yards. You will then try to obtain an exact reproduction of the pictures seen in your mind, when you finally put an end to the walk, sit quietly somewhere and *start to project the 'film seen' in your mind's eye*.

You probably know, that difficulties of concentration and

meditation also stem partially from the fact, that these exercises directly involve mental abilities and influence the surface of the brain, changing the form and numbers of convolutions. This is a biological, a physical process, and needs certain time for it, if the aspirant has not been endowed with sufficiently refined properties of his brain. It is from this that there comes that unpleasant feeling of powerlessness, which so often overtakes the beginner: the physical counterpart of the mind (that is, the same brain) is not ready. However, do not think that the aforesaid is a proof of insufficiency of an ordinary brain, for special development is required only for special purposes.

CHAPTER XIV

Introductory Exercises — Series III

IF we drew a diagram of the process of true meditation, it would be like a *straight line* (see Fig. 6), without any deformities or digressions, tending towards the aim, which is the theme or subject of meditation. Looking at such a graphic presentation of the idea, we see that there should be no deviations, or dissipation in our inner awareness, and no other thoughts should be permitted even to make their presence felt in your proximity. After passing through the course of concentration, you have most probably developed certain ability to 'see' thoughts, and if not exactly to see, then to 'feel' them approaching and entering your consciousness. You have fought these intruders, and have finally learned how the repel and obliterate them 'automatically', that is, by not devoting any corner of your awareness to them. This led you to a 'clear and successful' performance of concentration exercises, which, in turn, gave you power over your mind.

Now, our *'straight line meditation'* is the result of the former study, just mentioned. This is a 'text-book' example, or what could be called a theoretical exposition of success. In practice it may not be so rosy. The *'line'* may curve, twist and even be broken (see Fig. 2), and the results will be accordingly. I believe that we are seeking for something better. Therefore, let us start with new techniques for that purpose.

Exercise H : Look at Fig. 1 depicting the *straight line meditation*. Imagine it to be like a rail, or track on which you may travel, without words, or any other mental activities into infinite remoteness. There is nothing around you and your attention is concentrated exclusively on that straight, nameless line, running continuously before your mental sight.

At first, do this with eyes closed, as it will be easier for many students. Some successful aspirants say, that they first imagined the LINE as if starting from the middle point between their eyes, just at the base of the nose. I have nothing against it, although I was quite happy without this kind of visualization.

Now, silently TRAVEL ALONG THE LINE, not too fast, so that at all times you are aware of your mental movement. Do not allow any other imaginary pictures or impressions to arise in your mind, for this will compel you to stop the whole exercise and to start again. THE RULE THROUGHOUT THIS COURSE is, that *when you permit an interruption in meditation or an exercise, stop it and begin again, counting the time anew from this point.*

THIS RULE MUST BE MOST STRICTLY ADHERED TO, or your study will fail.

While typing this for you, I often stop and do the recommended exercise for a short time, in order not to omit anything useful which can be said about it. There was a time when I started these exercises with a certain uneasiness, as some unpleasant, but nevertheless necessary work. But it all passed away, and to the extent that as the mind became more and more obedient exercises began to be a pleasure, giving feelings of peace and strength, which no other experiences could ever bring. So it should be with you, because we are all human beings, and our essential nature is similar.

So now, I allowed myself to travel with you on that 'straight line' for a couple of minutes. It was wonderful. I wish it to be so for you.

The target of this simple little meditation will be the same FIVE minutes of perfect performance. All intermediary stages must be recorded in your notebook: the date, time, and length of exercises (the time reached of uninterruptedly following the line). The attempts ending with lesser results made during a session should not be recorded. Only: *'one minute and a half reached on the line'*, and so on, each day.

Exercise J: This is like (H), but instead of the straight line, imagine a very large circle, something like a big racecourse, and follow round it several times, according to your target time for that day. WHEN FIVE MINUTES IS REACHED, RETURN TO (H) and do it with your eyes open; then to (J) in a similar way.

Repeat both until you are satisfied with their performance. Apart from a *clean* performance, which does not allow any mental intrusion, one of the unmistakable signs of success and progress will be, the feeling of deep satisfaction and power growing in you. And you will need a lot of that power in your further study !

CHAPTER XV

Elementary Meditation — Series IV

Now we have a solid grounding in the theory of meditation behind us, plus introductory exercises. If they have been successfully performed, the time has come to attack the first degrees of meditation proper, although naturally, of an elementary nature.

A good definition of meditation will be useful for us at this stage: MEDITATION IS A PURPOSEFULLY DIRECTED AND HARMONIOUS APPLICATION OF OUR MIND.

In this world, dominated as it is by mind, we must start with something accessible to our present master—the mind, whom we finally hope to reduce to its proper role, AS THAT OF MAN'S SERVANT, BUT NOT HIS LORD.

We still have to wait for that blessed moment, when the roles of man and his mind will be duly reversed. A beginning has been made with *concentration*, but it was only a technical development of a certain form of domination of our thinking tool. It was a necessary and useful introduction to meditation, based on the control of ALL functions in our *consciousness*.

I will arrange the material in the chapters ahead, so that FIRST a mental theme of meditation will be given, and then this will be developed into a stream of controlled thoughts, which is just the first degree of meditation.

The conception of the role and importance of that THEME should be explained with all details and full clarity. A simile will help us in this matter. Imagine a vast territory before you, covered with fields, forests, scrub, hills and lakes. At a certain point, *which can be in its imaginary middle*, there is a large *intersection* from which highways go in several directions, thus creating a *star-like pattern*. You are on this intersection and you call it—the MEDITATION'S THEME. From it you can use any adjacent road you wish. The ends of these highways are not perceivable because of their length and the environment, which limits the perspective, and the visible horizon. In other words, when starting to meditate one cannot say where one will finish. Everything depends upon the time and effort the student devotes to his work. As is the case with the intersection, you may develop the theme of meditation in any direction, so that you can travel from the central crossing along any of the connecting roads. You have probably already guessed what my role is as your instructor in meditation, and how I can help you. I will explain certain highways of thought, starting with the *theme*, and giving you examples of meditation techniques and advice on how to use these roads.

But can I travel along them instead of you, so that you will reach the desired aim? Your common sense will say—NO! The means of transport, maps of the country, information about events likely to occur during your '*journey*', all of these can and will be delivered to you, during this course. However, the *travelling itself* belongs exclusively to you, and to no one else. If someone tells you otherwise and promises to take over all your work for you, in order that you may reach achievement '*for nothing*', then he is a dangerous deceiver, wasting your time and energy, neither of which is unlimited.

Read that part of this chapter, near the beginning, starting with the words: 'The conception of the role . . .', several times, the more the better, until the idea will be completely clear to you. It is a condition for a successful performance and an understanding of all the following material.

Exercise K: The *theme*, as short as possible for a start is—'I AM'. It is your cross-road. So now, let us look on all sides for as far as we are able to '*see*'.

(1) 'I AM' means that I am conscious of my *existence, here and now*, in the form of a being we call '*human*'. It is almost a bare definition, and therefore insufficient. So, let us go further on this highway of thought. My being functions in several ways. One of them is its mental consciousness, which I use for this type of meditation. I am thinking in a certain direction connected with the problem of 'I AM'. That is my aim. My being has the power to control that process of thinking, in which a twofold activity can be distinguished. *Firstly*, when I create certain short

thoughts, which are unimportant, as they do not have any basis in fact in the life around me. I can call them my thought forms, arising from my own mind. *Secondly*, I may contact certain clichés, which have become magnetized by the effort of my awareness to meditate on the theme of 'I AM', and which have approached closer to me. I cannot express in the mind's language any formal definition of WHAT I really am, but I may KNOW and FEEL the very undoubted fact of my existence. AND I AM DOING SO NOW!

Such may be your meditation, or rather, the start of it along the *first road*, leaving from the *intersection*. You should realize, that this is only a suggestion, and remember this in future work, so that you do not slavishly follow my ways, memorizing them and then substituting them instead of your own work. In this case I have made the task easier for you, as the *First Road* in its essence can hardly be changed, because of the special character of its THEME.

So now, let us follow *other roads*.

(2) My 'I AM' is not something immovable and definite. It came from that sub-division of relative TIME, which we call 'the PAST'. What do I know about that *'past'*?

Now start to work individually, answering the question of that *'past'*, which you alone can solve. Avoid theoretical and meaningless verbalizing, which does not have any real contents, nor provide a definition for you, such as: I came from my former incarnations, or, I probably lived in another form, perhaps here, or on another planet. This will not solve anything. Seek other, deeper answers. Of course, if it happens that a direct perception of your *'past'* (that is, a true cliché of it) appears in your awareness as a definite picture or idea, but *not* any guesswork, then the presence of that cliché should be considered. But, even so, it will be of no great importance: you cannot change the past and likewise the present, which is a result of the past. What matters here is the *experience*, brought about by *meditation*.

(3) Another *road* leads into the FUTURE. This is a more difficult part of meditation. For, the only thing which you may be able to project into the *future sub-division* of time will necessarily belong to your personality, your *ego*, which is unreal and mortal. Is it worth allowing it to be mentioned in your meditation?

Think about something better.

Explore the *road* paved with what you *would like to make* of your 'I AM' in the future, that is, what you wish it to become, wiser, better, stronger, more useful for other 'I AM's' belonging to your human companions in evolution. Do you wish IT to return to the ABSOLUTE 'I AM', which is the sum of all the separate consciousnesses? Are you longing for the *Father's House*?

Such are a few of the *highways*, which emerge from a chosen *theme* of meditation. Explore others and work over them, until you feel that at your present stage of development you have exhausted all possible material. A very important point you should always be conscious of is the method of *resting* between the '*roads*', or even during the actual travelling on them (in other words, meditating on them). This 'rest' does not harm your meditation, and you can use it as often as you wish, simply because it is the HOLDING IN YOUR MIND OF THE THEME OF MEDITATION and nothing more. So, for example, between the 'past' and 'future' phases of the present meditation of 'I AM', you simply insert these two words, and remain so, as if slowly repeating them in your mind. This may even 'magnetize' a cliché in your neighbourhood, attract it, and if a more advanced being had been working with this cliché before, your gain may be quite considerable, as you may get new and valuable conceptions, which otherwise would be hidden in your far distant future.

Exercise L : The THEME is—'MY LIFE'. Simple, but not so easy ! I am recommending it at this point because of its brevity and compactness, which facilitates concentration and prevents verbalization, unavoidable if there are many words, or sentences in the *theme*. You know that verbalization is something like a pair of crutches for the beginner, but they must, and will be rejected when you will stand firmly on your own legs. So, why dedicate too much time and attention to something so temporal and unreal? Remember that your ATTENTION is the magic water of life not only for you, but also for the innumerable beings around you, which you may recall from pervious chapters.

Road 1 : My life is what I am now living through : my awareness of it is manifested by my thoughts, feelings and bodily form, in which I act in the physical world. This is a kind of development of the previous *theme* which was 'I AM'. Indeed, both are bound together, although 'MY LIFE' may be perceptible for other egos, 'I AM' remains a mystery for everyone except the man himself. Nobody knows (among ordinary men) what there is in my *self*, except my 'I'. Now, take a step ahead, and MERGE into intense thinking about 'MY LIFE'. This road is too personal to be chosen for you by another person.

Road 2 : What was my life in the PAST? Here I have a broad field for meditation, for I believe that I know a lot about my past, at least, in this incarnation. I will now try to re-enact my life, that is, my conciousness during my past years, starting from the earliest moment I can remember, which will take me out of my almost unconscious childhood. I will follow the most important moments of my *past*, reconstructing them as pictures, not as words.

Also here, you have almost unlimited material for your meditation, but do not try to re-enact events in your life, but rather your *changing attitudes, convictions, beliefs, experiences,* and so on. Look at them from the present point of view, judging them according to their usefulness or uselessness for your present state. Take several 'rests' from the THEME, as was done previously.

Road 3 : With every moment I pass from the short-lived 'present' into the FUTURE. But I can stop for a while, in order to consider independently that future in my life. What can I expect from it? What do I wish from it?

Elaborate on these problems for a while, using different aspects of that future, in the realm of intellectual strivings, material achievements, and emotional life.

What should I perform and live through, before the page called the 'future' in my life will be closed by the hand of death? Will death be the end of my future life, or will it be only a transformation in form and environment?

Think deeply about this, taking a rest from the 'theme', which gives you a chance to contact a suitable cliché. When this happens, stay with it for as long as you can, remembering that clichés depart if a man pays too little attention to them. But with them also goes a valuable opportunity for advancement, associated with the realization of an inspired and highly evolved cliché. If an unwanted stream of thoughts tries to enter your awareness, or a false cliché of anxiety, deception, impurity, fear, blasphemy, and so on, repel them with your 'NOT INTERESTED' and in serious cases, with the great exorcism from Chapter IX (page 46) of my *Concentration*.

Exercise M : MY THINKING. I can discriminate between *two* kinds of thinking. The *first* kind is when I have some theme to consider, or purpose in directing my thinking apparatus to a certain aim. I would call this 'purposeful' thinking. If I have to solve a problem, for example, how to fill in my taxation return, it will be a mental process induced by the circumstances in which I live, and dictated by reasons arising from them. In brief, here I am using my mental powers in order to make my living according to the requirements of the outer world.

If I try to remember something which was of interest to me, it will be a very similar process. The first aspect belonged to the present time, the second to the past.

By delving into the future, I can plan my day's activity for tomorrow, today, anticipating what I have to do and how I will solve my future problems. Again, we may see, that by meditating with a purpose, no matter how simple and elementary it may appear to be, the *three sub-divisions of time* can be clearly distinguished and recognized.

Once again, I have given you only a framework for meditation, and you may develop it further according to your own ideas, but always be careful—NOT TO DEVIATE FROM THE THEME, and not to slip unconciously into something, having little in common with the actual *theme*.

During the first few days—perhaps weeks—there will be a lot of distractions and while starting with the idea to meditate about your thinking processes, you may finish with something very different. This must be avoided and eliminated. Remember, every exercise which is interrupted, or replaced in your mind by unrelated ideas, must be cancelled, and a *fresh start made from the beginning*. This must be repeated until you are able to perform everything clearly, without any deviations, but not necessarily for a long time. Better a good exercise for a minute, than a spoiled and confused one of five minutes.

The type of thinking just described, is rather a creative one, at least, in its early stages, that is, when you set yourself a

PURPOSE for meditation, related to your personal life. You start, so to speak, independently, but your following meditation may be based on a cliché, which is close to you. Do not believe, even for a moment, that you can have in your mind something which has never had any connection with the thoughts of other men, in this or another epoch. Also realize that they will be contacted by other men in the future, who will get them as ready-made clichés. Nothing perishes in Nature, and therefore no force is ever annihilated, but in the best case, is only transformed.

So, as you may see, the connection between our 'independent' thinking and clichés is a very intimate one, and it is often hard to distinguish as to where there are only thoughts and where there are clichés. Only practice will lead you to this ability of discrimination.

The *second* kind of thinking appears when I start without any clear-cut purpose, simply sitting quietly as if catching thoughts from the space around me. Then I am merely a *receiver*, without any *sending* apparatus, just like an ordinary wireless.

At this point, two aspects may appear. In one I am catching the thoughts created by people around, or even quite distant from me, which as yet have not had the opportunity to be fixed into clichés and are just 'freshly' floating in space. I may also note that the thoughts of those who are living under the same roof with me, especially members of my own family, are easier to 'catch' and re-create in my own mind. This happens because there exists a certain affinity between our minds and even our physical contacts, which makes mental ones easier.

The second aspect belongs to the exclusive catching of clichés and especially those to which our minds are attuned, in other words, with which there is affiliation with those ideas.

Such will be the draft for elementary meditation about one's own thinking processes, but, of course, you may elaborate it more and develop it according to your own needs and desires. But never become sleepy or dizzy during these kinds of mental contacts. If you feel yourself to be tired, delay the exercise until you have rested and then start again, with refreshed awareness and force.

It is true that these exercises may seem tedious to you, but it was the same with your elementary study of the alphabet, with its syllabication, and so on. Without it you would never be able to read these lines. So, without performing these basic, elementary exercises of meditation, how can you expect to realize and start the higher degrees of this art? Always be logical and full of common sense.

As a conclusion to this chapter, I will narrate to you my own experiences and those of others, in mind reading by the once famous telepathist and clairvoyant, the late Stefan Ossowiecki, about whom you can find many comments in the relevant occult literature. An interesting one can be found in the recently published *Exploring the Occult* by Douglas Hunt.

I knew Ossowiecki personally in the years 1930–35, then later we came into contact only rather sporadically. At the time I was lecturing in public on Hermetism and its adaptation in the Tarot. After one of my first lectures, a middle-aged gentleman came to me, presented himself as Ossowiecki and told me that he himself was interested in occultism and especially in its scientific application, which he could perceive in the Tarot's philosophy. Finally, he kindly invited me and a friend of mine, Dr S., who was also a member of one of my Groups, to visit him at his home, situated in a fashionable residential area.

On arrival we were asked to sit down on a large divan, and O. arranged it so that he was in the middle, with Dr S. on his right and myself on his left. Ossowiecki was a Pole by birth, but had spent his youth in Moscow and had apparently brought from there, his cordial custom of holding his welcome visitors by the wrist. He was one of the most pleasant and sincere type of men that I have ever encountered.

To start with, he began to speak about his numerous telepathic and clairvoyant experiences in Paris and other places. But at the time I was less interested in them, than in his scientific attitude to phenomena, which he was so well able to exhibit. So, I thought to myself: 'I have heard a lot about all of these stories, but does he possess any philosophical explanation of them?'

At the same moment O. interrupted his talking and threw me a sharp look. 'O yes!' he said, 'I too possess my yoga, perhaps a little different from yours. I too am seeking an explanation of the powers manifested in me.' A flash of intuition passed through my mind. 'It was through the contact sir,' I told him, nodding towards my right wrist, which Ossowiecki still held in his hand. 'Oh! Yes!' he answered with a smile. 'You certainly know that it is the easiest way in which to read another's thoughts!'

He was able to tell the whereabouts of any man, providing he was given an object, which belonged to that person. It was sufficient for him to put it to his forehead in order to start to speak, in a clear, quiet voice, mentioning places, surroundings, and stating whether the person was living or dead, and if the latter, in what circumstances death had occurred.

On a later occasion Ossowiecki complained that his wonderful powers seemed to vanish, because of the burden of family and society life he was compelled to carry, since he was a member of his country's upper class. Our contact was broken a few years before the start of World War II and at its end, in 1946, a friend wrote to me from Europe, advising that Ossowiecki had perished during the last year of the German occupation of his native city of Warsaw. Apparently, at that time, there were frequent street raids by the German Police, which always followed on after some aggressive acts by the Polish Underground. Therefore, it was dangerous to stroll on the streets.

One day Ossowiecki went for a walk away from his house, and never returned. It was accepted by his family, that he had been arrested by a flying squad and executed together with other hostages. Not even the slightest trace of him remained, as the body was probably thrown into a common grave somewhere on the outskirts of the city.

Evidently, he could not foresee his own fate and the danger connected with leaving his home that day.

During his lifetime he was a most kind man, with a compassionate and sincere heart, ever ready to help anyone in any manner he could, advising and spending his money and time on those in real need.

His unusual talents were discovered during World War I, when he was a young student in Moscow. His colleagues took him to see a wise and famous Rabbi, who had the name of being a clairvoyant. When the old man saw Ossowiecki, he embraced him and said: 'This man has been given a talent and power by the Almighty, which no one else possesses. He can see the human aura and thought.'

Another striking example of a perfect reading of clichés by

Stefan Ossowiecki, happened in the autumn of 1941. A lady, whom I had met years ago before the War, wrote to me, asking me to introduce her to Ossowiecki. He was then living in Warsaw under the German occupation and was very careful about meeting strangers, for fear of inviting suspicion from the occupation authorities. The lady's husband, Mr Oledzki a high official of the Polish State Bank, had left the capital in a car, accompanied by a friend and colleague, shortly before the Germans arrived, and headed for Rumania, as did many other Polish people at that time. They only got as far as a few miles before Lemberg, where they then stayed with another friend of his, who was a landowner. This was because Russian troops were already pouring into the country. Finally, both men decided to leave for the city, because of the apparently greater danger of being found with a landowner, who was sure to be robbed and perhaps even killed by the mob. Nothing more was known of the two missing men by their relatives, as Lemberg then came under Soviet occupation and was cut off from Warsaw.

I then wrote a letter to the lady, from Paris, enclosing my personal introduction to Ossowiecki. And here is what subsequently happened.

She was allowed to visit the famous clairvoyant, taking with her a gold watch, which her husband had worn for many years before the war. Ossowiecki took the watch, pressed it to his forehead and then started to say to her:

'I see your husband and another man travelling in a cart. Then four armed bandits come out from the bushes by the side of the road, two of them being in Soviet uniforms. They stop the cart, order the men out of it and rob their belongings. Then a few moments later they find a car cushion with a Browning pistol sewn in it. They immediately put both the men into a trench beside the road and shoot them. The killing was performed by the bandits in civilian clothes, both of whom had swarthy complexions. The two soldiers merely watched. Finally, they dismiss the boy who was driving the cart telling him to return home and not speak about anything he had witnessed. Don't seek the body of your husband. I see it thrown into a common grave with many others, who were so lawlessly killed at that time.'

When, in 1941, the Germans occupied Lemberg during their summer offensive, Mrs Oledzki was able to contact the headman of the village from which had come the boy, who had driven the cart, in which the luckless men had travelled for the last time. He confirmed every word of Ossowiecki's vision, which had taken place more than a year previously and about which, he quite naturally knew nothing.

May these few lines be a modest tribute to an unusually gifted man with a crystal-clear heart, whose remains lie in an unknown grave in a distant country. If he had lived amongst us in the West, and if his premature death had not cut short the possibility of scientific investigation, with his usual kind assistance, many of the powers that lie hidden in everyone of us, could have been explained in a scientific and useful way.

While there can be some doubts regarding experiments conducted with 'professional' clairvoyants and telepathists, Ossowiecki would have been not only able to produce phenomena, but also to collaborate in their investigation and explanation.

* * *

This fourth Series, containing elementary exercises in meditation as given in Exercises K, L and M may serve as preparation for the next, more complicated ones. But without that preparation we cannot pass successfully to the more advanced work. The mind must be trained to a certain degree, before the student will be able to 'read between the lines' when he reaches the chapters treating of the meditation proper. And this is because true meditation, beyond words and the thoughts connected with them, reaches into the realm of the supermental activities of the human consciousness which, naturally, cannot be depicted exactly in language based on the same words.

If you wish, you may add some other *themes* to this chapter and then work with them as has been done in this Series. There is no question that it will be very profitable for your further study of meditation. For example, develop such subjects as: MY SPEECH, MY BELIEFS, MY BODY, and so on. As you see, I recommend the most 'personal themes', because you are developing your own abilities and you try to influence—by direct means, as was previously explained—the functions of your own brain. So it is only logical that in the beginning, you should operate with material closest to your own personality. Abstract themes will come later, when the elementary ones have been assimilated and dominated.

CHAPTER XVI

Intermediate Meditation – Series V
(Dealing with the Mind)

PRACTICE shows that we can never spend too much energy when we are dealing with the primary tool of meditation, that is, our mind. The more we know this power, which is ours but not US, the better the results which can be expected from our endeavour to obtain a real ability to meditate. In this Series of exercises I will use themes and definitions taken mostly from certain Great Souls, or true Masters, who themselves attained the peaks and therefore can advise us better than anyone else. Even on a much lower level, when one remembers one's own hard climb to an understanding of the nature of *mind*, this reminiscence helps one to understand one's present difficulties, which are unavoidable and the sole purpose of which is to give experience and knowledge. The reading of this book will not lead you to domination of your mind, nor the mastering of the art of meditation. This is what you have to realize and thus spare yourself disappointment and bitterness.

'What a statement!' someone may say. 'Of what use then is the whole of your present book?'

I was expecting this query and am ready for it.

This book, as every other manual, can be likened to a PLATE OF FOOD OFFERED TO A HUNGRY PERSON IN ORDER TO FEED HIM. The food spread on it, will not solve the whole problem of saving him from starvation. There is a certain definite and positive condition to be fulfilled if he really has to be fed. And twofold action is necessary for that purpose: TO EAT THE FOOD AND DIGEST IT PROPERLY.

No matter how simple and true this is, many people are unaware of its truth and expect a simple glance into a book to be satisfactory. To such people I say: IF SO, THEN WHEN YOU HAVE TO TAKE YOUR NEXT MEAL, LOOK AT IT, SMELL IT, CALCU-

LATE HOW MANY CALORIES OR VITAMINS IT MAY CONTAIN, ITS APPROXIMATE TASTE, THE MARKET FROM WHERE IT WAS BOUGHT, EVEN THE NAME AND PARTICULARS CONCERNING THE COOK WHO PREPARED IT, THE PRICE, and anything else you like, *everything except the last and only essential activities*: TO PUT THE CONTENTS OF THE DISH INTO YOUR MOUTH, CHEW AND SWALLOW AND SUBMIT THEM TO THE LIFE-GIVING DIGESTIVE PROCESSES.

Now it is my turn to ask you: 'What will happen if you continually do everything else with that food, but eat it? Will you be saved from starvation?' I am afraid NOT! Even the good cook who prepared the dish for you will not help if he does the eating and not you!

To return to our book, you will agree that the cook is the writer, and the prospective diner (but not any mere ONLOOKER!) is you. I hope that by now you will realize the meaning of the beginning of this chapter: it was to convince you that you have TO EAT and not merely LOOK! And this is still not enough. Even the best food, properly chewed and swallowed will not always bring the expected result, of feeding the body. There still remains a most important factor—TO PROPERLY DIGEST THE FOOD SWALLOWED. If the digestive functions are faulty, the food, as any doctor will tell you, will not be assimilated as it should.

If the ability of the student does not reach the art of digesting the contents of this book, he will not master meditation. But I have provided something for that purpose, and it is just the *preparatory material* contained in the first fifteen or so chapters of this book. Perhaps these have been rather tedious for some readers, but all who have passed through similar processes of preparation and then of right digestion will KNOW that it is an indispensable condition. In the world of philosophical and mystical literature there are many good works, providing us with quantities of material for meditation. I will use them widely in the following chapters as basic themes for your study. But this book has been written as a manual, giving not only a framework for the inner work you have to perform, but also all introductory data, so that when you reach the texts, you will know HOW TO HANDLE THEM.

But that is not all, it would be insufficient. So, to fill your '*plate*' the following method will be adopted.

FIRSTLY, the text or, as we will call it, THE THEME FOR MEDITATION will be given, and SECONDLY, there will be the DEVELOPMENT of that theme by the writer. It then remains for you to PUT THE LIVING FORCE OF YOUR ATTENTION AND ABILITY TO HANDLE MEDITATION into such *developments*, live them and *digest them in your own individual way*, without merely following them literally and slavishly. Under no circumstances should you commit such an error. DO NOT ASSUME EVEN FOR A MOMENT THAT YOU CAN DELEGATE THE DIGESTION OF YOUR FOOD TO YOUR COOK. No matter how kind and friendly this 'cook' (that is, the writer) may happen to be, he cannot do more than he is really able to do. So, if you come across a book, or a person who tells you that 'you have only to read, or listen and, by this fact alone, you will master your problems', tell him what he deserves. I do not need to make any further suggestions, as you will find the proper way to deal with such a case for yourself.

Exercise N:

THEME: *What is mind? It is only a bundle of thoughts. Stop thinking and show me then, where is the mind?*
(From Maharshi's Teachings)

Development: The inherent quality of our mind is the thinking activity. It is vastly different from any other subject we may take for the purpose of comparison. The foremost ability of say, a fish, is swimming in water. We cannot imagine a fish without this. But, if a fish stops its movements, which is quite possible (at least, in theory), or is removed from its native habitat—the water, it still exists as a fish and does not lose identity with its species. The cessation of activity does not deprive any object in the material world of its existence. When a man sleeps without dreaming he is unconscious, as if non-existent for himself, but for others he is still the same person, only unconscious of his surroundings.

Then what is the position with our mind? It is NOT identical with our brain, which is only its physical instrument. When our mind is inactive in deep, dreamless sleep, our brain still exists and is the same organ as it was in the waking state, only inactive, for its motive power has been withdrawn from it. Therefore, learn to discriminate between the *mind* and the *brain*.

139

If the mind is NOT identical with the brain, where then is its real, inherent realm, without which there cannot be any concept of mind? IT IS THE THINKING PROCESS ALONE, or, as the Sage *Maharshi* said, its THOUGHTS. Let us experiment a little. When I am eliminating ALL thoughts (which implies the same fate for my feelings) from my consciousness, there is no THINKING PRINCIPLE at all. Nothing manifests it any more, and no one can see my mind from the outside and so say to me: 'Look, although you are not conscious of your thinking principle. I can still perceive it!' Or do you expect someone to say something like that to you? I hope NOT!

To proceed, I start to learn that if I can extinguish my mind like a candle, I can also light it at any moment I wish. In other words, I can always re-start the activity of my mind, and then I can watch this activity, which is—as I now know—inseparable from thinking.

So, was the Maharshi right or wrong? I shall not indulge here in impracticable and useless deliberations and theories, for example, that someone would like to say: 'Well, although you could not find your mind when it was silenced, at least, it still existed in a latent state.' This is merely *empty verbalization*, without any real essence, for it is too much to expect a sane man to believe in something which he knows has ceased to exist, just because someone wants him to. I do not agree with such an attitude. From this, it is not far to the second statement of our *theme*: '*the mind is only a bundle of thoughts. Stop thinking and show me then, where is the mind?*' It is like the sealing of a finished process, for no one can ever show me any real trace of the mind other than its function, as was possible with the fish, once it was pulled out of its watery realm. It still remained, but mind does not.

This axiom of the Maharshi's also has another important consequence: when I extinguished my mind, WHO was this I? Did I cease to exist, passing into a state of unconsciousness, blankness, or swoon? NOT AT ALL! I still felt my life, although beyond the material world, which surrounds me in the physical state of awareness. It is true that this life is hard to describe, for, in annihilating my mind for a certain time, I also annihilated the language of words, being themselves the outer expression of thoughts. And still I lived, but with a different, more ethereal life, which seemed to be FREE from *Time* and *Space*. Quite definitely, there is *something* in me which is above and beyond the mind and the senses.

*   *   *

This will end our framework for the '*development*' of meditation for the present. The research after THAT, which lies beyond the mind will be approached in the final chapters, when you will know much more, and consequently, be more able to understand the things which transcend the realm of mind. This realm seems to be the only real one for the majority of the sons of man in this period.

We can now resume the exercise.

I hope, that by now, the method we will unswervingly follow in later chapters dealing with meditation proper, is clear to you. It is not by any means a simple one. The THEME must be well memorized, just like any other important formula, and slowly repeated SEVEN TIMES in your mind. Whisper it if you find this helpful.

Then slowly read the '*development*' SEVEN TIMES, until it is quite clear to you. Do not listen to anything else from your mind, for it is the mind itself which will exert every effort to prevent you from extinguishing IT even for a moment. Realize that this power wants to live, and your obliterating of it means its temporary death. But this power lives *only at your expense*, occupying the living energy of your ATTENTION (see former chapters about this), and its life is not your life, but only that of certain vibrations, without which your consciousness is purer and greater, as you will soon discover. So do not feel any false sense of 'guilt' when I tell you that by silencing your mind you cause it to die temporarily. Anyway, it must die when its time comes, so what is wrong in your temporary liberation from something mortal?

To conclude this first and basic exercise of meditation on the human mind, I may add, that if we ban it for a short while, and later, for any length of time we want, WE ARE GAINING INCOMPARABLY MORE THAN WE ARE APPARENTLY LOSING BY SUCH A PROCESS. Happiness does not exist in the world when mind is the overlord. But it exists after the revolution, banning that overlord, for then comes SOMETHING, which is close to EVERYTHING and was formerly hidden from us by the muddy waves of that same mind.

When I typed all of this, the 'mechanical' work was performed by my mind, it is true, but—NOTHING MORE! It ceased at the same time as the typewriter's keys stopped. How great is that PEACE, when the mind is silent and still!

Exercise O:
THEME: *The mind is the great slayer of the real. Let the disciple slay the Slayer.*
(From *The Voice of the Silence*)

Development: From the previous exercise I know about a certain role that uncontrolled mind has in my life. It has a delaying and binding influence. What good does such an attitude of the tool I call 'the mind' bring me? Most certainly, no good at all! I know that tools are necessary, for without a screwdriver I cannot extract or drive home a screw. But is it the screwdriver which really acts? Of what use is it without a living hand behind it, to move and direct it? Isn't it the same with my mind? Yes, if it is an obedient tool, but not while it is an uncontrollable contraption. When the mind vibrates incessantly and when I have no power to stop it, I see only what the mind allows me to see. I am a slave, without any inner peace and happiness. From the previous exercise I know that the REAL is beyond the mind, and if that mind prevents me from seeing that REALITY, isn't it a killer, a mean, pitiless killer? I see it now, the naked Truth!

If so, I am entitled to put an end to such tyranny, in the words of the *theme*—to 'slay the Slayer'.

I know what that slaying means: it is *making the mind still*, and setting myself FREE from any inhibition from outside, which is basically foreign to me, for I can be happy and alive without it. So be dead, my mind, for as long as I order this of you. I will call you to life as soon as I have need of your services. So be it!

* * *

When performing this meditative exercise, do not forget the rules from the former exercise: to read the *theme* slowly until fully memorized; then to read the '*development*' SEVEN TIMES, after which, to hold its contents before your inner eye, trying to make it your PERSONAL meditation, to *live it* in the depths of your true Self.

I shall not mention these rules again after every exercise, for they are unchangeable for every meditation, until such time as you advance to the MUTE MEDITATION, sometimes called—CONTEMPLATION.

Exercise P:
THEME: *The mind is a good servant, but a cruel master.*
      (From *The Voice of the Silence*)

Development: Before I started to practise *concentration*, my mind was a source of incessant difficulties in my inner life. It refused to obey, but since I have realized that it is only a power lying outside my true Self, and learned to use this power according to my needs, the mind has become my servant, instead of the former master, who compelled me to act according to its own whimsies, but not on the orders of my true Self. I could not concentrate my thoughts at times when I urgently needed to do so; I suffered mental agonies, being incapable of using my mind in a reasonable and dispassionate way, dictated by my common sense, when fateful decisions had to be taken.

Lack of concentration brought me insecurity and instability in my actions, which in turn caused suffering, defeats and errors committed at my expense. My will-power, weakened by the selfish egotism of the mind, which caused it to vibrate instead of being at peace when I needed that peace, was unable to make and realize logically sound decisions. This again was a continual source of suffering, all because the mind played its usurped role of my master. And how cruel that master has been!

But now that I have reduced it to its proper level as my servant, I can see that the mind is a useful tool, without which I could not perform very much in this world, including my study of meditation.

What was the deciding factor in that change in the relationship between myself and my mind? A simple, but enormously important one: THE REALIZATION THAT MYSELF AND MY MIND ARE TWO DIFFERENT THINGS, AND THAT I AM ABLE TO RULE THAT THING—THE MIND.

This understanding stopped the former continuous drain on my will-power, caused by disorderly thinking (vibrating) of my mind, which literally gave me no time for any life *for myself*, that is, when I no longer wanted to contribute to the passion for vibration inherent in an unsubdued mind. Together with the submission of my mind, I can see that submission of my desires has become much easier and more realizable, as, being able to stop thinking, I am also able to stop the astral vibrations, which are, in other words, the same desires and emotions. As a conclusion to this meditation exercise I can say that: THE ABILITY OF VOLUNTARY CESSATION OF THINKING IS THE KEY TO IT ALL.

CHAPTER XVII

The Creation of Clichés

THE subject matter of Chapter XVI having been concluded, we can pass on to the use of the powers arising in us, as a result of the *solution of our mind's problems*. By 'conclusion', as regards the study of every chapter in this book I mean the mastering of its exercises, in this case, the satisfactory and oft repeated performing of these exercises, while meditating along the lines recommended until the truth of the *themes* of the meditations become OUR OWN TRUTH, inseparable from our newly acquired attitude towards, and understanding of these themes. In brief, we have moulded our minds into the shapes we wanted, and not into their own wilful patterns.

One of the most important activities for a genuine occultist is the CREATION OF DESIRABLE AND EVOLUTIONARY CLICHÉS. You know from former chapters that we humans, as well as innumerable other intelligent beings in the immense universe, invariably possess (or, much better and exact, are possessed by) the sparks of the immortal, omnipotent POWER, which we have tried to explain by the term HYPERCONCIOUSNESS. The student will do well if he now interrupts this lesson and returns to the chapters dealing with the concept of that HYPERCONCIOUSNESS. Presuming that you have followed my advice, I shall continue.

We know, that the immense cliché of the universe has been created by the PURE IMMATERIAL CONCIOUSNESS, which it is not wrong to call the 'HYPERCONSCIOUSNESS' in relation to normal human awareness. Our ambitions cannot go so far, for a spark cannot do what is done by a FULL FIRE. So, I will not teach you how to create a new world, and I hope that you fully understand this, thereby rejecting all rubbish and nonsense, so often (and so regrettably) spread by the false self-styled 'prophets' and 'masters'. We have to know our possibilities and our limitaions, thus allowing the mother-Truth to dwell in us.

Well then, what sort of clichés are we able to produce, with which of the already existing ones can we associate ourselves? The answer is a simple and unequivocal one: THOSE WITHIN OUR REACH. Already the elementary ability of meditation, which you should have started to realize from the material you have so far studied in the foregoing chapters, should make you able to perform certain things in that direction. For *clichés are the direct result of clear and intense meditation, with full power of concentration,* used for that purpose. By these words you are initiated into this problem, which so far has been held in secret during the past ages. Your meditation is the real *power*, a creative power, and there is not, and cannot be any substitute for it. Now you may understand why I wrote this book. I hope it will reach the right hands, and be used as intended, for the CAUSE OF LIGHT, but not for that of *Darkness*.

Actually, I disagree with those 'over cautious' people, who can be found in certain pseudo-occult associations, and who have never been able to practise anything belonging to the art of inner development of man. Most of such people hypocritically, of course, try to dissuade others from any practical use of the occult laws. They do so, simply because they themselves have never been able to achieve any true realization, and hence egoistically dislike others attempting to perform something, in which they have failed. Look attentively around you and you will be able to unmask the hypocrites.

From the contents of the preceding fifteen chapters you can see, that high moral and ethical standards have been set as conditions for Achievement. If someone with impure intentions will try to obtain certain faculties, connected with the *art of meditation,* he will be compelled to satisfy these standards, which means that he must then cease to be a low and egoistic individual. Moreover, for any successful achievement, as is supposed in this work, you will invariably need help from the *Above*. It will be given to you only if your attitude guarantees the purity of your aims, not otherwise. The Supreme sees through us and no cheating is possible in this case. That is the *safety-valve*, of which we are well aware. I am not ignorant of the possibility of also using occult powers for evil, that is, egoistic purposes, but their range is very limited and the results too ephemeral to be taken too seriously. No doubt, a 'black magician' might be able to arrange certain troubles for a few persons he hates and who are not of too high standards themselves, but, in any case, he is only an instrument in the negative karmas of such people. But he will never be successful in his attempts to harm any true white occultist or a saintly man. Even a simple and sincere belief in God and His goodness on the part of an ordinary man is a sufficient guarantee against dark influences. Know, that NO EVIL CAN EVER TOUCH US IF WE DO NOT POSSESS WITHIN OURSELVES THE GERMS OF THE SAME KIND OF EVIL WHICH MAY BE THROWN AGAINST US. There is no room here to expand on this point, but if you are interested in it, you can find a full explanation and advice in the chapters of my *Tarot*, dealing with invultuation and other astral crimes.

So, we will create positive and useful clichés, of course, rather elementary at first, and then later more highly developed ones.

Examples:
(A) Imagine that you have some special business, or a project, and so on, and you want to do everything you can, in order to secure its success, quite naturally, apart from every kind of necessary physical preparation. You have to give a convincing speech in company, upon which depends decisions favourable to you. You know that, as a rule, even ordinary speakers, who do not use any occult means, prepare their speeches in advance, and then even practise before a mirror, so as to exercise the maximum influence on their audience. There is nothing wrong in this, but we should go further, by creating a FULL CLICHÉ of the forthcoming event.

Remain alone in your room; study the text of the speech well; imagine yourself standing on the rostrum, and visualize the people before you as clearly as you can. If you know some of them by sight, include them in your mental picture with as much exactness as possible. Then, with eyes closed, look around several times, in your mind, as if seeing the future surroundings in which you will act and mentally pronounce (even whisper if you wish)—'I AM!', with full confidence in your power to reassure yourself. Finally, start your speech, slowly, clearly, injecting the firm intention of being heard and agreed with in every thought you express in words. Believe that everything will happen according to your plans, and that the minds of your audience are tuned to your conclusions and methods. The most deciding factor in the building of a successful cliché will be *your conviction that you are right, and entitled to strive after your aims*. A spark of the HYPERCONSCIOUSNESS, which is omnipotent, may be incarnate in this factor. Perhaps now, you realize, that if the intentions are impure, this deciding moment will inevitably fail, for, in the overwhelming majority, men have this hidden feeling of justice in themselves, which, in this case, will destroy confidence.

Of course, as everywhere, there are exceptions, but they only support the general law of the building of clichés. This explains the magic influence which some men, who are evil (from our point of view), have been able to exert on their passive audiences. I strongly suspect that, in their best years, the dictators Hitler and Mussolini, were sincerely convinced that they were fighting for a just cause, and this strange magnetism was passed on to the multitude of people around them.

(B) We can foresee desirable events by systematically meditating about them with considerable purity of concentration. Let your effort be similar to figure No. 5, or at least No. 4 given in this book. Here I mean, the uninterrupted stream of cliché-forming effort issuing from you. If you are to meet someone, say at a railway station sometime during the day, think about and SEE the accomplished event as clearly and sharply as you can, even mentally pronouncing what you would like to say to the person. Repeat this many times during the session. The efficiency of the cliché thus created will depend solely upon you, just as a good painter will create a valuable picture, while a less talented one will be unable to achieve anything similar.

(C) You are in need of a certain service or even the propitious fulfilment of a request of yours from someone else. Place yourself in circumstances similar to the real ones. Imagine yourself facing the person and beginning to act, speaking convincingly at first, then remaining silent while conveying a strong impression so that he, or she will understand your intention, see it in a favourable light and so be prepared to hear you when you really ask. You should realize that the preparation must be exact and intense, if the cliché has to be realized according to your will. Do you wish to know the real SECRET OF SUCCESS? It is your unswerving concentration and ability to hold your mind 'empty' between the different phases of your action. In brief, do not spoil your cliché by incoherent and unrelated thoughts. If you have been a good student of my *Concentration*, you will not encounter any unsurmountable obstacles at all.

There is only one *Power* which is superior to cliché-building, even of the most elaborate and clear-cut ones. It is the power of true PRAYER, directed with an open heart and for a worthy purpose. But this was the subject matter of my *Theurgy* and there is no room to say much about it in this work. Often such prayer, evoking the participation of the HYPERCONSCIOUSNESS and connected with clichés, may produce what we call '*miracles*'. They are not 'unexplainable' for those who know practically, what they read in this book, but I would not say that mental understanding leads to the REALIZATION OF MIRACLES! Such a conception would be utterly wrong. A *miracle* is always a TOUR DE FORCE, as Frenchmen say, and if you read parts of the Gospels of Christ, you will see this for yourself. Seemingly, the Great Teacher was able to produce miracles even without the participation of His will, as was the case with the bleeding woman, who touched His robe from behind.

Actually, a prayer is very often connected with the unconscious building of a cliché, which gives a picture of the desired result for the devotee.

But, as such a cliché is usually not too clearly defined and concentrated, and not every prayer sufficiently sincere, the results are not always as beneficial as expected.

*   *   *

The method of cliché-building, given here, can be applied to every *bona fide* problem we need to solve, providing you satisfy the conditions under which such an action should be conducted. And I have already spoken about it in this chapter.

*   *   *

There are different kinds of clichés which are not connected with physical events, but with more elevated meditative functions. In Chapter XVI we had three examples of meditation about the mind's properties and their handling (see exercises N, O and P). First read the themes. Then judge for yourself whether or not you could build clichés on them and if so, which ones. As there were no mental pictures, as in this chapter, nothing similar can be done. We have to be satisfied with this solution, for we are unable to describe anything beyond visualization, fitting to the language of words. Nevertheless, certain clichés must arise from abstruse meditation, as well as those of a higher order which visit us, when we are ripe enough to accept them. When, for example, I meditate on TRUTH, there can be two different causes:

(1) The cliché comes to me, magnetized by my mind and allows me to penetrate deeper than mental conceptions. Then I become occupied with it, lend it that *living force* of *concentrated attention* and so we both become enriched: the cliché is fortified and I myself receive some spiritual experience, which can never be lost.

(2) The idea of TRUTH, which might be congenial to me, is developed into a cliché during meditation, which later starts its own independent life, even after I finish my meditation. It then goes off 'into space' to seek someone, who can add something to its contents and so the chain has been started.

In either case I cannot give you any further explanation, for there are no words available for that purpose and approximations, or similies would be of no use in this matter.

In our innermost recesses, when the *Peace* reigns supreme, we even KNOW about such formless creations, for we ourselves are in essence, the FORMLESS SPIRIT.

When you too pass through these experiences, the same cognition will be born in you, which will then allow you to convey the gist of them to your fellow men. That is why so many spiritually awakened men have spoken of the SILENCE, as being the peak of every initiation.

The Maharshi once said, that: 'Speech is the great-grandson of Truth.' Then, when we want to reach that Truth, we must transcend feelings and thoughts. We will encounter the problem of SPIRITUAL SILENCE when we come to MUTE MEDITATION and its relation to MUTE PRAYER, as practised by the great Saints and Masters.

CHAPTER XVIII

Meditation in Diagrams

IT may be useful if attempts to meditate, along with elementary meditation and further experiences in this field ending in regular and successful meditation, will be presented in the form of diagrams. This will help you to understand the patterns, which may be formed by your initial efforts and from subsequent developments of this study. Every beginner thinks that whatever happens to him is known only to himself, and that his experiences are almost unique. Of course, this is not so and, just as with conventional study in our schools, teachers know a lot about the difficulties encountered by their pupils during their years of learning.

It is no different with occult studies, if undertaken earnestly and if the aspirant has really abandoned the idea that, *in this kind of knowledge he may dispense with certain conditions and much effort*: an attitude not permitted even in conventional schools.

In the diagrams following (Figs. 2–6), I have shown the general lines which follow on from the beginning and the subsequent study of meditation.

Meditation, as we have already defined it, is *concentration in movement*, attention directed to living ideas and clichés. Therefore, I can represent the ideal course of meditation as a *straight line* and it is shown in all diagrams as line X–Y. The curves on both sides of it are the patterns of our meditation.

Fig. 2: We start from point 'X' and if our abilities are as they should be, our path will lead directly to the final aim, marked by 'Y'. Of course, so far this is impossible and after a moment your mind dissociates itself from the ideal line X–Y and thought comes taking us to point 'a'. Let us now follow the curve with full attention.

If the line X–a still shows the desired direction moving towards the aim, or 'Y', the next stage will probably be bent back a little and then raised at 'b', but you can see that this point, although aiming at 'Y', is much farther from the *base* line of X–Y. Our thought wandered somewhat astray. At this moment we may catch the error and make an effort to return to right thinking.

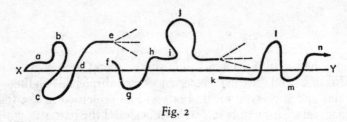

Fig. 2

The new part of the curve between 'b' an 'c' depicts this activity. But, because of the lack of training we are unable to stay on the ideal line and overshoot it, reaching only 'c', instead of 'd'. From here we again direct our attention ahead, pass through 'd' and arrive at point 'e'.

I hope that after this short explanation you are able to orientate your mind according to the meaning of these diagrams, so I will not repeat the same deviations again, but simply describe them by drawing the *line of meditation* as it was.

Another faulty step occurs at 'e': here the mind went completely astray, forgot the theme of meditation and started to occupy itself with thoughts having little or nothing in common with the *theme*. This is represented by the short, dispersed lines radiating from 'e'. A sad and depressing sight.

Finally we again remember what we have to do and return to the line X–Y, somewhere at point 'f', and then start to move ahead. The next deviation leads us to 'g', from there to 'h', then a long step in the true direction, which is finally transformed into a backward movement at 'i' and from there it proceeds in a long curve of unco-ordinated thinking to 'j', again ahead and. . . Once more unconsciousness interrupts meditation, deforming it into a bundle of incoherent thoughts, marked by dispersed debris.

After a while, our consciousness recovers and takes us to 'k', which is again in the direction of 'Y'. But not for very long. A new deviation occurs at 'l', corrected by movement to 'm', then a new ascending curve starts, which crosses the base line. Then begins an effort at improvement and so our time has run out.

It was, of course, only a general pattern and individual cases may vary considerably, but the central idea of unsuccessful, initial efforts will be very similar to the diagram in Fig. 2.

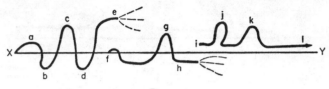

Fig. 3

Fig. 3: This presents another pattern of meditation, evidently a more advanced one, for in it thought all the time proceeds in the required direction, although still with many vibrations and deviations from the true line of X–Y. Also, at a certain moment 'e', the mind of the aspirant goes astray, forgets the theme and follows its own whimsies. Duly rebuked and compelled to return to 'f', it follows on to the peak 'g', until a new break-down interrupts meditation at 'h'. Apprehended at 'i', awareness does not disengage itself from the true direction, but passes through 'j', 'k' and 'l' and then the meditation ends.

The next problem to solve will be to carefully study both diagrams, while inserting your own thoughts, as was done during your attempts to meditate and then repeat the effort again and again, each time trying to avoid and cancel the irregularities just described.

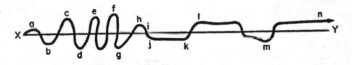

Fig. 4

Fig. 4: Here is presented the next, much more advanced degree of meditation. In it we see that the aspirant is able to eliminate completely the unconscious moments he had in the former diagrams and follows an uninterrupted curve, without any

153

definite backward movements, continually striving towards 'Y'. Naturally, vibrations still occur at points like 'b', 'c' and 'd', but their amplitudes are now not so wide and so sharp. This means that the meditating person has held his mind *not very far* from the base line of X–Y.

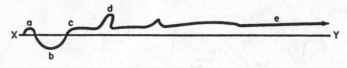

Fig. 5

Fig. 5: Still better progress! Although still not able to reach X–Y for any measurable length of time, the meditating student can say that now he is really finding the right technique and his concentration improves, together with will-power. For you should know, that *interruptions* to meditation, as described previously, are the most convincing proof that the will-power of the aspirant still has serious weaknesses and is unable to secure the continuity of the inner processes in his consciousness.

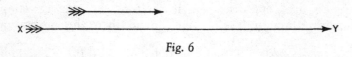

Fig. 6

Fig. 6: This diagram, as you can obviously guess, depicts the meditation of a Master, who has nothing more to learn on this earth and who has left all of our human weaknesses and imperfections behind him. Such a straight meditation must invariably lead directly to the Aim and that is why we say, that a spiritual Master lives continually in the Supreme. In other words, he and the Father are united in the ONE UNIQUE SPIRIT, REALITY, TRUTH and LOVE.

Perhaps you may now see where meditation actually leads its faithful adherents and students.

Upon reading all of the foregoing again, I have the same feeling, that all of it is only a framework, or draft of the future perfect CONSTRUCTION. Everyone must insert his own living force into it, and thereby build the indestructible TEMPLE, in which he will find his final Peace.

CHAPTER XIX

Japa

THE more we know about our subject the better the outlook we will have for a successful conclusion to our study. Therefore, in this present course, I will not omit the very old, but proved and practical method of JAPA, borrowed from the occult arsenal of our Hindu brothers. But first we must have a full explanation of what it really is, its method, range and aims.

Actually, *Japa* is midway between *static concentration* and *meditation* and from the book *Concentration*, which is a technical introduction to the *art of meditation*, you will know all about the exercises used for reaching one-pointedness of the mind.

Now we are approaching the end of Part II of this work, dedicated to the techniques of meditation, and have before us Part III in which we will start to practise real meditation, based on the abilities (those of concentration) and knowledge (as given here in Chapters I to XVIII), which the student is supposed to have gained so far.

Therefore, let us finish Part II with knowledge of *Japa*. The core of this method is a continuous mental (sometimes even oral) repetition of a short sentence, mantra, or maxim, and so on, which is supposed to OCCUPY THE WHOLE OF THE MIND OF THE STUDENT, *during every minute he is not compelled by his worldly duties to attend to the current matters of his everyday life*. In India there are men who devote all of their time to spiritual searching, or to Yoga, limiting their worldly activities to unavoidable ones like eating, sleeping and bathing, plus praying, or meditating. This category of 'professional' mystics, often called 'Swamis' and occasionally 'Sadhus' has no, or very few counterparts in Western society, except in monasteries or convents. But we will not speak of the latter organizations, as they belong to a different category of men and women, who follow purely religious paths, although some methods used by them are pretty close to those of the Eastern Yogas (in their Bhakti, or even Raja forms).

In my *In Days of Great Peace* you will find a detailed description of how I used *Japa* myself, in 1946, when preparing to leave for India.

As I have already said, you may choose almost anything you consider to be suitable as a text for Japa, under the condition that it will not be too long or cumbersome. The shorter it is the better. Therefore I shall not give you too many examples so that you may use something different, if you find it more suitable for your mentality. If you want to know the truth—IT IS OF LITTLE IMPORTANCE WHAT FORMULA YOU USE. This is because Japa is a means, a technical method, having no other aim than to help you to overcome the wandering of your mind, to discipline it and to strengthen your will-power. As you may see, its range is quite a large one and that is why I recommend this ancient, but proved method as suitable for the transient period between 'concentration' and the practical use of earnest meditation.

Here are some suggestions: 'I AM'; 'WHO AM I?' (the Vichara); the GAYATRI ('Let us meditate upon the glory of the ONE Who created this universe: let Him illumine our minds'); and 'AUM MANI PADME HUM'. For those who are religiously inclined, we have excellent short prayers which will suit our purpose well: 'GOD THE HOLY, GOD THE HOLY AND MIGHTY, HOLY AND IMMORTAL, BE GRACIOUS UNTO US! BLESSED BE THOU, O LORD!'

Sometimes a shorter formula, like 'AUM' (the same as 'OM') is very suitable. I repeat, it is the way in which Japa is performed which counts, not the words of the formula itself. Of course, if an aspirant chooses a short prayer and uses it with due devotion he cannot miss obtaining additional benefit in the form of a response from Him, Whom he worships. For those who have an intuitional devotion to Christ the following verse, originating from the early days of Christianity, can be recommended. As you may see, it is also a powerful invocation, which will strengthen your Japa spiritually: 'CHRIST IS RESURRECTED, DEFEATING DEATH BY DEATH, AND GRANTING LIFE TO THOSE WHO ARE IN THE GRAVE.' Of course, you may realize that the expression 'who are in the grave' is similar in meaning to the words which Christ used when He commanded His disciples to:

'Follow me, and let the dead bury their dead.' Then the 'granting life' to them would mean *spiritual resurrection*, from the deadly sleep in matter, as occultists say.

As I mentioned before, Japa must fill all of our waking state, which is not occupied by our professional and other bread-winning activities, and so on, of the mind. It is amazing how much time humanity wastes on unnecessary and meaningless activities of the mind, from which no one derives any profit or benefit and only acquires a weakening of the ability to concentrate, or to use will-power.

In practice, the day of a Japa performer will look something like this: immediately upon awakening start pronouncing your 'AUM' or other chosen formula, not too fast, but just so that NO THOUGHT CAN SLIP IN BETWEEN JAPAS! This is the condition and everything else is of secondary importance. When someone speaks to you, or you have to speak to somebody, interrupt the repetition and use your mind and speech as usual. If you are accustomed to reading your morning newspaper during breakfast, or on the way to work, and so on, allocate whatever time is necessary for that purpose, always being conscious that your exercise with Japa is much more important than satisfying the curiosity of your mind. Let this concession to it be as brief as possible, *it is in your own well-understood interest*, and nobody else's.

When you work or perform other compulsory activities during the day-time, you will most probably find, that not all of that time is really occupied, for mind can still find its fractions of a minute or even much more, for its own whimsies. Here is where the decisive action of your Japa comes in: instead of allowing your mind to be occupied with indifferent matters, order it to perform Japa and nothing else. You will be amazed at how quickly and convincingly your power will grow and with it—inner peace.

SO, I WILL REPEAT: THE CARDINAL RULE OF JAPA IS TO FILL YOUR MIND WITH IT EVERY FREE MOMENT WHEN THE LATTER IS NOT OCCUPIED WITH ANY COMPULSORY ACTIVITY, from early morning to bedtime. It is a very commendable habit, to fall asleep with Japa in the mind. Then you will see what can happen during your sleep and how it will influence your dream state. I will purposely not give you any intimation about this, as a result of rigid and faithful performance of *Japa*, which is always highly beneficial, takes different forms in different individuals.

There is another very important rule: DO NOT TELL ANYBODY ABOUT YOUR WORK WITH JAPA, OR IT WILL BE DAMAGED OR EVEN DESTROYED. Too many cases of this are known, so that the breach of this rule is ABSOLUTELY FORBIDDEN for every student of meditation, or even for anyone using *Japa* for any other purpose. The only exception is in the case of a faithful friend or companion, WHO IS HIMSELF ENGAGED IN SIMILAR TRAINING, AND IF YOU KNOW THAT HE IS MORE ADVANCED THAN YOU ARE. For all other cases the RULE IS absolutely binding and unbreakable, if you really want to get profit from your work. In brief, if speech is silver, then SILENCE is pure gold. Naturally, if you feel that you need some additional instruction, and so on (which actually should not be, as everything has been so arranged in this course, that you have all necessary information and instruction in this book, and if you follow my advice, to read the book at least SEVEN times first, you will not have any problems at all), you may write to the author, who will be glad to assist you, provided that you do not ask something which is already contained in this book.

How long should you work with Japa? Again, no definite time can be advised, as there is a personal rule for every student.

It is the flexibility of *Japa*, which is one of the reasons why it has been so admired in the East for thousands of years.

AS SOON AS YOUR MIND STARTS TO BE AUTOMATICALLY FILLED WITH JAPA IN ALL PERIODS WHEN IT IS FREE FROM ANY COMPULSORY ACTIVITIES, WHICH ARE ACCEPTED WITH YOUR CONSENT, YOU MAY CONSIDER IT CONQUERED TO A SUFFICIENT DEGREE TO ALLOW YOU AN EASY TRANSITION TO THE NEXT STAGE OF YOUR STUDY, THAT IS, REGULAR MEDITATION, as expounded in Part III of this work.

From my own personal experience (and I do not write anything apart from such experience), I know that *Japa* is an excellent method. It is a simple, comparatively easy and fast means for reaching the most important inner knowledge about the *difference between man and his mind*. It gives a man such a wonderful feeling of freedom and certainty, that there is hardly anything better, or even comparable to *Japa*. However, it must be *used as a means, but never as an aim,* as some ignorant aspirants (mostly in the East) seem to believe and practise. Do not commit this error. *Japa* should not be confused with some important prayers, or mantras, which certain Saints and yogis used throughout their lifetimes. Such formulas were the constant themes for their MEDITATION, but NOT exercises aimed at the transformation and subjugation of the mind, which they had long since left behind them.

PART III
REGULAR MEDITATION

CHAPTER XX

An Ethical Group of Meditations – Series I

OUR work of preparation finished, we can now pass on to regular meditation, involving all the knowledge and techniques, which we have been able to collect from the first two parts of this Course.

The easiest and most attractive themes will be those from renowned ethical texts, starting with Neo-Platonic and ending with contemporary ones. The techniques to be used in Chapters XX and XXI remain as before:

(a) First read the *theme* several times until you have fully memorized it.

(b) Then try to penetrate into its contents without looking at the *development*, provided below the theme. Do your best in order to understand it, always remembering that it is *only the cross-road*, from which you have to start your travelling.

(c) After some ten minutes (more, if you feel is desirable), slowly start to read the separate sentences of the *development*, thinking deeply about each of them and adding your own version, which arises in your mind. Under no circumstances deviate from this work, and if you catch yourself thinking about something unrelated and not intended to be in connection with the *theme*, start the work again from the beginning, that is, 'a', then 'b', and so on.

(d) In this way work through the whole text of the *development*, until you finish it completely. Then go through it, as much as you can memorize, another time. The first stages of this type of meditation may be performed with the eyes closed and, for better concentration, with the eyeballs turned upwards, as if you were looking at something on the ceiling. It helps to overcome the lower kind of attacking thoughts and the physical feeling of the body. Of course, you will not forget to perform a few prana-yamas before starting, while seated in the right position, described along wih the techniques of pranayama in Chapter XV of *Concentration*. While pranayama is not an unavoidable accessory (although very useful and helpful, as you most certainly will experience for yourself), the correct sitting posture (called a 'Westernized asana') is a definite condition, if you do not wish to have additional difficulties from the side of your body, which sometimes even affect health. To sit for a long time in an unhealthy and uncomfortable position is obviously harmful.

1. THEME: *Withdraw into yourself and look. And if you do not find yourself beautiful as yet, do as does the creator of a statue that is to be made beautiful; he cuts away here, he smooths there, he makes this line lighter, this other purer, until he has shown a beautiful face upon the statue. So do you also; cut away all that is excessive, straighten all that is crooked, bring light to all that is shadowed, labour to make all glow with beauty, and do not cease chiselling your statue until there shall shine out on you the godlike splendour of virtue, until you shall see the final goodness surely established in the stainless shrine.*

(From *The Enneads*, Plotinus)

Development: I am entering into my invisible 'I', composed of feelings and thoughts. First, I look at my feelings, emotions. Is each and every one of them always gracious and pleasant? What feelings did I have when I arose from my rest of last night? Was I anxious and irritated, or had I a quiet feeling of contentment and peace?

(Analyse all of this and then proceed to the next part.)

Are my feelings towards my fellow men good or bad? I know that no conditions justify my inner ugliness, when it appears in me. Therefore, I have to remove the evil and repulsive emotions from inside me. They are destructive, no matter whether or not my mind tries to convince me that in certain circumstances I could not inwardly behave in a different way. I could and I should!

I will no longer forget that the Lord dwells in every form, no matter how imperfect it is and I have no right to offend the

Lord's home. If men are unjust towards me or even malicious, that is because of their ignorance. Should I be ignorant also? Do I wish to be so? If not, let me remember this during the coming day, so that tomorrow I will finish with a better account than today, and my inner statue will then gain in beauty and charm.

Now, my thoughts! Do I always think what is reasonable, enlightening and beautiful? For I also have to ennoble this side of me, otherwise my image will remain imperfect as it is now. But I want to create BEAUTY, in which Truth will dwell. Do I direct my thoughts towards certain persons with envy, contempt and impurity? Let me look into this. I will remove this harshness from the statue, so that new harmony will start to radiate from it. When peace and harmony are in me, the outer world reflects them and becomes more beautiful. I have no right to make the world uglier or unhappier by my own example. This is my final decision for today, tomorrow I will do more.

*　　*　　*

This classical example of ancient ethics can be worked with for as long as you feel it is adding value and beauty to your inner nature. You may develop it more if you have the inspiration to do so. When in this, or another way you feel that you have done your best, then, for the last session with this theme, evoke the text of it in your memory and look at it, remembering your development work, which you have previously performed. You should then have a much deeper understanding and feeling for the beauty of Plotinus's meditation.

2. THEME: *A craving for the objects of the senses rises out of the illusion caused by ignorance of the real nature of the* SELF; *just as the illusion of silver in the mother-of-pearl causes an attachment for it.*
(From *The Ashtavakra Gita*)

Development: This ancient teaching reaches into the deepest causes of human misery on this earth. The craving for physical possession is the main reason for my inner imbalance. How free I would feel, if there was no attachment to material objects in me! Let me look and find out now, how things are with me: what is dearest to me on this earth? How will I react to the loss of all my possessions and property? Will I be unhappy? If so, then know, my truant, little self, that the moment of abandoning everything I now see around me, and not only what I possess, cannot be avoided. Therefore, is it worth attaching oneself to anything, which must be unavoidably lost? The fact itself of 'possessing' certain commodities of material life is not an evil in itself, it is my attachment and fear of losing them, which is the danger and a forecast of future suffering. That is with what I have to deal!

The Great Ones never attached any value to earthly possessions and They were actually poor from the material point of view. Hence, do I believe myself to be happier than They, simply because I have a home, a car, some money, and so on?

It is the innate illusion which makes men believe in such a way. I no longer wish to be a slave of illusion, I want the freedom of Truth!

Lead me from darkness to the Light!

3. THEME : *Lust is radically opposed to knowledge. How strange that one who is physically enfeebled and has reached the end of his life, is still eager for sensual enjoyment.*
(From The Ashtavakra Gita)

Development: Knowledge includes the element of foreseeing and forestalling. I know that every sensual enjoyment finally leaves frustration and disappointment. I am now indifferent to the objects of my lust in the past and former sensual ecstasies are dead and cold. Will I seek others in order to experience the same grief and regrets when they too are lost? Moreover, they depend entirely upon the most fragile of all things—the human body, my own body. When it grows older, former achievements become impossible, and inner fire starts to consume me when I cannot satisfy them any more.

When will the time of wisdom and discrimination come for me? For only then can I steer my soul into the haven of peace and happiness. Therefore, self-control is the surest way to Peace.

4. THEME : *Knowing the objects of perception to be nought by nature, that steady minded one neither accepts this, nor rejects that.*
(From The Ashtavakra Gita)

Development: If I know deep within my conciousness, that everything which can be perceived by the senses, felt by the emotions, or thought of by the mind, is only temporary illusion, can I attribute any reality to them? Should I associate with them inwardly when I am receiving outer impressions, or try to reject them when they come and wait for my attention? No! I shall pass alongside without minding them and so their absence or presence will no longer affect me. Thus do the sages: they live in this world, it is true, but they are not of this world. And in this lies their eternal serenity and bliss. Their words are intended to create the same in us. Is there any better Path than that of following those who KNOW and who TEACH the TRUTH?

Now I am thinking deeply about this problem, so as to realize the wisdom of non-attachment in my heart.

For changeable is the mind, and one cannot rely on it. When it rules, it is the source of suffering. When it is ruled, it is a useful tool.

5. THEME: *Look upon friends, possessions, wealth, mansions, wives, gifts, and other good fortune, as a dream or a magic show, lasting only a few days.*
(From *The Ashtavakra Gita*)

Development: This deep reflection on absolute ethics needs little commentary from my mind. The crux of the theme is the realization of the illusory character of everything around me. Therefore, the lack of the things described, if such is my destiny in this life, is rather a blessing, for the pain of breaking of attachment may be spared me in this way. Will I crave for them, when I have realized their nothingness?

There are moments when I see this clearly and it seems that then some higher Self is in me. Sometimes I feel enchanted by earthly attachments and achievements, but isn't that the voice of future suffering?

Steadiness in discrimination, that is what I need and for what I pray!

6. THEME: *Bring to an end wealth, desires, and good and pious deeds, they will not bring rest to thy mind in the gloomy forest of the world.*
(From *The Ashtavakra Gita*)

Development: This looks like an ultimate step on the path of spiritual discrimination and non-attachment. The root of evil is desire: fulfilled—it dazzles and blinds; unfulfilled—it makes one suffer as if from a deadly thirst. Both aspects finally bring suffering and the moments of false happiness during the satisfying of desire, are so short and easily forgotten, that even the memory of them is like the dead, yellow leaves, fallen from the trees in late autumn. I realize that when the words of the theme of this meditation become truth for me, I will be free from the misleading paths that cross the forest of the world.

I can see that suffering is self-inflicted, so it can be discarded only by my own Self.

Whoever has realized this has achieved the highest possible ethical peak: he will not create disharmony, anxiety, fear, lust and anger either in himself, or in others. That is my aim.

7. THEME: *Transform your mind into controlled intuition, let everything in you be the Light. For such is your destiny.*
(Sri Aurobindo)

Development: The striking beauty of this aphorism makes meditation easier. I know that intuition is cognition without and beyond the thinking process (mind). I will not confuse this higher power in me with emotional, or mental ecstasies, which are valueless for an earnest seeker. Nothing permanent, or of assistance on the Path can come from either. By controlling them I will be able to distinguish them from *true Intuition*, which is Light in itself. To be directed by genuine Intuition means to dwell in Light.

And Darkness will not embrace me, when I am in the Light's Orb. I know that at the end of the Path everyone enters the realm of Light, which enlightens every man who appears in this world. That is my destiny.

8. THEME: *Transform your efforts into the controlled and powerful stream of your soul (true Self). Let everything in you be a conscious force. For such is your destiny.*
(Sri Aurobindo)

Development: During this course I have been able to see that much effort is necessary, in order to develop the art of meditation in me. But I also know that these efforts will not stay forever. When the Aim is reached the stream of meditation grows from an irregular rivulet into the majestic river, flowing incessantly and surely into the *Ocean of Truth*, in which I will find the *Silence, Light,* and cessation of all effort, which is unavoidable only in the state of *separateness*, that is in the realm of Untruth. Thus transcended, the consciousness becomes immutable and unchangeable, and destiny is dissolved in Bliss.

However, I will not believe the fallacy of expectation, that these peaks are within easy reach, or attainable in a short space of time. I shall not hypnotize myself with the false belief that I am already on the very threshold of Attainment. I am able to face the truth, and see the ages of toil and gradual progress, which lie ahead of me.

So, until the River gives its waters to the Ocean, there will always be struggle and effort before me. The guiding star will always be the awareness that the Search is certain and Attainment sure.

9. THEME: *Transform your joy into the continuous ecstasy without any object. Let everything in you be bliss. This is your aim.*
(Sri Aurobindo)

Development: Joy comes and goes in me. When I am far away from my mayavic sheaths, there is joy in me. But as I cannot yet experience continuous joy, shadow envelops my awareness. Knowing the cause, I can reduce the moments of Darkness, transforming my Path into the bliss of ecstasy (the fore-runner of Samadhi). As in true Samadhi, there cannot be any vision of objects, the words of the *theme* are the Truth. When there is no shadow, everything in me is Bliss It is the eternal inheritance of Man.

A Master said, that the chief obstacle to Achievement, which is the ultimate Bliss of Realization, is the *uncontrolled* and *disorderly mind*. That is why I cannot enjoy perpetuity of the inner Joy, which is my aim. Now I can see the enemy. It is both inside and outside of myself, as it is the mind, which distracts my meditation from my interior and attacks me from the outside.

The more I am free from its interference, the closer become the periods of Joy, which one day will be transformed into the final Bliss.

10. **THEME:** *The Joy of Being is not limited by time, for it has no beginning nor end. God is leaving one form only in order to enter into another.*
(Sri Aurobindo)

Development: After the former meditation, this one is open to me: the Lord is Joy Itself, and therefore It cannot be limited, just as He cannot. It is my purpose to enter into His Joy. The Great Teacher of Humanity told us: '*Enter into the Bliss of the Lord!*' It is the bliss of eternity in my conciousness. Everything which tries to limit it is a shadow, the unreal Maya.

Should I spend my life as if dedicated to shadow instead of Light? My existence, limited to the physical form, is opposed to my spiritual Joy, but I know my Path and can distinguish truth from untruth.

In the great inner Silence there is neither the world nor its noise. Therefore the Silence is one of the gateways to the temple of Joy. I will develop this Silence in me until it becomes my true nature, for it is the destiny of all manifested Life.

11. **THEME:** *So long as we live in this world we cannot be without tribulations and temptations.*
(Thomas a Kempis)

Development: How much time can I dedicate to meditation, in which alone I can find the inner Light? I must confess that worldly affairs absorb the greatest part of my time. Tribulations and temptations have their source in our attachment to this world, which is beyond all necessary measure. I often forget to render to God what belongs to God, and am occupied with the things belonging to Caesar, as was told us by the Great Teacher. Under such conditions I am only exposing myself to troubles from outside, as well as from inside, because I cannot be perfect in my relations with the outer world, thereby attracting trouble and expiation of errors.

Temptations are sent to me in order to be overcome and rejected. During meditation I am close to understanding and agreeing with this idea, but as soon as the world catches up with me again, I fall into the same old errors.

But realization of the cause of misery bears within it the roots of the tree of Wisdom. When one ceases to be subject to something which, in one's most lucid moments (as in deep meditation), one recognizes as false, the step to liberation has been made.

12. THEME: *The beginning of all temptations is inconstancy of mind and little confidence in the Lord.*
(Thomas a Kempis)

Development: How strikingly similar is this saying of the saintly Christian monk—who lived about six hundred years ago —when compared with the words of the contemporary Sage Maharshi, who defined the main obstacle to Attainment exactly as the '*wandering mind and perverted ways of life!*' The words become true when they come from true experience, and I can see that great souls have similar spiritual experiences. So I was right when I realized the necessity for domination of my mind, when starting my study of concentration, which alone can prevent the mind from its wandering and unsteadiness. Confidence in God does not admit of any perverted ways of life, for they are an offence to Him. When we have little confidence in the Lord, we are liable to be engaged just in perverted ways. Now I see that Truth is universal and manifests itself in every epoch through the great Souls, who are the vanguard of humanity.

13. THEME: *Often we do not know what we are able to do, but temptations show us what we are.*
(Thomas a Kempis)

Development: There is no such thing as something happening to us without any reason or purpose. I am able to realize this now. Therefore temptation, which comes to attack me, contributes to my self-knowledge, showing me my weaknesses and undoing. Sometimes I may imagine that I am much stronger than I really am and thus try to omit certain necessary experiences, as being obsolete as far as I am concerned. But in moments of temptation, when I have to fight with all my power against the impure stream, which tries to swallow me, I can see through myself much better.

Temptations are like a whetstone, which makes a blade effective by improving its cutting edge through friction. Inner friction in me does the same. So I will not avoid, but rather combat and overcome the tribulations.

Hence I will not complain because of them, but accept them as a necessary means, leading me to the development of inner strength and steadiness.

14. THEME: *Acts performed without any attachment, in the spirit of service to God, cleanse the mind and point the way to Liberation.*
(The Maharshi)

Development: The above teaching is identical with others given in this Series I of meditation. The Great Rishi, who lived in our own epoch (1879–1950) supported the spiritual instructions of his fore-runners and contemporaries, like Sri Aurobindo Ghose. Attachment is the source of misery and can be likened to a weight on the feet of a swimmer, which causes him to sink. Moreover, a very important statement of the Sage tells us that selfless acts directed to service of the Lord are an efficient means for the cleansing, or, in other words, the controlling of the mind. They lead to Liberation, which is the end of all tribulations in matter. Looking around me without any prejudice, I can see my limitations, even my slavery to conditions and surroundings, which stem from my ego-centred (that is, full of wrong attachment) activities in this world. They are the causes which create the results, reflected in destiny, or Karma in my incarnations. And Liberation is the lofty peak shown to us by the Sage.

The fourteen meditations you have found in Series I, have come to an end. They are the material you have to work through and so develop certain new abilities and inner experiences. Accept them in a right way, that is, as your *personal* work, from which you may profit and obtain more light. Should you go through all of them? If you intend to get the best from this course, your adherence to the recommended texts will be essential.

I trust that you do not imagine, that you can pass successfully through this course in a few months' time. It will not be so. Always have in your mind a clear distinction of the difference between 'reading' and 'studying', and know just what you can expect from both. If you read a novel, you do not need to study it, for such work is not usually intended for that purpose, as really it is rather entertainment.

But, with a book such as this, *reading* alone will definitely not be any work at all. Here you have to learn about something of which you knew nothing, or very little before, and for learning, a mere glancing through its contents will be useless.

This Series is called 'Ethical'. But the ethics in it are of a different kind, by comparison with the superficially accepted meaning. They do not touch so much on things turned outwards, to the surrounding world, as to the inward ones, in the realm which belongs only to you and to nobody else. Accordingly, your meditation work is your own and nobody can do it instead of you, as I have already mentioned in former chapters.

The development of harmonious and wise inner ethics in you is the problem and this work is intended by the writer as a contribution to the solution of it. I know that not everyone will accept this system and if someone can build a better pattern suitable for himself, it is his own business. It is not an easy task and knowing how many experiences, failures and recovery from them, the forming of a logical and practical structure and finally, spiritual assistance are needed for such an undertaking, I cannot be sure that many people will have the time, or take the trouble to do it.

This Series of meditations still leaves you a lot of freedom and does not bind you to a strict and literal adherence to their texts, but only directs your attention towards certain currents of thought, connected with the *themes* chosen for you.

In following this course you will see that material for meditation has been freely selected from many different sources. At the present time, there are innumerable good texts, available in book form for men of this twentieth century. It is impossible to collect ALL OF THEM together in one book. Moreover, it is quite unnecessary and impracticable. The real TRUTH cannot be exactly expressed or explained in any human language, for It by far transcends the mind. Hence, there is no book written by man, which could contain the whole of Truth, which is not knowledge, theory, or teachings, and so on.

In this work you will find a special Series of meditations dealing with different aspects of Truth, but it is unable to express that Truth, so that nothing remains to be added. Truth can be found in ourselves, we may be aware of It, feel It, live It, merge in It and all of these will be right for us. But we will never be able to literally 'transplant' It into another being.

The real fact is, that by the way of suitable meditation, men are able to come to the realization of the Truth in themselves. Therefore it is logical and sound to suppose, that what has been good for many will also be good for others in the future including yourself, provided you follow the proved Path.

How can you tell if you are progressing during your present studies? Because there will be certain indications. If you obtain more peace of mind, if fewer questions disturb your meditations, if a wonderful feeling of inner certainty grows in you, if fears recede, giving place to faith based on experience and if you become more patient and compassionate towards the outer world, these will be a few of the signs which will show you you are advancing. But do not think much about yourself, just work and hope! This may be the surest proof you can get. The inquiry —'How quickly am I progressing, how far am I from my starting point?' is not dictated by your true Self, but by the anxious mind. To silence this ego would be one of the most decisive victories for you. A man who has overcome his ego-personality is no longer interested in the fallen enemy, and allows him to be buried for ever.

*　　　*　　　*

I feel that this collection of meditations should not lack certain texts taken from the Buddhist *Dhammapada*. Some students, whom I have had the opportunity of observing and assisting, have a peculiar inclination towards the holy texts of Buddhism and their approach to the intimate ethics in a man, which lead to a further development of spirituality in him. The philosophy of Buddha is practical 'par excellence', expressed in the simplest words and does not require much explanation or comments. Therefore, my role in the concluding pages of this chapter will be limited to giving the best selection from the verses accompanied by brief comments, when the necessity to clarify the meditation may call for them. All of the Dhammapada is based on a deep knowledge of human psychology and it is just as well applicable to present-day man, as it was many centuries ago.

174

Another proof that the basic human psyche does not change much even over such a long period.

After all, who knows whether or not some of you listened to the original Preacher, or his disciples, or contacted the living philosophy of the *Perfect One*, in this or another way? This remembrance cannot dwell in your mind-brain, but it is, and must be preserved in the spiritual spark, the fulcrum of your lives, which leads you through innumerable material existences to the Final Liberation called—Nirvana by Buddha. Similarly perhaps, many of the present-day sincere followers of the Great Teacher—who taught in Galilee almost twenty centuries ago—may have trodden, at the same time as He did, on the soil of the land to which He came to bring to us the imperishable LIGHT.

The aim of this manual is to assist a possibly larger circle of earnest *seekers*, and concentrated selections are being given here for that purpose. They are more than sufficient for you in order to serve as a firm basis, on which you can weave your own meditative patterns. If your mind tells you that 'peharps there are still better and different texts', be ripe enough to find the right answer for that deceiver, who tries in every possible way to deflect your attention and so prevent you from subduing him. He is acting in his own interest and trying to remain your boss for ever. At the moment when you realize the truth about this tragic play, which prevents you from attaining Liberation and Bliss, you are truly entitled to discard him as leader and duly make him your servant.

*   *   *

SELECTIONS FROM THE DHAMMAPADA

1. THEME: *He abused me, he beat me, he defeated me, he robbed me—in those who harbour such thoughts hatred will never cease.*
He abused me, he beat me, he defeated me, he robbed me—in those who do not harbour such thoughts hatred will cease.
For hatred does not cease by hatred at any time: hatred ceases by love—this is an old rule.

Development: When reading these lines, I recall the eternal words of Christ, regarding how to treat our enemies and those who injure us, with their so often hard to understand and mysterious advice 'to turn the other cheek', that is, to be unresisting to evil or apparent injustice. When I call forth a simile from this lower, physical world, I can see that no fire can be extinguished by applying any fuel in order to put it out. Oil poured on to a fire will only feed it. What we need is something else which alone can help by acting like a stream of water. This water is forgiveness and dispassion. These liquidate the karmic struggle of the affected egos, which we all are on this earth.

The knowledge that nothing comes to us without reason and that no one can harm us without it being a result of our former actions is most essential here. It will bring peace amidst the most intense of troubles. But the harming of others must be resisted.

2. THEME: *He who wishes to put on the yellow robe without having cleansed himself from sin, who disregards also temperance and truth, is unworthy of the yellow robe.*

Development: How often it is that true asceticism is misunderstood, and people like to change their labels—religions, or sects, in order to advance spiritually, as they wrongly believe! To accept the outer signs of asceticism means nothing more than a kind of very dangerous hypocrisy, which is hard to eradicate because a misguided man is then able to believe quite sincerely that he is right. The Maharshi clearly condemned such an attitude, when pointing out that no 'change of labels' (his own words) is of any use. It is the inner attitude alone which counts and that is why this contemporary spiritual Teacher insisted that Realization is possible 'even in a noisy London flat as well as in a secluded Indian Ashram'.

3. THEME: *As rain breaks through an ill-thatched house, passion will break through an unreflecting mind.*

Development: Now I realize why the author of *Concentration* and *Samadhi* insists so strongly on the training and domination of one's own mind. The idea is age-old and always true. Seeking once again for the most understandable parallel in the outer world, I find, that even the most gifted engineer will be unable to tighten a vital screw in his motor, and so on, without a proper screwdriver. His knowledge will be of no avail if instruments are not provided, as his finger-nails will not be a substitute for them. Fuel or cooling water will constantly leak from a loose valve, until it is repaired.

And so it is with the human mind, which is, as I already know, an important tool of my consciousness. No spiritual giant was ever a fool and everyone of them was a master of his mentality and not a slave of wavering thoughts, or feelings. Because feelings are ruled and can be subdued only by the *higher power*, which, in this case, is mind *in relation to them*, this *power* must be trained and operated according to my needs. Moral purity is therefore impossible without a pure and well-ruled mind.

4. THEME: *As rain does not break through a well-thatched house, passion will not break through a well-reflecting mind.*

This is simply a stronger assertion of the previous theme (3), so it does not need any further development.

5. THEME: *Those wise people, meditative, steady, always possessed of strong powers, attain to Nirvana, the highest happiness.*

Development: Here I find a beautifully strong emphasis placed on the necessity for meditation, as the highest function of the human consciousness. We should dedicate as much time as we can to it, for no other means will ever put us closer to the Attainment, described by Buddha as the 'highest happiness' (or beatitude and peace). Endurance in meditation is the assurance of success.

6. THEME: *Fools follow after vanity. The wise man keeps earnestness as his best jewel.*

Development: Once again this is an underlining of the law, that for meditation there must be study and understanding. Without them we are only fools, destined for defeat, which will inevitably bring disappointment and frustration, of which it is very hard to get rid. And still, even now, one can hear in certain pseudo-occult societies, based on ignorance, that 'everyone can meditate', that everyone is 'invited to meditate', and so on, just

177

as if everyone could be invited to use a complicated computer or other machine, which requires special training and knowledge.

7. THEME: *As a fletcher makes straight his arrow, a wise man makes straight his trembling and unsteady thought, which is difficult to guard, difficult to hold back.*

Development: Little can be added to these words of the Master. The idea is clear, but a method must be adopted to put it into a workable form. The author recommends his contemporary manual for control and development of the mind—*Concentration*.

8. THEME: *It is good to tame the mind, which is difficult to hold in and flighty, rushing wherever it listeth; a tamed mind brings happiness.*

No development is necessary.

9. THEME: *Those who bridle their mind which travels, far, moves about alone, is without a body, and hides in the chamber of the heart, will be free from the bonds of Māra, the tempter.*

Development: Domination of the mind brings freedom for consciousness, which is actually the Man himself, but not his body. The *Tempter* is just that mind, fighting for supremacy over him, to the disadavantage of the man.

10. THEME: *He who knows that this body is like froth, and has learnt that it is as unsubstantial as a mirage, will break the flower-pointed arrow of Māra, and never see the king of death*

Development: The perishable body should be looked upon for what it is worth and not as something substantial or permanent. It should be reasonably treated, just the same as is a horse owned by a good rider, but no more. Identification with the mortal body brings one under the terrible power of Death, that is, suffering fear and frustration.

11. THEME: *Death subdues a man who is gathering flowers, and whose mind is distracted, before he is satiated in his pleasures.*

Development: This is only a further statement about the fate of those who consider themselves—consciously or subconsciously—as being their bodies. This is the worst possible fallacy.

12. THEME: *'These sons belong to me, and this wealth belongs to me,' with such thoughts a fool is tormented. He himself does not belong to himself; how much less sons and wealth?*
The fool who knows his foolishness, is wise at least so far. But a fool who thinks himself wise, he is called a fool indeed.

Development: The perishable character of all possessions is here, once more underlined, and the old truth, that 'the fool, who starts to realize that he is a fool, through that realization becomes a sage' is again reaffirmed. Whoever, while being foolish and immature, that is, believing in his wealth, and so on, thinks he is wise, falls into the deepest pit of ignorance.

13. THEME: *If an intelligent man be associated for one minute only with a wise man, he will soon perceive the truth, as the tongue perceives the taste of soup.*
If a fool be associated with a wise man even all his life, he will perceive the truth as little as a spoon perceives the taste of soup.

Development: The important doctrine of ripeness in man is here proclaimed. It is so simple that the theme itself works as well as does explanation and development.

14. THEME: *As soon as the intelligence of an immature person develops for his own ruin, it destroys his bright side, bursting his head.*

Development: This is a warning, that 'learned fools' are worse than ignorant ones, for they can bring more harm by their partial learning in certain branches of knowledge (material, of course). Destruction follows, just as learning of dangerous things, such as our nuclear discoveries, hangs like the sword of Damocles over the foolish community, or the whole of humanity.

15. THEME: *Do not have evil-doers for friends, do not have low people for friends: have virtuous people for friends, have for friends the best of men.*

179

Development: In our 'enlightened' age we know enough about the influence, which one personality can exercise on another. Good will radiate good, evil only darkness. Christ warned us very firmly about the same, and the inspired poet-king David said that: 'Blessed is the man that walketh not in the counsel of the ungodly, nor standeth in the way of sinners. . .'

16. THEME: *As a solid rock is not shaken by the wind, wise people falter not amidst blame and praise.*

Development: The winds of human recognition, or reproach are not essential for the one who knows himself. He is aware how difficult it is to know oneself, so he is also aware of how ignorant are those who try to judge others, before they possess the most important knowledge of themselves.

17. THEME: *Few are there among men who arrive at the other shore (become Arhats); the other people here run up and down the shore.*

Development: This is a statement, which is well known to the Christian world: 'Many are called (that is, born and reincarnated), but few are chosen' (that is, those who attain Truth in spiritual consciousness). This shore or side is the material, mortal existence, which always brings more suffering than happiness. The other, the immortal side is the realm of the pure, enlightened CONSCIOUSNESS, beyond incarnations and suffering.

18. THEME: *Forests are delightful; where the world finds no delight, there the passionless will find delight, for they look not for pleasures.*

Development: The outer side of things is often pleasant, but their roots are bitter. We strive, we find, and then we lose. The approaching suffering of separation is greater than the short pleasure of possession was before. Which is the path of the WISE?

19. THEME: *If one man conquer in battle a thousand times a thousand men, and if another conquer himself, he is the greatest of conquerors.*

Development: Here the Lord Buddha is speaking about the Realization of the true Self in man, following his mastery of his lower, perishable functions and bodies. This is the true and perennial conquest.

20. THEME: *By comparison with the hundred-year long life of the one who does not see the Path to immortality, one day of a man who does is greater.*

Development: We see a similar truth expressed by Thomas a Kempis when he speaks about the 'vanity of desiring a long life without living it virtuously.' All spiritual Masters are ONE, said the Maharshi. Again and again we see their unity in Truth, when they speak the same language to us throughout the centuries so distant in time. A long life may well be frustrated and a short one enlightened by right discrimination and deeds.

21. THEME: *If a man commits a sin, let him not do it again; let him not delight in sin: the accumulation of evil is painful.*

Development: Here the Law of Cause and Effect, or, as our Eastern brothers call it—Karma, is again emphasized. Justice in Hermetic philosophy also gives the same idea. As man sows, so will he reap. Buddha's warning is repeated here.

22. THEME: *Not in the sky, not in the midst of the sea, not if we enter into the clefts of the mountains, is there known a spot in the whole world where death could not overcome the mortal.*

Development: What had a beginning must also have an end. How often we forget this truth, an inexorable one, which frightens the fool and brightens the sage, who does not believe in the illusion of this temporary existence in matter. While the former tries to avoid or delay death, the wise one is not affected by it: he does not want to die before his time comes, nor does he want to prolong his physical journey here by any means. This is what I have found within myself by meditating deeply about it in the Silence of my Heart.

23. THEME: *Not nakedness, not platted hair, not dirt, not fasting, or lying on the earth, not rubbing with dust, not sitting motionless, can purify a mortal who has not overcome desires.*

181

Development: In this verse the Teacher is speaking about the uselessness of outer means for cleansing the soul. Of course, this applies only when the physical actions just mentioned are not accompanied by spiritual enlightenment and sincere striving. Spiritually minded men can easily neglect outer appearances to a certain extent, but they will never make themselves appear disgusting or ridiculous. Simplicity and the conquest of desires does not mean monstrosity, or nonsense. All exhibitionism is only a proof of the lack of any inner values in such a person.

Unfortunately, how much exhibitionism in all its ugly and treacherous forms is around us today? Take, for example, the false yogas with their equally false exponents, and their ridiculous and nonsensical theories propagated for naïve and foolish people, gullible enough to be unmercifully duped and robbed of their money. As if anything true could be bought! I shall meditate deeply about it, so as not to allow myself to fall into that old, but still dangerous pit.

24. THEME :   *But now,*
Thou Builder of this Tabernacle—Thou!
I know Thee! Never shalt Thou build again these walls of pain,
Nor raise the roof-tree of deceits, nor lay fresh rafters on the clay;
Broken Thy house is, and the ridge-pole split! Delusion fashioned it!
Safe pass I thence—Deliverance to obtain.
(From *The Light of Asia* by Sir Edwin Arnold)

Development: In this last of our verses taken from Lord Buddha's Teachings, we see the crowning of the results of the efforts attained by the wise man in his struggle for Freedom. The Master compares the physical and emotional factors to a house, built of illusion and desires. Isn't this so? If I look at all of my actions, and those of my fellow men around me, I must concede the truth of this verse, a realizable, living Truth, bringing the bliss of Attainment.

'KNOW THE TRUTH AND IT WILL MAKE YOU FREE' is the supporting teaching of Christ. Striving for what is perishable is foolishness, bringing only bonds and suffering. Sri Aurobindo rightly said that: 'Men call for freedom, but are still enamoured of their own bonds!' What a paradox it is! And a very tragic one.

There is no 'ultimate desire' which, when fulfilled, would set me free, for there is no desire that will not create yet another one, still more deceptive and cruel.

To cut it here and now is the only way of setting my foot on to the Path, leading to the Bliss of Liberation. The first step must be made, so why NOT TODAY?

*   *   *

You now have a good many themes for meditation and are supposed to perform them as prescribed. If so, then you are undoubtedly coming closer to the SYNTHESIS of all meditations, as proceeding from one and the same SOURCE, which we may call—WISDOM. Your purpose now, in the advanced course of meditation ahead, is to consolidate the present achievement for further steps.

CHAPTER XXI

Sankaracharya's Meditations — Series II

1. THEME : *Who is there on this earth with soul more dead than he who, having obtained a human incarnation and a male body, madly strives for the attainment of selfish objects?*

Development: The Sage Sankara here puts the question quite boldly. He voices the deplorable and tragic error of the one, who devotes his life to searching for unreal, perishable and evanescent aims. Should I follow this unhappy pattern? Should I deposit my only treasure, my true Self, in a bank which I know must go bankrupt? Should I hunt for material objects and aims directed to egoistic achievements, which will not last beyond my grave? Hard as the problem may be, for an individual and practical solution, it must be dealt with. Therefore I will seek in my innermost depths for the silent answer, which transcends the ephemeral life of today and which enlightens my path into Infinity. The Infinite is my fatherland, not this small speck of matter thrown into space as a temporary dwelling-place for those who are passing along with me, through the hard school of separate existence. Now I am trying to find the solution.

(Think deeply about what you have read, then try to remain in the silence of the mind and senses. The solution comes without any words.)

2. THEME : *One who has a strong intellect, who is a learned man and who has powers of comprehension, is a man qualified for such an (a spiritual) investigation.*

Development: Now I understand well why the development of my power over my mind was a condition for the study of meditation. There is no better method, or keener means to achieve the required intelligence, than the training of my mind accord-

184

ing to my will and making it one-pointed by concentration. Meditation is the weapon which conquers the toils of spiritual search and investigation. As with every weapon, it should be sharp and clean and able to pierce the hardest core of any problem arising in me. Therefore, let me think about my spiritual duties.

3. THEME: *Among the instruments of emancipation (liberation) the supreme is devotion. Meditation upon the true form of the real Self is said to be devotion.*

Development: I see that the ultimate aim of meditation is the approaching of the Lord. The Sage Sankara supports this in the verse just quoted. No spiritual progress is possible without an intuitional and firm recognition of the Supreme. My beginning and my end will be in Him. My real or true Self is His reflection, the true *form* of the Self is the object of progressive meditation. What is that form? In any case, it has little in common with anything I can see in the manifested world of matter. This '*form*' must be inexpressible, but I feel that I shall be able to approach it, to merge in IT! I cannot *see* it as something apart from me, for then there will be a binary: IT and myself! And WHO would then be me, apart from IT?

I believe I can conceive that Truth, which unveils Itself only in perfect Silence. I am merging in It.

(Stop thinking, forget your surroundings, merge in Silence.)

4. THEME: *Some say devotion is meditation on the nature of one's Atman. He who possesses all these qualifications is one who is fit to know the true nature of Atman.*

Development: My Atman is another term for my true Self. Therefore this meditation may be identical with the former one. I feel that the 'knowing' of the true nature of the Atman means merging in it, excluding all the shells of material consciousness, of feelings and thoughts. It will lead me to the Silence. When I come into It, I shall be IT. I cannot be apart from IT. This is the greatest mystery, but it must be solved and can be solved I will do it. I am the SILENCE!

5. THEME: *One who has attained rest in spirit, like the flame which has obtained rest when the fuel is consumed, and one whose kindness is not actuated by personal considerations, and who is anxious to befriend those that seek for help, (he is the Guru).*

Development: I see that the fire of the egoistic life must first be extinguished before rest can be obtained. The searching for the perishable must be stopped before the flame ceases to burn. Then only will I be able to become one beyond all personal considerations, for I will see the unreality of the ego in myself as well as in others. And if those people, who are still unaware of this truth, seek my help, I shall give it as something quite natural and without expecting any recognition or reward.

6. THEME: *Salutation to thee, O Lord, full of compassion, O friend of those who bend before thee. I have fallen into the ocean of birth and rebirth. Rescue me by thy never failing glance which rains the ambrosia of sincerity and mercy.*

Development.: I feel admiration for the Great Souls, who enlighten the world's darkness by their presence and action. I know how hard it is to dominate one's lower nature, so I can see how powerful and beautiful are those Great Ones, who have already performed the great task! What could I feel for them if not devotion, esteem and love? Such a Being is a true friend, for he understands everything, he knows my difficulties and is eager to assist me, if only I am willing to accept his help. The ocean of Maya cannot be crossed without a guide, who knows its treacherous currents and hidden rocks. The ambrosia of sincerity and compassion, which comes from the final, achieved Wisdom flows from such a spiritual Master. May I encounter him, in any form he may consider as suitable for me.

7. THEME: *The great and peaceful ones live regenerating the world like the coming of spring, and after having themselves crossed the ocean of embodied existence, help those who try to do the same thing, without personal motives.*

Development: Around me I see different people in very different degrees of development, wisdom and virtue. The scale extends

186

both up and down. Those who are closer to the top are the Great Ones, of whom the Sage Sankara speaks. They are an irrefutable necessity and there is certainty of their existence in the gradual progress of men. Advancing beyond personality, the Great Ones extend their mighty hands for those who are eager to follow in their steps. This is the mystery of mastership. Blessed are the seekers who are privileged enough to meet such a Master on their path, for they will then have all doubts, which destroy so many honest souls, eradicated in them for ever.

8. THEME: *Constant fixing of the mind on the pure Spirit is called Samādhāna (true concentration). But not amusing the mind by delusive worldly objects.*

Development: In these great words we have the ultimate Truth of Achievement. Everyone gets that for which he strives. Distractions of the everyday materialistic life stick to human karmas like leeches and are very hard to remove. They suck a man's life energies, wasting them on ephemeral and short-lived aims. This is a dispersion of forces; this is the preparing of countless sufferings for the unwise person.

To concentrate one's attention on things which today appear to be alive, but tomorrow will inevitably be non-existent, is to assist one's own death. Everything in the material world is subject to death, after a short period of illusory 'existence'.

Life is indestructible consciousness, that is, Spirit. To participate one's awareness in it means true and uninterrupted Life.

Now I see why the fixing of the mind on pure Spirit is right, hopeful and the only salutary attitude.

How can I do it? For Spirit cannot be described, nor defined as can be other factors in my life! Spirit is pure consciousness and pure consciousness appears when the vibrations of the senses and mind are stilled. Now I can see where lies the Path to the Indescribable: to separate oneself from everything that is outside, and to enter into the *Silent Shrine* of one's own innermost awareness. It comes of itself when the vibrations stop. Then remains the true *Essence of Life*, simple, silent, pure, indestructible and omnipotent.

Then the Hyperconsciousness may appear, showing the way to the final Achievement. I see that there is no complicated terminology, no memorizing of things in the mind and there are no laborious exercises. Achievement is really so close, so simple, that men pass beside it and cannot perceive the Truth within their very reach.

Why delay the attempt to realize the Eternal in me? Who seems to prevent it? I see it clearly now. It is my mind, which is frightened of being pushed aside, of being dominated and made into a slave instead of a dictator. Now I recognize the Enemy, and will not let him deceive me any more, as Lord Buddha said when he reached his enlightenment. I am silent both outside and inside: I contemplate the Real. No more thinking, all is at peace in me.

9. THEME: *'What is bondage? Whence is its origin? How is it maintained? How is it removed? What is non-spirit? What is the supreme spirit? How can one discriminate between them?'*

Development: In this verse of Sankara's I see that the basic questions are being put to me. But now I can answer them.

Bondage is the desire for change, for separateness in mind and feelings and the occupying of myself with these two throughout all my life, as do millions of others. The *origin* lies in myself, in my hidden desires, extroversion, curiosity about perishable things, sensual enslavement and lack of discrimination, will-power and peace.

If I call these malefactors before the tribunal of my true awareness and condemn them, they will be removed and not maintained. They are non-Spirit and my sentence against them removes the unreal, which is that non-Spirit.

The supreme and only Spirit is within me, in my innermost depths, where no vibration, or 'enemies' dare to enter. This is discrimination. My eternal aim is to enter into that Inner Temple inside myself, for no outer one can substitute the True Spirit in me.

I now see the road leading to it. Will I make my first step today?

10. THEME: *Sons and others are capable of discharging a father's debts; but no one except oneself can remove (his own) bondage.*

Development: How clear this meditation is, now that the preceding one has been mastered! Who else can eat my food, or drink my water? My salvation is in my own hands.

11. THEME: *Others can remove the pain (caused by the weight) of burdens placed on the head, but the pain (that arises) from hunger and the like cannot be removed except by oneself.*

12. THEME: *The sick man is seen to recover by the aid of medicine and proper diet, but not by acts performed by others.*

The development of both meditations nos. 11 and 12 is now fully within the reach of the student himself, so I will not give any advice regarding them. But do not be deluded by the apparent easiness of finding such a solution. The main aim of meditation is not any mental agreement with the obvious truth of a *theme*, but a firm grasping of the consequences from the understanding achieved and its practice just from the moment of that realization. Be wise and act accordingly.

CHAPTER XXII

From the Maharshi's Wisdom — Series III

WE now come to meditation themes taken from the teachings of the contemporary Sage and Spiritual Master—Ramana Maharshi.

A Hindu of Brahmin origin, he happily combined the age-old classical Vedantic tradition of his race with contemporary ease of expression and terminology. In fact, his philosophy, which has nothing in common with the useless brain-based theories and logical concoctions of official Western pattern, *can be lived*, unlike the abstruse matters just mentioned, which can only be recognized by the efforts of the human mind. I do not wish to undermine the role of the human mind in the slightest, for it would be utterly wrong. Without that mind I could not even write these lines which you now have before you eyes!

The difference, and it is a basic one, is that the Sage taught us to assign the mind to its PROPER PLACE in our consciousness, in the role of a tool, directed by the higher Power in man, his spiritual awareness, his true SELF. When I am typing the pages of this book, I am not guessing and blindly searching with my mind as to *what I have to say* and whether there is something 'better' to seek for in my mind. But there is a very realistic and sure realization, that ideas do not come from laborious thinking and consultation within the mind. And this makes me certain that my mind is co-operating: there is no doubt about it, and just in the way that I want it to. It is forming '*the stream*' into thoughts and words when ordered to do so. But it is *silent* and unobtrusive *when the current stops*. I hope you will understand what I mean and hence I will abstain from any further explanation. The Maharshi said openly, that his mind was, according to his teaching, *dead*. And still in his words we can find depths and wisdom not encountered in those of people who sublimate their mentality and set it on the throne, which rightly belongs to the spiritual and real SELF of man.

Read this short introduction several times before you start to meditate on the following paragraphs of this chapter. The more you know, the better for you and nothing is so useful as vast knowledge about oneself and one's mental processes, for the development of a true and successful ability to direct your consciousness into the paths of controlled activity, which we may call MEDITATION.

1. THEME: *The highest goal of spiritual experience for man is Self-Realization.*

Development: The Sage Maharshi believed that the full knowledge of our own Self, or the immortal essence, is the supreme means for the achievement of all the other qualities inherent in us like Love, a high moral code, peace of mind, devotion to the Supreme, and so on. He emphasized that all evil and lack of development are a direct result of man's ignorance. Whoever KNOWS, will not commit stupidities, or evil and selfish deeds. The final wisdom in man enlightens his whole nature, removing the stains of materialism and egoism, both of which come as prodigal children of the basic ignorance. If I *know* what I really need, I will not rob, or injure others, for my *supreme good* lies beyond the reach of the ego-personality-mind, of that unholy trinity, which rules the lives of non-realized men.

There is nothing beyond true Realization of the Self, for it is the final Achievement, after which there is nothing more to learn, or experience. One's evolution then comes to its blessed end—'The dewdrop slips into the Shining Sea!' thereby becoming one with the WHOLE, or, as Christ told us, comes to dwell in the Father's House, where there are mansions for every Son of Man.

2. THEME: Work performed with attachment is a shackle, whereas work performed with detachment does not affect the doer. He is, even while working, in solitude.

Development: In this meditation is resolved the problem, which so often affects and embarrasses many otherwise able students. They often think that the work in the outer world, which they are compelled to do as their bread-winning occupation, and so on, is just an obstacle to spiritual Achievement. Here the Master removes this fallacy and gives an exact explanation as to how we should 'Render therefore to Caesar the things that are Caesar's. . .' Never again will I complain against the conditions of my life, for it would be an unwise misunderstanding, opposing every spiritual path. I remember another saying of the Sage, expressing the same truth: 'You can attend to your worldly duties and still obtain SPIRITUAL ENLIGHTENMENT.' Certainly Maharshi knew what he said for he showed it by his own example. Therefore I cannot have any doubt about it. If my mind tries to embarrass me with its usual treachery, by putting in doubt everything aimed at its domination, I will know from where such unwanted doubts are coming.

3. THEME: *If one can keep quiet, without engaging in any other pursuit, it is very good. If that cannot be done, where is the use of being quiet as far as Realization is concerned?*

Development: Here I can see the cardinal virtue necessary for Attainment. No man can progress spiritually until he quietens his lower nature and so deadens the noise of his surroundings, visible as well as invisible. The voice of Spirit-Truth can be heard only when I cease to listen to unnecessary worldly noise. Or better still, when being amidst any kind of noise, I will no longer hear it, but will listen to the soundless voice, which incessantly speaks in every human being, even though they do not wish to, and so cannot hear it. Most certainly I can recall moments in my own life, when loud noises surrounded me, but I was so intensely merged in inner problems, that I was as if completely unaware of all the outer bedlam.

This is a milestone on my Path. Instead of listening to unimportant and empty things, I will hear the salutary voice speaking deep within me.

Refraining from engaging myself in any other pursuits except that of my Path is wisdom, as revealed by the Master Maharshi. In other words, according to another Great Teacher: 'Be in the world, but not of it.' There lies the solution to everyday life. Simple as it is, it is perhaps one of the most difficult things for the beginner on the Path. The world has a powerful attraction for human ego-life. Realization puts my ego into its proper place: as a temporary, lower expression of myself. I am really far beyond and above it. This is what I have to realize and meditation about it will bring me wisdom of myself.

4. THEME: *The ego is the source of thought.*

Development: Here is the most important solution of the mind's problem: the thinking process, if not firmly directed, becomes the source of the ego, which I am now trying to fight. So a student must be done with allowing his thoughts to wander just as their master—mind likes. Every moment that I am over-powered by uncontrolled and aimless thinking, I am destroying a vital bridge on my Path. I will only have to build it again later, with much toil and pain. Hence it is better for me not to allow the inimical powers to put obstacles on my Path now. But the initiative must come from myself.

5. THEME: *Change of environment is unnecessary. It is the mind which suggests this wrong idea. Your efforts can be made even now, whatever the environment.*

Development: This teaching of the Sage Ramana strikes right at the very centre of human weakness: the idea that the present conditions are not suitable, and that one should first create a propitious environment for one's spiritual advancement. How wrong this is! And yet this fallacy prevents millions from taking a decisive step and thereby taking their destiny into their own hands.

It is not the conditions and surroundings which prevent our meditation, it is our slavery to our mind, which invents every-thing possible in order to divert us from the Path, because the Path will bring about mind's submission. If I am really able to undertake a practical study of meditation, which alone can raise my consciousness beyond the level of death and suffering, it is NOW, JUST TODAY, and not tomorrow! The power in me which compels me to delay the start, is within myself, and it must be fought from the INSIDE, not from the OUTSIDE. Now I realize this. Delay simply means that I still consider certain things more important than my inner development, my inner, true life. Some-times I do not wish to confess this, but I know that it is so, for it cannot be otherwise. One cannot serve both God and Mammon at the same time.

I am now taking a fateful decision. Only I can do it.

6. THEME: *Attending to the Self means attending to work. It is because people believe that they are the bodies, they think that work is being done by them. But truly, the Self alone is the real motive power behind all our activities.*

Development: Another cardinal problem is solved. When I believe that it is my little ego-personality which performs any work, it can be tiresome and binding for me. But when I realize that all activities have their roots in the *real Self*, which is not my body and has little in common with anything at all, then I am able to work, and to look on this process as if *apart from it* and not feel myself to be the doer. This makes any kind of work easy and not depressing, for then I am APART, observing the working machine—my body, with its brain and muscular power, and so on. I remember this idea even from the study of Western occultism, when I taught myself to 'separate' from the impression, that it is 'myself' who is toiling and tiring. I remember all the positive results achieved since the time when I first accepted this attitude.

It is now time that I became ripe for important decisions, one of which is expressed in the present theme of my meditation.

7. THEME: *You must get rid of the idea that you have yet to realize the Self. You are the Self here and now.*

Development: I now see why so many people hinder themselves by wrongly imagining, that they have to perform something, or to act in a certain way, in order to realize their true being. No action will do this. It is inner change, that of awareness, which alone can lead to my aim. I have to go deep into myself and merge in my innermost consciousness, forgetting thinking and all the surrounding world. Then the condition will be created by myself, which may allow me to dive into the depths, where there are neither conditions, nor environment, simply LIFE alone. It seems to me that I now understand what many Saints spoke of when they insisted on inner peace and the merging in God! For He is just in this ultimate, unperturbed Peace, of which even the Old Testament speaks.

The Reality can neither be born, nor die : if it were otherwise then it would not deserve the name of Reality. For the Real is only THAT which exists beyond our *three mortal sub-divisions of time*—past, present and future. There is no time for Reality. A tremendous conclusion then arises : I am ALWAYS the Self, and there never was, nor will be a time when the SELF was non-existent. And that is just what the Sage says to us. So why can't I realize the Self immediately, here and now? Because I am NOT looking into IT, but into the unreal appearances of the outer world, *which was created*, as Maharshi says, *by the mind in us.* How can I see the REAL if my whole attention is directed to MAYA; if I dedicate all my thoughts and feelings to the APPEAR-ANCE, but not to the ESSENCE of things? This meditation may be an *initiation for me*, if I reach the right conclusion. I see it now. I also see what powerful means meditation is, opening new vistas and horizons for us.

8. THEME : *Solitude is the* INNER SILENCE. *It is in man's mind. But man attached to the things of outer life cannot get solitude, for his mind is not controlled nor silenced.*

Development: The first sentence of this meditation is not new to me, now that I have passed through the previous chapters. I now see how the Self can be attained, or, properly speaking, how I can allow my true Self to descend into my awareness of today. It is by REMOVING EVERYTHING ELSE except the Silence in me. This is the required SOLITUDE. And I realize now, why the attachment to outer things must be curtailed, at least, for the periods I dedicate to meditation. But if I am absolutely merged in the material world throughout the whole day, without any voluntary and deliberate retirement into meditation about the Silence, it will be immensely hard for me to create the required attitude just for the comparatively short duration of my meditation's exercises.

I can see that meditation must be gradually extended into the periods, other than just the one or two meditations daily. The chief obstacle to detaching my mind from the unreal, is that I believe that the outer world is more important than my inner life. This is attachment to worldly objects, no matter how many and how different they can be.

But I see a ray of hope: in one of the foregoing chapters I was told about the influence of the CONSCIOUSNESS on the material world, which, in the language of the mind is equal to miracles. Why then should I not start to practise the approaches to the Hyperconsciousness?

I know about the necessity of achieving mind control, and that is why I studied concentration. The final aim of it is the *elimination of mind* (that is, of all thoughts), for a period desired and predetermined in advance. Truth can be found only when the mind has been effectively silenced, which is attainable by way of a practical study of concentration. I feel that the time will come when, in the inner *solitude*, I will find the solution to all my problems, including the most important, which is that of my own, true SELF.

From today I will attempt to practise merging into the Silence, not only during my regular time for meditation, as is now the case, but also during every appropriate moment of the day.

9. THEME: *The State which transcends speech and thought is called* MOUNA *(or Silence). It is meditation without mental activity. Subjugation of the mind is meditation: deep meditation is eternal speech.*

Development: I see that the very aim of meditation is firstly subjugation of the mind, so that it can no longer be an obstacle to a clear vision of the *Supreme cliché*. Secondly, it is the full silencing of that mind, so that consciousness becomes similar to the mirror-like surface of a quiet lake or pool. I can see the real Reflection of Truth in it then, but not otherwise. The Maharshi truly calls this meditation without mental activities, for then the mind remains in peace and is inactive. But my true I-Self is then closer to me, and so I have a chance to experience that SELF.

When in the 'normal'—which for me is of a lower type—meditation, the mind is directed into desirable channels, and can vibrate only according to my will and intention, while in the MUTE meditation mind is simply not present at all. And still I live and am aware of my being. Where could I find better proof that I am not my mind or feelings? I am now trying to engrave this great Truth in the deepest recesses of my memory, so that IT will always be present as a background to all of my spiritual work.

I know that two men, both using *mute meditation* at the same time, will understand one another immeasurably better than by means of speech. This Silence, as said the Master Maharshi, is our ETERNAL SPEECH.

That is why a true Master is never eager to speak. He only uses the language of the mind when asked and when the highest expression, like the just mentioned SPEECH OF THE SILENCE, is inaccessible to those around them, because of their insufficient development. And the Master KNOWS what is around him and acts accordingly.

Spiritual Silence has nothing in common with artificially induced inactivity of the mind, as in the case of a swoon, shock, hypnosis or defective brain. Spiritual Silence is only ONE, and it comes when man invites IT and is able to stand ITS power and peace.

My aim is to reach this Silence, through the gradual process of my inner development. That is why I am studying this book and performing the recommended exercises.

Let the river of my consciousness, that is, myself, never deviate from the paths of the Silence.

10. THEME: *Mind, body and world are not separate from the* SELF. *And they cannot exist apart from the Self, being like its lower manifestation. But* SELF *perfectly exists apart from and beyond those manifestations, which men confuse with reality in the world. They do not affect the Self.*

Development: From the theme of this meditation I see two important aspects of Truth. Firstly that all that is visible and sensible is unreal, for it had a beginning and therefore must have an end. But can I see the beginning, or the end of the Spirit-Self, that HYPERCONSCIOUSNESS of which I read in former chapters? I know that IT is omnipotent and beyond all limitations of time and space. It is truly the realm of the Self, and that is why I am immortal, being nothing less than this HYPERCONSCIOUSNESS.

Secondly, if I imagine the Self as a Seer, then the seen world will be like a screen, on which plays the light and shade of relative life. And WHO alone can see this play? It is pure, unmanifested SELF, the only Seer.

I feel that here lies the hidden solution of the problem of Life as the only immortal factor in Manifestation.

My immortality belongs to my deepest and truest Self, which is independent of everything else, from my bodies to the farthest galaxies, which are equally mere shadows before the immovable, unchangeable LIGHT OF CONSCIOUSNESS, purified of all conditions and aspects. I may call IT—Spirit, as Christ did.

When Buddha reached this Light, he immediately proclaimed his victory over the unreal and said that never more would the illusion be able to build any prison for the Light in him.

I look forward to the blessed moment, when I shall be able to express the same Truth, which will then live in me.

I can see more and more, that meditation can lead me to that Peak. What else can do so?

That is why I will continue my present study, for this work will produce results beyond my present incarnation, that is, I will take the fruit of my efforts with me into Eternity, which is my true Fatherland.

11. THEME: *If the mind is turned in, towards the Source of Illumination, the objective knowledge ceases, and the SELF alone shines as the Heart.*

Development: I can consider this saying of the Sage Maharshi as a direct technical instruction for spiritual meditation. The mind must be directed into its source, into its beginning, that mysterious realm where the first thought was born in me. Beyond this will be the REAL ME, unstained by thoughts, or feelings. I realize now the aim to which the present meditation leads me. It is the IMMORTAL Fulcrum in me, from which I project my bodies with all their attributes, into innumerable incarnations, until the Realization of the only real *Source* starts to shine through my every thought, feeling and deed. Then my Path will be approaching its end. THE DROP WILL FALL INTO THE SHINING SEA.

What can objective knowledge teach me? Only the wisdom necessary for living in the material worlds and yet for everyone of them a different kind of knowledge will be needed. I cannot see any reality in such knowledge. The wisest men died, and nothing visible remains of them on this earth. If they went into other, more perfect forms, they have certainly forgotten their elementary experiences here. And it will be the same with me!

This understanding brings me a true evaluation of the values in the world. Everything will be lost in the moment of my departure. I will never live through it again. So why should I be attached to the evanescent here and now?

The Light of the SELF is alone worthy to be sought after.

12. THEME: *The moon shines by reflecting the light of the Sun. When the Sun has set, the moon may be useful for displaying objects. When the Sun has risen no one needs or looks on the moon, although it may still be visible in the sky. So it is with the mind and the Heart. When we have only reflected light, we are compelled to use it. But when the Direct Source is high, it becomes the only Light we need.*

Development: This splendid simile is most enlightening for me It does not deny the partial usefulness of the mind, but it puts that mind into its proper place, showing that there are things which are much better and more real than the mind. I know that intuition, which is actually cognition without thinking, is much higher than ordinary mental processes. But humanity still does not possess the full ability of using that intuition, which, at the present time, is only a sporadic manifestation in a few men.

When it is night, the light of the moon is a blessed help for the nocturnal traveller. But nobody would compare our satellite with the source of all light, the sun. I feel that there is a deep truth in this comparison. While not denying the usefulness of the mind under certain circumstances, we are shown the inadequacy of the substitute as compared with the *Source*.

I can see that the idea of this meditation is to create a propitious ground in me for the true understanding of the relationship between the mind and the Spirit. Some rather narrow-minded seekers try to reject the whole conception of mind, even before they have learned to live in the Spirit. They land on an empty, infertile and uninhabited island. The wise one does not commit this folly.

Now I can see why spiritually advanced men throughout human history have been rather critical of the mind, having something infinitely better in their awareness—the Light of the Spirit, which shows them clearly the Path and the Goal.

They were not dreamers or unrealistic men, but just the opposite: most earnest and intelligent people, striving only for that which they knew was the real Goal and Attainment.

All of our materialistic science deals with earthly things and still it is unable to create really propitious conditions for the majority, but only for a minority of men. And these conditions cannot survive their own lives: they cannot take any discovery on to the *other side*.

While not denying certain values in the creation of a better environment for as many people as possible, I cannot compare it with the search for imperishable values.

Let the example of the Moon and the Sun provide me with true insight while I continue to live in this relative world.

*   *   *

You already have some series of meditation behind you and the question might arise as to what is the best way in which to operate with these themes, which are really not so very hard. They are not divorced from our old tutor—Logic and hence should not present any mental difficulties. But the problem I would now like to confront is of a different character.

It is that of the *method*, which will be the most useful for the earnest student. Experience shows that the success in a study of meditation depends upon our right use of the mind's powers, as an introduction and then for the transferring of the *development* back into the *theme*. It must be well explained.

(a) *Read the theme slowly and with full concentration* several times, until you have completely memorized it. As you may see, I am giving only themes which are short and concentrated and the idea of which can be encompassed by your mind without undue difficulty. Some students need to read only, say, seven times, but others will have to dedicate more time in order to impress the theme firmly in their minds. This is immaterial, for only the final result counts. The fact that you might need five, or fifteen minutes for that purpose at first, need not be a cause for any worry. What has to be avoided is the wandering of the

mind, leaping from one thought to another, and thus not allowing you to penetrate into the contents of the meditation. But
this will not happen, if you have honestly passed through the
recommended course of *concentration*, which should enable you
to cut short all the whimsies of the mind.

If you start with, say, Theme 1 from this chapter, dealing
with the value of Realization of man's true Self, and finish your
attempts to absorb it with thoughts about Indian fakirs, meals
served on banana leaves in Ashrams, or about the performance
of the latest jet fighters, and so on, then there is good reason to
be concerned about the state of your mind control. In such a
case, you must go back to the book *Concentration* and discipline
your mind, until you can use without interference from the
stream of unnecessary and harmful thoughts, which slip into
your awareness against your will.

However, we will presume that this difficulty has been overcome in one or another way, and that the contents of the *theme*
have been absorbed. And so we will pass on to the next step.

(b) Similarly as with (a), read the *development*, which follows
the *theme* several times, trying to tune your ideas along the lines
of the former, being aware all the time that it is only *one* of the
roads, radiating from the *theme*. Here you may encounter two
possibilities for further meditation. The *first* kind will be when
you recognize that this *development* satisfies you in full, and
that you do not feel any urge to engage yourself on any other
road. Then read every sentence slowly and separately, while
closing your eyes and thinking it through, until you feel that
you have done your utmost in order to illuminate the idea behind
the sentence, or, if you prefer this simile, that you have digested
it well. This process must be well controlled and should not be
transformed into whimsies of the mind, which have nothing to
do with the idea you are supposed to be working through. The
best method is to hold the sentence firmly in your mind, just as
if you were holding a full cup of water, which you cannot subject
to any strong vibrations or trembling of your hands, for fear of
spilling the contents. I AM PLACING THE UTMOST IMPORTANCE
ON THIS TECHNIQUE, AS IT IS THE BEST KNOWN AND MOST
REWARDING.

Do not think about any distractions, for they will lead you
astray along paths, which have very little, or nothing in common

with your basic THEME. Have no doubt that this WILL SUFFICE when you work in such a way. When you feel that your task is momentarily done, pass on to the next sentence of the *development*, and so on, until the last one.

The *second* possibility for further meditation will appear, when you are not satisfied with only ONE road, as given in the *development*, and feel that you have enough POWER to explore other roads, creating them independently of the *theme's cross-road*. This will, of course need more time and effort and will expose you to wider dangers of bungling and deviating from the real idea you have to operate with in your meditation. Nevertheless, you are fully entitled to follow this way and if successful, it may give you a faster approach to the Goal, but only WHEN YOU MEET WITH FULL SUCCESS ON YOUR OWN PATH, and NOT MERELY MENTAL ACROBATICS, which lead nowhere and do not assist in the absorption of the *theme*.

I do not actually need to mention, that further procedure with the 'roads' of your own creation should be exactly the same as in the *first* case, that is, working through every sentence as was done with the *development*, as given in this course. You will probably have to write down your own 'road', and then 'dissect' it according to the method given previously.

What would be my personal advice? While not hiding anything from you and recognizing your freedom of selection in the development of the given themes, I still believe that, in a very few exceptions (those concerning well-trained students, who possess full power of concentration) it would be better if you limited your efforts to the texts given here, without venturing on to other paths. Then, when you have grown stronger and more experienced, you will have plenty of opportunity and freedom to return to these Series (I to III) and to work with them again, with the addition of your own 'roads' of approach. It would be incomparably better for the student to perform exactly and clearly everything that he finds here, rather than to add more material and not work through it properly.

Well, in one way or another, you have worked through the *development*. What now? WITH YOUR CONSCIOUSNESS EN-RICHED BY THE WORK JUST DONE, AGAIN CONFRONT THE THEME, HOLDING IT FIRMLY BEFORE YOUR INNER SIGHT. You will be astonished and probably enchanted at seeing the difference between the light you were able to throw on the *theme* BEFORE you worked through the *development* and—NOW! You may see how much wiser your conception is and how much better you can now 'see' the real contents of the theme of meditation.

Finally, a last remark for this *Series*; which will be that, as you can probably see, the meditation, as prescribed, will most likely take more time than you guessed when you started. I think that every *theme* might well take you more than one session, before it is performed as intended. Neglected work will lead only to failure, be sure of that! In this course you will find several Series of meditations, and each covers twelve, or more items. It is not absolutely necessary to work through all of them, as you can choose only those from each Series, which you may feel most suited to and inspiring for you. But no Series should be abandoned as a whole, for this will lead to an inharmonious development of the student.

CHAPTER XXIII

Exercises Dealing with the Mind – Series IV

WE have now reached the point where we should consolidate everything that we know practically about our mind. It is necessary, for if there will remain even the smallest dark corner, a gap in our knowledge of all the activities of our mind, the more intense meditations may become unrealizable. Why so? Because the mind is a very intelligent and treacherous power, well aware of its gains and losses, but not possessing such manifold abilities as are hidden and potentially present in man's true awareness. Some occultists have compared the character of mind to that of a very well-developed, super-animal force, which knows quite well 'how' to act in its own interest, but lacks the ability to conceive 'why'. And just in this weak point of the mind's power lies our superiority and ability to dominate it. If it would be otherwise, no spiritual progress would ever be possible and even thinkable. You already know that the mind is NOT interested in man's development and looks on a human being merely as on a *source of power*, which, if dominated or deceived, can provide this mind with new forces, vibrations and experiences. Mind does not see anything beyond its own egoistic interest, its own life, expressed in incessant movement, and cares little about what is of benefit, or is disadvantageous for that SOURCE. But mind feels strongly, that if this *independent consciousness* in man becomes awakened, it will invariably put mind into its proper place, that is, make a servant of it, compelled to vibrate according to man's own will and even to cease all vibrations and merge in Silence. And this is the least desirable thing for it: that is why mind fights so cleverly and desperately for its supremacy.

If I can stop all thinking processes and eliminate mind's activities and vibrations, it can happen ONLY BECAUSE I KNOW

THE TRUTH OF THAT MIND EXPERIMENTALLY: IT IS ONLY MY INSTRUMENT, BUT NOT MYSELF, NOR SOMETHING POSSESSING CONSCIOUSNESS INDEPENDENT OF ME. Know, that your power over your mind is never more strongly manifested, than when you compel it to silence, and then observe what happens as a result of your action as ruler.

In this silencing of the mind we find an inexhaustible source of power and deep satisfaction, which approaches the *Peace beyond all understanding*. This means that mind does not, and cannot understand WHY man wants to dominate it and limit its activities, so far untapped and knowing no master. But the fact remains, that a well-dominated mind is the best possible servant. Many scientists would be amazed, if they could only experience the growing power of investigation, conclusion and intuition available to those, who, by their inner effort, achieve separation from their thinking principle, reducing it to a controllable factor in their consciousness.

In this Series IV of the exercises, we will practise meditative talks with ourselves, aiming at a final solution of the perennial binary: MAN and his MIND.

1. THEME: *I am ceasing to think. I do not need any thoughts to enter into, or to be emitted by my mind.*

Development: Do as you say. Sit in a quiet asana and close your eyes during the first stages of this exercise, but later learn to look into the space in front of you, as if aimlessly, without perceiving anything and being absolutely uninterested in anything lying before your eyes.

Do you live during this short period?

Of course I am living.

What do you think?

Nothing, as required!

So where was your mind at that time?

It seemed to be as if inactive, silent.

Well, there was no trace of its activity, and subsequently no trace of the same mind.

Yes, I was not conscious of my mind.

But were you conscious of being alive, or were you in something like a swoon, unaware of yourself?

No, I did not lose my awareness of life.

2. THEME : *From the foregoing you can see that your mind* IS NOT *an essential factor in your consciousness, that there may be states even apart from your mental awareness.*

Development: Logically speaking, I have to admit this possibility, but it seems that I will have more such experiences and more exercises to perform.

It is true, for only by practice can a man become firmly established in the new standards in his consciousness.

3. THEME : *Don't you feel, after such an exercise, as if something is arising in you, quiet, peaceful, sure of itself, eternally free and happy?*

Development: I have as if a foretaste of these things. They are not yet very clear-cut and definite, but the *feeling* is there.

From this 'feeling' will grow certainty, and from certainty, the positive KNOWLEDGE, that you and your mind apparatus are two different things. And from this will come your own awareness that when you are without thoughts you are close to your TRUE SELF and the other (the mental consciousness) can be subjugated, removed or accepted, according to the WILL OF THE NON-THINKING FACTOR IN YOU.

4. THEME : *What then is more important, real and independent? The thinking machine in you, or* THAT *which is above the thinking processes?*

Development: I can live without thinking, but the awareness of being alive must disappear, if I am going to lose *that which remained in me when the thinking was extinguished*. This may be so in a swoon, or under anaesthetics, for then I have no proof of being alive. The testimony of those who might observe my unconscious body does not bring any positive proof of my existence at that time, for I long ago established that MY LIFE is none other than the AWARENESS of that life. If it ceases, what then actually remains?

5. THEME : *Separation from one's mind gives a firm basis for the actual conception of immortality. The body, a perishable and temporary manifestation, is rather a proof of mortality, than of survival.*

Development: Truly, I cannot seek after eternity through the eyes of my body. The only thing which remains, is to seek after the other, less perishable element in me. In Item No. 4 I saw sufficient material for meditation about that search.

6. THEME: *What is the weapon used by the mind in order to defeat our attempts to dominate that mind?*

Development: The foremost weapon of the mind seems to be curiosity, the subconscious mental desire to place one's attention on every subject, which is presented by the mind's currents. I say subconscious, because there is no conscious choice of the clichés which approach. A man does not say to himself: 'Will I admit this thought, do I need it? Have I nothing better to accept into the light of my awareness?' Usually, such a selection does not take place, and so a man is then swallowed by the incoming currents.

7. THEME: *From where does the mind take all of the thoughts, ideas, mental pictures and theories, with which it assaults us during our attempts at meditation and concentration?*

Development: If we have attentively studied the chapters treating of cosmic clichés, then we already have the answer. Anyway we know that there is *nothing new*, or 'born yesterday' in the whole of Creation, or, better still, MANIFESTATION of the ONE WITHOUT A SECOND. His immense creative consciousness, which men call 'Spirit', operating beyond all the limitations of time and space (which He created Himself), *contains eternally everything which*, in our narrow and limited conception, WAS, IS and WILL BE. From this inextinguishable SOURCE, different manifested *Cosmic Forces* (and the *mind* is one of the foremost), draw everything they are allowed to. In this way innumerable clichés are reproduced and put before separate human minds. If accepted, they flourish and are strengthened, if not, they wander through the infinity of different kinds of space and time, seeking another opportunity to get a loan of new, vital energy from a living consciousness, not necessarily a human one. For I think that there are innumerable worlds which give haven to other incarnate beings, following their particular ways of reintegration, which perhaps are even similar to our own, but also vastly different and even incomprehensible to human imagination.

I feel that meditation about all of this may give me more peace and stability in my own consciousness, as then I may realize that nothing perishes and that I am not obliged to shelter every cliché and feed it with my own powers, those of ATTENTION and INTEREST. I feel that I may come to the realization, that the MOST IMPORTANT THING IN THE WHOLE UNIVERSE, AS WELL AS BEYOND IT, IS ONLY ONE: THE ENERGY OF MY PURE CONSCIOUSNESS, DEVOID OF ALL OUTER SHELLS AND ATTACHMENTS.

Summarizing all of this I find that: dissipation of my attention leads me to frustration, but *concentration of my innermost fulcrum* fulfils the design of the Creator of all the Clichés in the Cosmos.

Following on this, I see that my meditations may obtain assistance from the SOURCE, to which they are directed. As someone said: 'If we take only one step towards the Lord, He will take two in our direction.'

8. THEME: *The foremost quality of a progressive human consciousness is the ability of an effortless return of the mind into the Silence several times a day during daily life.*

Development: When I experience even a short moment of Silence in me, I feel that this State is supreme above all other manifestations of my awareness. If I cannot yet abide in this State permanently, it is only because of my insufficient development. But, as every child grows into an adult, so my infancy in spiritual experience (starting just with the Silence in me) will not endure for ever, it cannot be permanent. When the right time comes, the FULL SUN will arise in my consciousness, and all the present shadows, like thinking, with all its variety of manifestations, will recede for ever before the Great Light. I know that this idea may appear unrealistic, or even nonsensical to those, who are not on the Path. But does it and can it affect me? Everyone is responsible for only his own cell of Spirit, which lies hidden in him, in his different veils, or bodies. So there is no reason to be worried, even if the whole world disapproves of my convictions.

By means of a voluntary return into the inner Silence, I am

proving my superiority over my tools—the mind and feelings. There is no other equally convincing method and experience. Knowing this, I shall do my best in order to come as often as I can into the true SOURCE of my being, which reposes in the perfect SILENCE.

9. THEME: *The Spiritual Teachers of humanity, who have attained the peak of inner development, are said to be in eternal Silence, using their mental powers only when necessary to communicate with earthly men.*

Development: Although I cannot judge about the probable truth of the above theme of meditation, because I may not have any personal experience with such a spiritual Master, I feel that it is only logical and acceptable, because thinking processes are NOT the highest activities in man, nor the only ones. When I am tired of thinking, I seek some inner peace. Some day I may obtain this Peace, and one of the first manifestations of it will be freedom from all outside intrusions from my mind. My thinking cannot change my fate, so it can be discarded, when I am ripe enough.

10. THEME: *The human mind is not an independent power, developing itself IRRESPECTIVE OF ALL OUTER CONDITIONS. An untrained mind is unlikely to perform much in this world, if it is dependent only upon SURROUNDING CONDITIONS. The power which arranges training and development of our personal mind is certainly different from that mind. This power has the freedom of choice, which is not always the case with the human mind.*

Development: Of course, education and environment are very potent factors for the development of our mind. The fact that few geniuses had initially, very favourable conditions does not destroy the rule. They too were finally able to direct their minds where they wanted.

On the other hand, no one would deny that many people, while being in the best possible conditions, still have not raised themselves beyond triviality and average abilities.

The problem is solved when we understand the Law of Clichés.

The choice of clichés belongs not to the mind alone, but in still greater measure to that 'unknown' core in man, which is above and beyond his mind. It is in this 'core' that there repose the seeds of the real FREEDOM and certain aspects of the HYPER-CONSCIOUS, of which more has been said in Part I of this work. The realization of the essential *freedom* of our awareness is one of the most powerful means to develop regular and true meditation. Without that freedom nothing could be achieved. But, as we have many examples of superhuman and also beyond average achievements in our fellow men, the truth of the freedom in man is incontestable. Someone may say that the majority do not actually feel that Freedom and act as if led exclusively by their destiny, as they say. But the *highest* human attributes do not belong to the *lowest* specimens of man and it is that fact, which many aspirants of philosophy fail to realize.

11. THEME: *We often hear about the so-called 'unity' of all men. And as a logical consequence comes the conviction that everything which* UNITES *us is right and that which separates is wrong. However, truth is somewhat apart from this statement. It depends with* WHAT *we would be united and which manifestations of life we are to join and from which to separate.*

Development: Discrimination should show us the way. I know from previous meditations that SEPARATION IS ESSENTIAL when applied to the lower and finite powers in man: his mind and feelings (astral sphere), for otherwise no inner freedom, nor spiritual progress are possible. Can I meditate while being at the mercy of my mind and emotions? So, I will separate from them and in this way make achievement possible. Because lower factors, as previously mentioned, are NOT capable of uniting men, they are so different and tend towards still greater differentiation. Nobody will insist that men have exactly the same *feelings* and *thoughts*, although the lines along which both work are similar. The only truly uniting factor is the one in which there is no differentiation nor opposition.

It is the SPIRIT, manifesting Itself in Silence and the SILENCE is and can be—ONLY ONE! No sane being will speak about 'different' Silences! Now I see where there is perfect UNION. It is in SPIRIT-SILENCE, which is mysteriously identical with the Hyperconsciousness. It is useless to try to express it in words, for in the very moment when speech begins, the SILENCE disappears and the HYPERCONSCIOUSNESS degenerates into the mind's activity. I will try never to forget this discovery, made today during meditation.

12. THEME: The final one for this Series will be—*meditation about one's right attitude towards one's body, emotions and thoughts. What should it be?*

Development: Should we 'kill' all emotions and mind's functions in our consciousness? Even if this were possible, such an attitude would transform a living being into a soulless automaton. If in the 'Garden of the Lord' (that is, the whole universe), there exist certain powers, conditions, phenomena, and so on, there must be a deep reason for it, and we cannot reach the CAUSE of all of them. We have to be realists and not try to change what cannot be changed, since it is far beyond our powers and possibilities. HE KNOWS, but we do not. Nevertheless, we can choose the best paths and flowers in the GARDEN, and this will not displease the GARDENER HIMSELF. That is the solution! Not to annihilate, but to take what we need and leave alone what we know is useless.

Coming now to the concrete problem of *mind and heart*, I see that my own solution will not be a denial of what cannot be denied, but will be a separation from unwanted manifestations, unwanted and unsuitable for me, but probably of use to other participants in the great evolutionary march! What is wrong with a tricycle when used by a seven year old boy? Nobody would condemn it, in fact everyone would probably be pleased to see the child riding the contraption. But no one will admire me, as an adult human being, attempting meditation and ruled by laws different to those for the child, if he sees me riding the same small toy on the footpath outside his house!

What is good for one, may be wrong for another.

Animals, unlike us, cannot control their emotions and their primitive mental activities. They react instantly and rather automatically. In the same circumstances they would behave according to the inherited habits and reactions of their species. They still have to develop the ability to perceive many astral and mental vibrations and without being able to do so, they may simply perish, as unfit for survival.

Man's problems and destiny are different, and this is what I have to know and meditate upon. The understanding, previously mentioned, of the necessity to discriminate between the powers which act in the universe gives peace. I feel this peace now.

An old proverb comes to mind: *'Everything is for the best in this best of possible worlds.'*

*   *   *

This Series is now finished and I consider that the student should by now have obtained a solid foundation for dealing with his mind. He knows what the mind is; the laws through which it works; how to use certain properties of the human mind; how to dominate it; how to make it useful in its own realm and finally, how to separate from that mind, passing into the higher and better consciousness—Life.

We are now going to face other aspects of meditation, loftier and more effective in their approach to the Highest.

They will also be more difficult, but, after all, who would expect a ticket for a virtuoso's concert to be cheap?

PART IV

ADVANCED MEDITATION

CHAPTER XXIV

The Sermon on the Mount – Series I

IT has so happened that during my lifetime I have faced 'The Sermon on the Mount' only twice. The first time was during the usual religious instruction in high school and the second time, after I had returned from my journey to India, where I had met the Great Rishi Ramana, better known as the Maharshi. I believe, and I have good proof of it, that everything happens in our lives at the right time, although not many people are able to realize this. And it was exactly the case with 'The Sermon on the Mount'. The presence and initiation of the Maharshi opened new vistas for me and made many inspired texts from the Scriptures understandable from the spiritual point of view. This applied not only to Indian Scriptures, but also to the Christian. The Great Rishi was also a sincere admirer of Christ and who could better understand the Great Teacher, if not another Teacher, sent to us in our own period? I spoke about this fact in my *Theurgy*, quoting in full, the sayings of the Sage Ramana concerning Christ. Consequently I will not repeat them again. In any case, the Gospels appeared to me in a different, much brighter light than ever before.

As a result, *The Sermon on the Mount* came to the fore. Its value for meditation is unsurpassed. The LIVING WORDS supply the Living Truth to the hearts of those, who are able to realize them and one of the foremost means for that realization is, of course, true meditation.

You have not come to this chapter as raw beginners, for three Parts of this work are already behind you. Therefore you are in a better position to take full profit from that inspired text than those who have had no opportunity for any scientific dealings with their tool of cognition, the human mind. Still, this will not be entirely sufficient for a spiritual merging in Truth, spoken of by Christ. A proper attitude, a spiritual attitude is necessary!

The more advanced our meditations will be during this course, the more spiritual they will become. Probably you feel this even now. So, how to acquire this spiritual attitude for reading the initiatory texts in the same spirit, in which they were originally told to us?

You know that there is no way in which to express SPIRITUAL TRUTH in words. All that we may read and hear are rather just inducements to IT. The first condition on the part of the student would be to accept the following words of the Great Teacher with sincere humility. In them alone there is the Light which can dissipate the mist and dust of the ordinary human mind. And it is in this attitude that I will attempt to present this chapter to you.

Therefore, before I pass on to the actual 'Sermon' itself, I will give you two introductory and initiatory texts, on which you must work with all your attention and concentration.

'A. THEME: *Heaven and earth shall pass, but my words shall not pass.*

Development: No other lips have ever been able to pronounce such a profound statement and no other human words contain such power and truth, giving enlightenment to the sensitive student.

Now you may see which attitude is necessary when dealing with this text: humility, and enthusiasm for the Truth expressed in our mortal language, the only one understandable for us. In listening to the words of the Great Teacher of humanity we are laying the foundations in ourselves for a spiritual temple in our innermost awareness, a sanctuary which is non-material, and therefore, indestructible in both time and space.

If you have heard mention of the 'other flocks, which are not of this world' and which Christ also has to bring to Himself, you may get a flash of intuition about the immense depth of meaning in these words. There is no need to be exceptionally intelligent in order to realize that our human family on this little earth is not, and cannot be the sole, or even the most advanced one. The infinite universe does not exist merely to please our eyes, imagination and fantasies. It is as alive as our own planet is and then the simplest calculus will show us, that there must be millions of planets with perhaps, conditions providing existence for intelligent beings and many of them must be higher than our own.

This is the light in which we should understand Theme A. The conclusion? Must you *believe* these great words, can you understand them properly? The matter of believing belongs entirely to you, to your degree of spiritual development. This development may give you the sole and best answer. Listen then, to what comes from your silent Inner Temple, when you hear the words of the Teacher and *know them*, not for me, or for others, *but just for yourself.* I shall not interfere with that, which should not be interfered with.

B. THEME: *You are the Light of the world.*

Development: When absolute confidence in the words of the Teacher has been established in you, another decisive injunction is ready to be assimilated. This is Theme B. When it says that the Light of the world is in us, it refers to the immortal element in man, about which we already know a lot from former chapters of this book. Certainly not the whole man, as we see him, is related to this Light. That which is only temporary and mortal in us does not participate in Eternity. But we know that in truth we are just that perennial element, the Spirit of Christ, the True Self of the Maharshi, the Reintegrated Adam Kadmon of Hermetists, and so on. When the Great Teacher spoke about that Light in us, He meant the Immortal. But how many are conscious of IT? We are all called, but only a few are chosen. They are the 'realized' souls, in whom the Light has passed through the material sheaths, the veils, which envelop the consciousness of an ordinary man, and has started to shine, no longer impeded by anything.

And those *great souls* are the actual Light of the world. But for us, there is a more profound fact: that this Light is EVEN NOW IN US ALL, only the majority does not know about IT, nor have any experience of IT. However, the fact remains that IT is in us and it is our business to let IT shine through the shrouds of matter, as the sun shines when the clouds are dispersed. There is no hope, but CERTAINTY, as Christ states categorically and in this certainty lies the whole secret of the final Achievement. Do not let us be deluded, it is not a matter of today or tomorrow for the majority of human beings. It cannot be measured in our limited concept of *Time* and here all guesses are rather delaying than forwarding factors, because they are creations of our mind, which can never participate in the Light, nor is it willing to assist in ITS unveiling. On the other hand, mind does and will do anything in order to prevent a man achieving spiritual status, independent of that mind and thus putting an end to its rule.

But for a spiritually-minded person, the time separating him from Achievement is not an important factor. Even in the advanced degrees of meditation, man learns to live beyond time and space, although he unavoidably returns to his physical consciousness after that high flight.

We may see how strong this certainty of Achievement can be from the numerous examples of Saints, martyrs and advanced Eastern souls. All of them despised the earthly life when confronted with abandoning the physical body in order to reach the higher state of existence. Some of them went joyously to their so often terrible deaths, while others showed unswerving faith in Spirit, whom they referred to as the only true Reality. How does it happen that such people are in the minority? Is the majority always right?

Look around impartially with a cool mind and pure heart and ask yourself whether the World is right, or the Teacher, Who taught us to 'be in the world, but not of it'.

Analyse the aims for which humanity is struggling in your own lifetime. Observe human history in the process of actual creation during these days of this twentieth century. If you are able to observe from the ideal position of Theme B, your answer can be clearly anticipated. If you look, like the millions around you, from the same materialistic point of view, which is devoid of any Wisdom, you will be unable to perceive any solution at all. Such a state is called 'LIVING IN IGNORANCE'.

*   *   *

As I have mentioned before, the two Themes A and B are a useful preparation for meditation based on *The Sermon on the Mount*. From my own experience, I firmly believe that we should always try to be prepared for every new step ahead, and not to start walking as if into an unknown and impenetrable realm. For this is the main cause of so many failures, even if the search has been brought about by the most idealistic and elevated intentions. Just as no sane traveller would venture alone into an unknown forest without any roads, so no spiritual 'travelling' should be undertaken without previous exploration and 'mapping' of the way. Now, knowing that the words of the Great Teacher are Truth Itself and that they can be realized in ourselves, for we do possess the necessary Light in us, we can start the meditations proper about *The Sermon on the Mount*.

1. THEME : *Blessed are the poor in spirit: for theirs is the kingdom of heaven.*

Development: *The Sermon on the Mount* is opened by a single assertion, which begins every part of the Teaching. It is the statement regarding the usefulness and sublimity of a certain inner quality in man ('blessed are. . .') and is followed by a description of the kind of 'reward' awaiting the lucky souls, who possess this spiritual quality.

The blessing of this quality is an indication of the necessity for possessing it, if man is to be saved from the spectre of death, threatening every creature, which as yet cannot transfer its existence, its awareness into the immortal region of the Spirit. I have to hold this in my mind during all the meditation about particular verses of the 'Sermon'.

For me it is a beacon, showing me what I have to develop in myself. But first, I must know the exact meaning of the virtue, mentioned by the Great Teacher.

To be *poor in spirit* cannot mean the absence of true Spiritual consciousness, for then it would be a sheer deception and absurdity. The meaning is different: under the word '*spirit*' there lies its *shadow*, so often mistaken for the Spirit itself. In some languages there is even a dangerous identification of the same word Spirit with that of the Mind! Apart from both the ancient languages of Greek and Latin, it is even now in the living ones. So, for example, in French—'*l'esprit*' may well mean the mind, the mood and intention in some cases, while in German —*Der Geist* has an exactly similar significance. Also, the true meaning of that which, in English, we accept as SPIRIT, is in some other languages only *one of the possible and usable expressions*.

Now I can see the truth in this verse from the 'Sermon'. One should not be 'high spirited' in one's mind and moods, but one must dominate them and put them in their proper place, as controlled servants, but not as one's lord! The mind cannot lead us to immortality, nor to 'salvation', which means, as we already know, the attainment of the eternal, uninterrupted consciousness, the immortal LIFE. In this epoch, humanity places almost all of its emphasis on the mind and its derivatives. The Great Teacher knew of this error in His time and, as a being in full control of all clichés, of those belonging to the past, present and future, He also saw the times in which we now live and His words, as always, have retained their actuality and freshness for men of all periods, in which intelligent beings will spend their physical incarnations, their lower classes of the great SCHOOL OF LIFE.

Those who are 'poor in spirit' are men who understand the temporary role of the mind and emotions, with their vanity and inability to lead them to any final Attainment. They control their thoughts and feelings and DO NOT ASCRIBE ANY PERMANENT VALUE TO EITHER KIND OF VIBRATIONS. They may use them, if necessary, but do not confuse them with their own immortal core, no matter how deeply and tightly it can be enwrapped, at the time, in the two veils just mentioned. Those who are 'poor in spirit', lack self-admiration, self-sublimation and the tragic acceptance as the true Self of its caricature, which is the ego.

The 'poor in spirit' have no pride, or contempt for their fellow men. They do not strive for riches or worldly power, for they well realize their nothingness. They are meek, for they are able to see the greatness of the ONE WITHOUT A SECOND, and through that meekness they acquire the Wisdom, beyond all ordinary knowledge, and this Wisdom is one of the brightest blessings, which can be bestowed upon a man.

Those who are 'poor in spirit' possess incomparably more true FREEDOM than those, who are attached to the ephemeral, illusory lights of the unstable, perishable life, which binds them as if with heavy ropes, composed of their passions, desires, egoistic feelings and similar things. Nothing of these illusions can ever persist, since they unavoidably abandon the men whom they hold in submission, leaving behind them the bonds of frustration and despair.

During meditation about all of the foregoing, I am applying the findings I am obtaining from it to myself. Let it shed more Lights on my paths!

*   *   *

As you can see, the short sentence of the first verse of the 'Sermon' develops into a protracted meditation, if it is to be used as intended by the Great Teacher. You will see the same process in the following sections.

2. THEME: *Blessed are they that mourn: for they shall be comforted.*

Development: What is the mourning about which the Great Teacher speaks here. Another interpretation of the translated word 'mourn' is *'are sad'*. Because of what? Sadness and mourning are states in which man suffers. I know that suffering is the main form of repayment for evil once done, no matter whether or not we can remember it. Some would probably say that it is a liquidation of karmic debts. In one or another way, suffering sets us free from certain parts of our erroneous past. Throughout human history, Saints and spiritually advanced men never tried to avoid suffering in the way that ignorant, average people try to do . They must know the true meaning of suffering. I am trying to know it now in the same way.

A debt is always a burden and if I am greatly indebted, there may be reason for my sadness, when I cannot find any explanation for it. When the burden is thrown away, a man is free from it. When the karmic debts are paid, we are comforted, the conditions of our lives become more propitious and less difficult. That is what those who mourn and are sad should know: there are deep reasons for all suffering. In the great account of human life no error is possible: what has once been paid will not be repeated again. I can now see the *wisdom* of not repulsing and the wrongness of instinctively shunning all suffering. Many of the prominent sons of man like the martyrs and other sufferers for Truth, even willingly and deliberately accepted suffering when persecuted by ignorant people.

Were they wrong? No, in the final reckoning they were right and in their attitude I see the correct example for myself. Let the bright beacon of HOPE, lit by the concluding words of this verse in the Great Teacher's Sermon, enlighten my Path.

* * *

Go through this 'development' and if you can, add to it yourself and see how more light comes from your own efforts. Such a method will be a very effective one. Do not cling tightly to only the writer's personal experiences, for you have the same Light in you, and if you are sincere and strive after Truth, the Spiritual Master will see your efforts and His holy assistance will reach you.

Many people have been astonished at how exact and sure is such help, which is given to us when our hearts are simple and filled with sincerity.

3. THEME: *Blessed are the meek; for they shall inherit the earth.*

Development: In a previous meditation I had a good explanation of the meaning of 'meekness', as a result of the Wisdom growing in a man. The understanding of the true relationship between the spark of spiritual consciousness enclosed in every human being and the WHOLENESS, or the infinite, eternal ocean of the ABSOLUTE CONSCIOUSNESS, which men call—God, creates wise meekness in an advanced man. P. Sédir, in quoting his spiritual Master, the mysterious Monsieur *Andréas* says that, 'we rub shoulders with death many times during every day, but we are not aware of it, nor does anything really happen to us until our hour comes.' This is a very enlightening statement, describing how small we are as mortal, incarnate men and how unreasonable is the pride and boastfulness, so often encountered among our fellow men.

Another famous spiritual Master of the end of the nineteenth century—Philippe Nizier of Lyons (France) pointed out directly to those, who asked him for an explanation of his superhuman powers that: 'I am a *very small one* and the Almighty always supports such people, but not those who feel themselves to be great and wise.' Thus spoke a man who could cure any sickness, knew the past and future of every man approaching him and who professed that all his deeds were exclusively due to God's Will.

The second part of this verse of the *Sermon* seems to be more complicated. *Inheriting the earth* needs deep insight, for it cannot be taken only in the physical sense. The meek possess inner Wisdom, which is agreeable to the Creator. Possessing the planets may mean the ruling of them and their population, in fulfilment of the Lord's designs. That is to say, that the Almighty uses the services of His enlightened children and we can see it even in the history of our own human race, limited as it is by time and space.

As the *Preacher on the Mount* constantly used the term 'Father' as being suitable for our attitude towards the Lord, the subsequent term 'children' is fully justified for us.

We know that Christ sent His disciples to visit all lands and to preach the *Good News* (the English translation of the original old Greek word as now used is—'Evangel'). And the Children served the *Father* well.

4. THEME: *Blessed are they which do hunger and thirst after justice, for they shall be filled.*

Development: Another quality, which initiates man into the Kingdom of God is his striving for righteousness, or justice. Deep in our innermost recesses there is the desire and hope for Justice, in all its manifold manifestations. Not everyone, at every moment has ready access to this hidden treasure. It depends on the intensity of the sincere inner search in man. I remember the profound words of the Great Teacher when He said: '*Ask, and it shall be given to you: seek, and you shall find: knock, and it shall be opened to you.*'

In these words there is the joyous certainty in the Search for eternal Justice—righteousness. The second part of the present verse of the 'Sermon' confirms them with the unconditional statement that *the holy thirst will be quenched* before we return to the *Father's Mansions*. This is the central point of my present meditation.

To fulfil my destiny, as just shown, I should practise justice in my own everyday life, so that there will be no contradiction between words and deeds, for such disagreement will only delay

223

the fulfilment of the Teacher's promise. And the responsibility will rest with myself alone.

Humanity, in dealing with its social and moral problems, has produced a crude substitute for true spiritual justice, of which the present verse tells us. There are different codes and laws, created to fill the gap between the evil will of some individuals and the 'common good' of human society. I see the reason why such 'outer' justice had to be applied: because of the absence of the 'inner' desire for righteousness in some unripe souls.

From time immemorial the thirst for true justice has been alive in advanced men. And of old, Ovid gave expression to it, in his description of his alleged 'Golden Age' when there were no courts, or police, and so on, simply because the people of that supposedly blessed age, spontaneously observed moral rules of their own good will, without any coercion by law, or fear of punishment. There must be a way to return to this state, and it leads only through the hearts of all men, when the time is ripe for it.

It depends upon myself when it will come for me.

5. THEME: *Blessed are the merciful: for they shall obtain mercy.*

Development: What is mercy? When I, in my worldly life, fulfil my duty arising from my obligations, I am only doing my ordinary work, which I am supposed to do, according to laws and conditions. There is little of spiritual merit in it. When people pay me what they are supposed to pay it is the same. And in both examples there is no spiritual element of sacrifice.

Mercy is something much loftier. When the Samaritan stopped, although he could easily have passed the injured man, as did others, he showed just this higher quality of his soul. For he did much more than he was 'obliged' to do. He sacrificed his effort, time and money, arranging both cure and care for the luckless traveller. He could not expect any reward for any of that, except in his own conscience. It was a typical act of pure mercy and it is about such that the Great Teacher tells us, invoking blessings on those of us, who have the spirit of mercy and compassion, realized not just in words, but in actual deeds.

I have no doubt that in every being there is hidden an element of merciful compassion, but often it is covered with the thick veils of egoism, laziness and even thoughtlessness, so that it cannot manifest itself in actions. So merciful people are those in whom the hidden fire of compassion has been allowed to develop into the burning flame of *active love*, which is the other name for mercy.

When this flame appears in our hearts, spiritual beauty starts to shine through it, enlightening the whole awareness for that time. The more such moments and hours a man has in his life, the more merciful he becomes, and then we come to the second part of the truth, contained in this verse: he may be sure that he will obtain mercy himself, in his need, far beyond trivial human justice.

The obtaining of mercy means something beyond that which is actually due to a man: it is a surplus of grace, which does not come from any codes or calculations, but directly from the realm of the Spirit, which is perfect in Its very essence.

Mercy is peaceful, as is the Spirit. It may be silent, for spiritual manifestations do not call for much, if any, speech. Its sisters may be understanding and love.

Let us now meditate about it in inner silence.

As with everything in this world, all of which can have light as well as shade, the virtue of mercy may be corrupted and deformed. When can this happen? When some human vice, like a subtle poison, is allowed to leak into the pure virtue. And no virtue is ever secure from it.

Immaculate mercy does not seek to gain any advantages from its actions, nor fame, nor recognition from the outer world. But how rare is such a pure manifestation of it! And how often the desire to be known as a benefactor, to be praised and revered, despoils mercy of its highest radiance! What then will be the reward for such deformed virtue? We can find it in the very words of the Teacher when, in speaking of such men who like to see popular recognition of their deeds, He said that: '. . . *they have received their reward*', that is, human praise and admiration.

But Christ was not speaking about such recompense when He promised an abundance of mercy for those, who practise it towards others: for—'. . . *when thou dost alms, let not thy left hand know what thy right hand doth.*'

Well then, does active mercy give no reward at all to the man, who has been able to preserve pure virtue in himself? Those who have experienced it know: peace of mind, certainty of attainment and moments of the influx of Grace, for which such a man would not take all the treasures of the world. These are just a few of the many spiritual delights, known to the merciful.

But *mercy* is neither blind, nor unwise. It knows without thinking when to act and towards whom to act. *Spiritual discrimination* must always accompany its actions, so that a man does not become *like the fool, who casts his pearls before swine*.

There is little that can be added, for it is INTUITION, which directs our steps towards mercy. As such, it is beyond the mind, which means that it is beyond words.

*　　*　　*

Afer carefully studying the DEVELOPMENT, tune it to your own understanding of the problem, add or subtract, if you feel this will bring you more light and then, return to contemplation of the THEME alone.

6. THEME: *Blessed are the pure in heart: for they shall see God.*

Development: I know, that purity of heart embraces everything: purity of feelings, thoughts and deeds. What is THE HEART? Certainly not the fleshy organ on the left side of my chest. I have found a very beautiful, exact, and inspired definition, among others, by the Great Rishi Ramana, who often spoke about it. The HEART is then the ultimate, the innermost core of man's awareness, without which he is nothing, a void. It transcends, of course, every manifestation of mind and feelings (the mental and astral of occultists), and the Sage also calls it the *true Self* in man.

Comparably, Christ defined the *heart* as the source of everything which emerges from man's activities, his thoughts, feelings and deeds. In this way we can see the identity of both conceptions, concurrent in their superiority over everything else in us.

Now I can come closer to the words of the verse: '*pure in heart*', as being the purity of the SOURCE of all human activities in all the three planes (or worlds) in which man lives. Now I see unmistakably that the man who is pure in heart is *absolutely pure*, for he is unable to give rise to any outward uncleanliness and likewise to retain any stain in himself. Several true paths to inner development give the methods for reaching this sublime state of purity of heart.

The *occult schools* like the Eastern ones (the different kinds of true, traditional Yogas), as well as the *Western Sources of Initiation* (the late Rosicrucian practices, which have now been inactive for about 200 years, or Martinism, Neo-Martinism and certain really secret occult organizations, which therefore cannot be mentioned, and so on), have a similar approach. It is that of gradual development, *from below to above*, similar to the normal teaching methods used in the outer world. Knowledge and powers are then granted by teachers to their pupils, according to their progress and developing abilities. In brief, through accelerated karmic travelling and having the distant lofty peak of ATTAIN-MENT before his spiritual sight, the disciple climbs higher and higher, aided by his instructors, if they so choose. On some of these paths, at a certain stage of development, the disciple may realize, WHO is on the *peak*. From that moment he may participate in the *Grace*, which will accelerate his climbing and shorten the time for it.

But there is another kind of Attainment, which discards all the minute practices of the Eastern and Western yogas, and uses a different method. On this Path man has only ONE GOAL and ONE WAY: straight to his creator, concentrating every effort toward the top of the Peak, ignoring all technicalities and elaborate systems previously mentioned. Instead of a gradual acquisition of the necessary virtues and powers, the *theurgist* (for such is the name for one who follows that steep but sublime Path) believes, that with Attainment of the Lord's Grace, everything else will be simultaneously reached. The Power of the Almighty, Who responds if approached, is then joined to the efforts of the pious man, attracting him like a magnet to the point of the final merging (the drop slips into the Shining Sea). Purity of *heart* is also attained along this Path, for the only approach to the Supreme leads through the purification of man's inner core.

Which way is better and faster? All depends upon the man himself, that is, from which level he starts his journey to the Peak. On the traditional path (Yoga and occultism) there are still many traps and the disciple, if not aided by a true spiritual leader, can fall, and painful indeed is such a fall.

And it is not easy (sometimes simply impossible) to find an experienced leader and to secure his assistance, for not all of them accept pupils.

On the way of Direct Ascent, which we call—*Theurgy* (see my book of the same title), the toil may also be enormous and it is usually so, but the possibility of failure is infinitely less dangerous, for then the Master is the Lord Himself. Do I need to explain further? Let us meditate on what we have just read.

* * *

Attained in this or another way, *purity of heart* solves everything. The Great Teacher tells us, that then we may be able to *see the Lord Himself*. This is difficult to grasp. However, these words should not be taken literally, for the simple reason that then, the process of the SEEING would imply an impossible consequence: when we see something, *we are apart from it*. Now, how can one be apart from the omnipresent and omnipotent Lord?

In his usual way of describing the Supreme as the *True Self*, which he called equal to God, the Maharshi said: 'WHO ARE YOU APART FROM THE SELF?'

Truly, no sane and reasonable man would contest, that there is not, and cannot be, any existence apart from the Creator.

What then, in the words of Christ, is the meaning of 'SEEING GOD'? Of course, it is the AWARENESS OF HIS OMNIPRESENCE!

Can there be something greater or loftier? And this does not contradict the unavoidable attribute of omnipresence, even if people would say that, in spite of this, they cannot 'see' (be aware) of God. That is their own fault, their impurity, just as one cannot see anything through a dark, or dirty glass.

I see now, that the words of Christ are marvellously simple and clear: only the PURE HEART enables a man to be aware of His Lord.

* * *

In Samadhi (the highest Superconsciousness) this lofty AWARENESS is also attained, but only in moments when the consciousness of the student is perfectly clear of all impurity. This is the 'temporary Heaven' of which some people speak.

Finally, I would like to mention a personal experience I had many years ago, when visiting the Parisian Headquarters of the Order of St Vincent de Paul, in the Rue de Sèvres. A large picture hangs in the vast refectory of the monastery and it is called 'The Presence of God'. St Vincent is seen kneeling, with folded hands, looking upwards and over his head there shines a light from above, penetrating the whole of the canvas. An attempt to imagine the unimaginable? Perhaps, but even in such a 'naïve' form the idea is 'catching' for those who can look beyond forms, right into the very core of things. The artist was able to visualize something which could arise in the soul of the Saint, when he faced the SUPREME PRESENCE, that is, when he saw the Eternal Light of Being, reflected in his own consciousness. When trying to paint, or express, in any other way, these sublime moments in human life, the artist, may participate, to a certain extent, in what he tries to make visible to others and then inspiration assists him in his task. When looking at such a work, something of its idea may penetrate the awareness of the beholder.

7. THEME: *Blessed are the peacemakers: for they shall be called the children of God.*

Development: I have heard a lot about the idea of PEACE in the foregoing chapters. Peace is undoubtedly one of the attributes of Spiritual Attainment. Without *peace* there cannot be any spiritual consciousness in man. A troubled mind and feelings only show a man's unbalance, wrongness and state of suffering. How many times does one hear complaints about 'restlessness', nervousness and lack of peace in men. Nobody would ever envy such states and everyone would like to be rid of them if it can be done and as soon as possible. Now I see the great role of those, who are able to contribute to peace in their fellow men. They cure the most insidious and troublesome affliction in us. Peace makes us closer to the Lord, Who can be approached only in the perfect stillness of all our lower vibrations, which we call —feelings and thinking. The great saying from the Scriptures comes to mind: 'BE STILL AND KNOW THAT I AM THE LORD.'

Incidentally, this will be a theme for special meditation in the chapters ahead. In it the Lord gives us His own instruction on how to approach Him with certainty. It is by BEING STILL!

Now I can understand the greatness of the role of those, who are able to assist us in reaching this inner PEACE. Truly, few may be their number, but do we need many suns in order to transform our nights into bright days? *Light shines in the darkness and the darkness cannot swallow that Light.*

Then are not peace-shedding people performing a task for the Lord? No wonder that the Great Teacher mentioned them in His Sermon : they are true CHILDREN OF GOD.

In a sense, we are all such children, but it is not always manifested in us. But the Christ spoke about those, in whom the Light is visible and sensible, who radiate His Peace, which He brought with Him on to our planet. Can we see this Peace? Where is it? Nowhere, except in the most holy recesses of consciousness, in the spiritual silence of the *heart.* And so it is sown from the heart into hearts, and the Maharshi could not fail to express this, when he said : *'Of what use are words, when the heart speaks to the heart?'*

This is the way in which a son of man becomes a child of God. I shall meditate about the eternal words, which will not pass, even when heaven and earth will have passed away.

*   *   *

At this point I would like to tell you something of the way in which we can 'develop' the themes of our meditations, as well as how I was able to produce their examples in this work, which are intended to assist you in your study and realization of meditation. And I presume that some of you may know it, even before you read the following lines.

I have already explained to you enough about the teachings on CLICHÉS, in order for you to see their workings throughout the surrounding world. The 'developments' in this book have not been written in any other way.

I have strictly followed the rules and methods I am advising you about now. It is up to you to judge about the results of this work.

You know about the conditions, which make it possible for us to attract the desired *clichés* from the infinity of time and space and from THAT, which is beyond all time and space. It is your attitude, which is the primary motive force, and it is the training of your instruments which allows you to use this force.

Through *education* of your will-power, *domination* of your mind's disorderly functions and the *purification* of your emotions the conditions are created, which open the *'secret door'* in your awareness, and through this opening you can 'look' into the realm, where clichés abide.

The *'theme'* of your meditation is the key for opening that inner 'door', as you most certainly have already realized. But the opening alone cannot guarantee us the vision: for this it is necessary to satisfy the three *conditions*, mentioned in italics in the previous paragraph, that is, education, domination and purification. That is all that is required *to be able to open and see.*

The THEMES in meditation are also like the crossing about which you already know a good deal. Now you may summarize what is required for stepping on to other roads starting from that crossing, apart from the examples given here as my own 'developments'.

Fulfil these requirements, and you may trace new and even better paths than you find here. Nobody is forbidden, or prevented from such pioneering, if he really wants to try it. And all such efforts will fortify certain clichés, making them more available to our fellow men. No energy is ever lost and no effort remains without result, if it really was an effort and not just an imaginary mental or emotional concoction, lacking the substratum of power and knowledge. Let us now pass on to the next verse of the *'Sermon'*.

8. THEME : *Blessed are they which are persecuted for righteousness' sake: for theirs is the kingdom of heaven.*

Development: Everyone knows that at this time and on this planet righteousness is not always recognized, or revered. There are too many cases, when just the opposite occurs. Then those who profess righteousness are persecuted and suffer from the vindictiveness of men, who prefer darkness and shadow to light and brightness.

Let us be frank: even if, at the present time and with our present means of cognition, we are unable to solve the enigma of the universe, we can still discern some great patterns, which show themselves in the web of creation. For those who are acquainted with the Initiatory Tarot, that is, Hermetic Philosophy, there is no doubt about one of these broad patterns in Creation:

the Law of Light and Shade. Can we, with our senses and our mind's cognition abilities, imagine the idea of *Light*, without even subconsciously, if not explicitly, having an idea of the *opposite*, of the background, which is *Shadow*? This is even more astonishing and hard to reconcile with the realization of something, like eternal coexistence and the mutual interdependence of both of the apparently opposite and mutually excluding conceptions, that is, of Light and the Darkness behind it. Light penetrates the darkness and darkness and shadow recede before the light. This is certain and cannot be denied. But at the same time, as light goes or disappears, darkness automatically and inevitably takes its place, although it cannot face that light. And so it is in the manifested, visible and sensible Creation, connected with Time and Space. What lies beyond is not accessible to all and sundry and therefore our language is unable to express it in suitable and exact terms.

Nevertheless, the problem remains with us: on which *side* do we have to be and to remain? All Spiritual Teachers have advised us that it is the right, the luminous side and warned us about the left, or shadowy realm.

In the great binary—Light-Darkness, the opposites are inimical, and so it is with virtue and vice. That is why Christ taught us to be on the right side and at the same time let us know that we may expect onslaughts from the Darkness and suffer from them. But He also underlined the reward for those, who persevere and do not yield to such onslaughts. His great words assure us, that Light will finally win the battle and the fighters on the right side will enter the blessed state He called the 'Kingdom of Heaven'.

From the examples of so many advanced souls, as are the different promoters of the Light on this planet, like the Saints, eminent White occultists and philosophers in the West, as well as in the East, we know that they all had to fight hard before they reached victory. There is no victory without a fight, and no flight from the battle-field was ever able to secure victory.

The glorious cliché presented to us by the Great Teacher is clear and unmistakable: *'Whoever will persevere to the end will be saved.'* This means that he will reach the *Final Peace* of perfection in which there is no more change, for change only means the necessity of amelioration. But once the Aim has been reached nothing even happens any more and the Kingdom embraces us with the eternal embrace of Peace.

In referring to the 'practical world', I can see that this world is by no means always right and a majority does not automatically mean truth or righteousness. Under certain circumstances a unit may fight and rebuff the world around it. In this we are supported by the second part of our present theme of meditation, assuring us of the necessity of endurance: *'But I have vanquished the world!'*

As in all our meditations, our *Theme No.* 8 has a deeply spiritual background and it is the assurance of the prevailing of the spiritual over the temporary, evanescent facts of the outer world.

One may feel, that, even in our next transformation, connected with the shedding of our physical shell, which we call 'death', Truth may be brighter for us, because the main cause of illusion—the body and the idea of the 'body am I', which is related to it in so many ways, is irrevocably destroyed and proved to be only dust. And above it all shines the immutable Light of the Mansion, in which there is the final rest and bliss.

9. THEME: *Blessed are ye, when men shall revile you, and perse-cute you, and shall say all manner of evil against you falsely, for my sake.*

Development: This verse actually deepens the explanation of the preceding one. How many devoted and inspired idealists have been ridiculed, not recognized and charged with crimes never committed, and so on. This happens because, embedded deeply in the human egos, there is still the sinister desire not to have around them men who exceed them in moral and intellectual qualities, especially those of moral superiority. For sometimes it is impossible to fight and defeat people with high mental qualifications, as their knowledge and skill are necessary in too many branches of human life. Education makes our degrees, and so on, defendable and incontestable. But not so with the *imponder-abilia* of moral elevation. Here everyone considers himself to be a competent judge, and for the criticizing of ethical values he is unlikely to put himself into serious difficulties, as would be the case with official science.

When one is devoted to a high spiritual ideal, like that of

Christ, no written law would defend one against one's 'agnostic' opponents. The Great Teacher knew it, and so we have this ninth verse of His Sermon.

The suffering of such offences from the outer world will be rewarded by the far higher happiness of the BLISS, promised by the Teacher. For an occultist this is no wonder at all, for he knows the *perennial law of balance*, which rewards everyone according to his merits, no matter how much time may be needed until that Law pronounces its verdict. Some call it by an Eastern term—the Law of Karma.

I know how hard it is sometimes to suffer unjust accusations and maliciousness from those around us and how evil these efforts are from the outer world, as they try to PULL DOWN EVERYTHING WHICH IS MORALLY SUPERIOR, because purity shocks uncleanliness and sanctity scandalizes the wickedness in men. There are few of the great Souls who escaped reviling when they were still present on this planet. But posterity has showed how right they were! The Maharshi, against whom there are no known accusations, told us that 'only the ego in man can be affected by gossip and maledictions'. The Sage remains unaffected for ever.

10. THEME: *Rejoice, and be exceedingly glad: for great is your reward in heaven: for so persecuted they the prophets which were before you.*

Development: The assurance of the final reward continues in this part of the Sermon. It is reinforced by the living example of other spiritually advanced men, such as the prophets, who were ridiculed and persecuted, because the Truth they preached was uncomfortable for the debased majority of their own people. This is the well-known story, and it does not need much explanation.

But it has a very profound meaning for us, when we encounter such open or hidden persecution in our own lives. It supports us in our critical hours. It gives us the firm conviction, that individual, single human beings, can be right and the mass can be wrong. Almost every student of meditation has been, or will be confronted by this problem and let him not forget this tenth verse of the 'Sermon on the Mount'. His sufferings were foreseen and predicted by the Great Teacher, it is true; but He also issued

His final consolation ('Rejoice and be exceedingly glad. . .'), for us and does the person, who has passed through a painful sickness and has subsequently been restored to the happiness of full health, remember much or regret the dead past, which disappeared in the ocean of irrevocable Time?

The gist of the present message is never to look back, but always towards the developing future. I already know that the most elusive thing is the philosophically conceived idea of PRESENT time. It is like a razor blade, almost without any thicknes on its sharp edge! What I am now seeing immediately becomes the past and then I enter into the time, which is coming from the FUTURE and by embracing it, I am transforming it into the PAST.

What meaning has pain, which was long ago drowned in the bottomless clichés belonging to that PAST?

Only neurotic and unbalanced minds would ascribe any meaning to that which WAS, but IS NOT now. It is not my path!

I shall meditate about this Truth, until it becomes a clear and irrefutable reality for me. I know that the final result will be the much desired BLISS.

11. THEME: *Ye are the salt of the earth: but if the salt have lost his savour, wherewith shall it be salted? It is thenceforth good for nothing, but to be cast out, and to be trodden under foot of men.*

Development: In this verse the Great Teacher emphasizes the importance and value of man. Actually, of all the visible creatures on this earth, *man* is undoubtedly the most advanced. With this goes the augmented *responsibility* for his activities, for nobody would expect such an attribute from an animal or other lower form of life. I have therefore, to think deeply about my own role in this world and of the responsibilities which are mine during my earthly life.

I shall not be like that salt, which has lost its true virtue and therefore become a useless substance, good only to be rejected into damnation's abyss.

I know that my life is not without a purpose and while perhaps, I am still unable to embrace the whole of its meaning, I am nevertheless, aware of its value. I dare not frustrate it, for I shall pay dearly for that. Frustration is the very fire, which burns, but does not consume us, after we have pronounced our own judgement about our incarnation, if unsuccessful, after release from the physical body.

But in this statement of Christ's there is also a tremendous force of hope and encouragement: WE ARE THE SALT OF THE EARTH!

I remember my former meditations from Part II of this book, in which I also dealt with the building of clichés. The essential pictures or clichés of my activities on this planet are not yet accessible to my everyday consciousness. Nevertheless, it is my duty to know what I can of them now. And the awareness, that I should not and cannot allow 'my salt' to become a useless, indifferent mass, is the final stage of the development of this meditation. I have enough experience of the sad results, coming from a frustrated and useless life, if a man is never awakened to the true aim of his existence. This world is too full of such examples. And its present impasse is due to just this fact, for the world is the sum total of its dwellers—men. 'AS YOU ARE, SO IS THE WORLD', the Sage Maharshi told us. In contributing to the positive side of the world, I am contributing to my own advantage and in improving myself, I am improving the world. This is the only way of real action, accessible to us.

12. THEME: *Ye are the light of the world. A city that is set on a hill cannot be hid. Neither do men light a candle, and put it under a bushel, but on a candle-stick; and it giveth light unto all that are in the house. Let your light so shine before men, that they may see your good works, and glorify your Father which is in heaven.*

Development: This verse has already been dealt with in the former text, so there is little to add. But, in order to complete my course of meditation on *The Sermon on the Mount*, I shall proceed with its details.

That we men, are the Light of this world, has been spoken of in the opening paragraphs of the present chapter. The example of the city built on a hill and of the candle set on high, tells us about the treatment of that Light in us. It should not be hidden, for the purpose of all light is to enlighten its surroundings. Little as I have of that light now in a developed state, it should still be made available to those, who tread the Path beside me. It remains the surest way, in which I can perform my duty! The Teacher does not leave us in doubt about this. *By seeing our good deeds, men will see the Light of the Father and glorify Him for that.* So, these are the *actions*, which enlighten our brothers around us, and it is these actions which bring glory to our eternal Father in heaven!

Some will probably say: 'But we were told, that we should first purify our feelings and thoughts.' That is perfectly right, for, if our feelings and thinking are pure and righteous, would we be in a position to perform deeds of evil intent? A moment of reflection will show us that it is impossible. The root of our actions always lies in our *heart*, as the Teacher said, and the HEART means the very CORE of man's consciousness, from which he radiates his feelings and thoughts. There is another, mostly unknown mystery of our inner life: a good deed produces good feelings and thoughts. I can experience this if I wish. After performing a selfless, good action, peace and comfort descend into us, if we do not indulge in any 'evaluation' of it: '... *let not thy left hand know what thy right hand doeth*'. There is *Something* much higher in us than the thinking process. Let my meditation teach me to turn may awareness to IT!

CHAPTER XXV

Meditation about Mastership – Series II

IN the previous Series No. 1 of our meditations we had twelve spiritual themes with which to work. In this chapter another kind will be expounded, having their basis in meditations about those, who are so spiritually advanced in their evolution, that they are usually called 'The Masters'. As with many other occult subjects, considerable confusion exists about Mastership and its relation to the rest of humanity.

The purpose of the following meditations will be to remove the nonsense and to promote a realistic conception of the great sons of humanity, from whom alone we can obtain true instruction in our strivings for spiritual attainment and final peace.

Who better can tell us about Mastership, than the Masters themselves? Hence, I have gathered together themes from the sayings of the Masters about their own paths and lives, as well as their direct teachings. In spiritual life it is the same as in the material one: one who knows more, instructs and assists those who know less and have no experience. Without the wisdom, which comes from the eminent Sons of Man, humanity would advance much slower and commit more errors, for which the retribution is—suffering.

Therefore it is a natural and wise proposition to turn for light to those who have possessed that Light.

It is a rare privilege and an equally great responsibility when a man is allowed to meet a true Spiritual Master during his physical presence on our earth. Nothing can ever compare with the facing of such a Man, who has passed all human experiences and obtained the wholeness of wisdom, for which achievement we spend our innumerable incarnations. Another remarkable factor is that such a Master teaches that: 'All Masters are essentially ONE', that is, the same Light of Spirit shines through them.

I have written chapters about the Masters as well as about the One, whom I was allowed to encounter in this my life.[1] But the Masters come on this earth very rarely and there are many false ones posing as genuine. They are easily recognizable for every man possessed of common sense and discriminative experience. An irreproachable and saintly life is the best proof of Mastership.

1. THEME : *I am the resurrection and the life and the path: who goes My way does not err.*
(Jesus)

Development : In these words the Great Teacher shows us the direct Path. Its name is the following in the steps of the Master. Who would show us the Path if there were no Master? One of His true disciples, who wrote the incomparable *Imitation of Christ* elaborated on this problem from his own experience. In that book I can find a treasure of spiritual initiation, summarized in the statement, that the Master will come to visit His faithful disciple, who has shown by his whole life that he had dedicated it to Him.

Before the spiritual awakening, or the start of preferring spiritual life to earthly existence, a man is as if dead, and so Christ told us to: 'Let the dead bury their dead.' Resurrection is necessary, and it can be found in Him. So many have already found it and I can find it too!

The Teacher refers to 'LIFE' as belonging only to those who have been awakened and that is why He says 'I am the Life'.

In an initiatory teaching from the East it is said: 'Thou canst not travel on the Path before thou hast become that Path itself.' That is why in our theme for this meditation we read: 'I am the Path'. On the road to Attainment everything melts together: the man, the Teacher and the Path. I shall meditate about it deeply in my heart.

On such a Path and with such a Leader, there cannot be any erring. That Path is enlightened by His Light.

[1] See my *In Days of Great Peace*, and *Ways to Self-Realization*, Allen & Unwin, 1957 and 1964.

* * *

In this Series, as usual, go through the development, first reading it several times and so memorizing it. Then add your own comments—but in short and precise sentences—if you feel that you may need something more than you find in this text. Finally, return to the theme, repeat it several times in your mind, then stop thinking and listen to the Silence arising in you. It will be calling for the related spiritual cliché. If your concentration is successful, and mind is stilled effectively, you may perceive the true cliché of the theme in your own awareness, without words, or movements of the mind.

2. THEME: *A Master is one who has meditated solely on God, has flung his whole personality into the sea of God...*
(The Maharshi)

Development: Here, in his own words, I have a definition by the Spiritual Superman about Mastership. All reason dictates that there cannot be any better definition than that made by the one, who has himself attained the lofty state of the Perfect Man. And thus it is with this meditation. I have to accept it as truth.

It means, that the Master's foremost activity is that of meditating about the SOURCE OF EVERYTHING, about OUR FATHER, if we use the inspired words of the Great Teacher Christ. The Master knows what is essential and he holds to it unswervingly. That is why he meditates constantly about God. I can presume that there cannot be any better purpose for a great soul, as is the true Master, who has passed through all human experiences long before us and who has acquired all Wisdom and is ready to shed his Light upon all, who are able to accept it and willingly allow it to burn in them for ever.

Here the Master compares God to the sea, in which the personality of a man has to be drowned. By this fact it becomes united with the SEA, just as in Edwin Arnold's lines: 'The dewdrop slips into the Shining Sea!' of Nirvana, or God.

The mind is powerless to express and to picture the full contents of God's idea, and comparisons and similes are the only way in order to awake the responsive fire in the heart of a seeker of the Supreme. In the Maharshi's description of the way, in which the Master (who he was himself) is related to God, the

240

simile of the *sea* is skilfully used. It is inspiring, solving all the problems. It gives a foretaste of the immense, indescribable bliss and final peace, which is the destiny of the 'drop' of human consciousness, when it attains the stage of ripeness for returning back into the OCEAN, from which it had been evaporated into the long process of evolution, through the aeons of time and the immensities of space. This is the basic wisdom which the Master possesses, and that is how he can be recognized. He is not occupied with anything else, but the dwelling in the Lord and the radiating of his Light, derived from that union, for those who have eyes to see it.

That is what, in the first place, I should know about Mastership, in order to be safe from all possible errors and deceptions.

3. THEME: *A Master forgets everything about his own personality being immersed in the sea of God.*
(The Maharshi)

Development: Here I can see one of the main differences between the Master and other men, no matter how intelligent and clever they may appear to be to us. All of them, including myself, are living principally in their personalities, or egos, and this is the most important thing in their lives. This is the reason why such men cannot 'see' (actually merge in) God. For that purpose, the Perfect Man, the Master, forgets and leaves far below his enlightened awareness that, which we believe to be ourselves, our individual being. Now I 'see' the cause of the apparent impossibility of men obtaining that experience of God in which a spiritual Master perpetually lives.

The limited, wide fence of ego separates us surely and efficiently from perceiving the Supreme.

I see that all the efforts of some philosophers and occultists to prove the existence, or non-existence of God are for ever condemned to be fruitless and vain. It is because they try to pull down what cannot be pulled down to the level of their minds, that is, the *Supreme*, and even Its reflection. When they cannot perform the impossible of lowering the Sun into their little vessel, they say that 'HE DOES NOT EXIST'. As truly said the Maharshi: 'IGNORANCE IS THE ROOT OF ALL EVIL AND SUFFERING!'

And that is why Jesus told us that: '*You cannot serve God and Mammon (at the same time)*'.

241

May the Spiritual Master, invisible but real, who is in charge of my soul which is seeking Truth, help me to cross this difficult bridge, separating the illusory, egoistic life, from the Land filled with the true Light in which I and my Creator are united, like a drop fallen into the illimitable ocean.

He knows my troubles, for he has passed through all of them, conquered them and so obtained the mastery of life.

4. THEME: *The Master becomes only the instrument of God, and when his mouth opens it speaks God's words without effort or forethought.*
(The Maharshi)

Development: Here I see the Master in another light, in his true role in this world of relativity. The Maharshi tells us, that the Master is an instrument of God, acting as a transmitter of God's will and teaching. In this he is in full agreement with all the Scriptures, revealed to humanity from time immemorial. There have always been inspired men of God, teaching words of truth and wisdom despite the fact, that men often refuse to accept the lofty speech of the Initiates.

And I see that the way in which the Masters utter their words of wisdom is different from that of the speech of ordinary men, who carefully prepare their important talks, make notes and plans, and so on. It is the mind which operates in such men, not the Spirit-God, Who speaks through the Masters.

It seems as if the Lord opens His clichés—which are inaccessible to ordinary men—to His faithful children, and they can then read them and let us know something of their wisdom.

When a 'philosopher' concocts his theories and guesses, no matter how clever their outer form may be, such things are spiritually dead, and seldom survive their creators—the human minds. By survival I mean the fact of living according to those theories. Look around! How many people are doing this even in our own day? But there are *words which will not pass even if Heaven and earth pass away.*

To read from the clichés, which are beyond time and space, is like reading an open book, where there is no doubt about the authenticity of the text. That is why the words of a Master are uttered without forethought, or effort.

The Maharshi knew this truth well and he allowed us to participate in its benefits.

5. THEME: *When the Master raises a hand, God flows again through that, to* WORK A MIRACLE.
(The Maharshi)

Development: In this sentence the Maharshi again makes an attempt to explain for us the way in which the *Supreme* acts through His 'Instruments'—the Masters. The raising of the hand signifies an act of will, of power. The role of God is like that of the current, passing through a conductor. This simile, as given to us by a Sage, who well knew what he said from his own experience, is extremely enlightening for me. It removes the clumsy anthropomorphic conceptions, still ruling in many religions. But the same Maharshi never condemned any such concept, because he knew that it is actually immaterial how men imagine the Supreme. It is the WAY in which they turn to Him, which really matters. But for many more intellectually advanced men, anthropomorphism is now like a mental *taboo*, and for them the Master Maharshi gave this inspired and acceptable comparison.

At the same time, it explains the way in which *miracles* are worked. This world which we think we know, the *manifested Creation*, is evidently subjected to the law of CAUSE AND EFFECT. But can He, Who imposed these laws, be bound by them? Even our imperfect mind tells us that it is most unlikely. The Lord is FAR ABOVE AND BEYOND any laws, those which we know as well as those about which we have not the slightest premonition.

We are acquainted with the fact, that in our limited existence, which is subject to definite laws, everything happens according to them. But what lies beyond them is like a miracle for us. However this does not apply to those who know other, more subtle and basic laws and, beyond all, not for the POWER WHICH IMPOSED THOSE LAWS ON THE MANIFESTED AND CREATED UNIVERSE. This is the true explanation of the possibility and existence of 'miracles'.

We make wide use of the physical laws known to us, and we are still acquiring more knowledge about the application of such laws, as well as discovering new ones, which rule matter. Let us only compare physical science of a hundred years ago and the knowledge of the twentieth century. Our present inventions might seem like miracles to our ancestors, if they could see them. And, in the future, the discovery of new laws might seem to be miraculous to our own generation of today.

6. THEME: *The Master takes on the occult powers like clair-voyance, clairaudience, and such things only as a form of* SELF-SACRIFICE, *because far greater illumin-ation and peace are possible without them than with them.*
(The Maharshi's Teachings)

Development: This is a striking statement by one, who should know the matter best. And yet, when I enter into the deepest recesses of my consciousness, I instinctively feel that the Great Soul was right. Properly speaking, what is the use of 'Siddhis' as our Eastern brothers call the psychic and occult powers? To whom do they belong, and for whom are they needed? If developed through the special efforts and toil of an individual, they are only another manifestation of that arch-enemy—the human *ego*, trying to sublimate itself over 'others'. I see in all of this, a deepened sense of separateness, which is, as the Great Rishi told us, just that mysterious 'primordial' sin, which spoils every effort of a man to raise himself closer to the Truth of his own being.

The manifestation of occult powers will not convince any-one not ripe enough to take the first real step on the Path of spiritual Achievement. And those who are ripe will enter on to the Path even without seeing any exhibition of Siddhis. On the other hand, even the most incredible and powerful examples of those powers will not convince unripe people, and often they will turn against the one, who displayed his superior develop-ment and strength. The example of Jesus and of the Saints and Prophets are too well known to be quoted. How wise the Maharshi was in telling us about it!

He possessed all those powers, but so rarely manifested them that even in his genuine biography, written by one of his true devotees, we find only a few instances, which can be ascribed to the Siddhis possessed by him (see—*Self-Realization, or the Life and Teachings of Ramana Maharshi'*, published by his Ashram, Tiruvannamalai, South India). Now I may have better insight as to why the Master spoke about the 'sacrifice' connected with the use of his occult powers.

Also, the thing which attracts men to these unusual powers is sheer curiosity and the desire to profit from them, without any personal effort on the part of such people. Is this right and desirable?

In this period, when there are so many rogues trying to exploit human weaknesses and lure men to them through their allegedly possessed Siddhis, this statement by the Master should be remembered.

7. THEME: *The idea that a Master is simply one who has attained power over various occult senses by long practice and prayer or anything of the kind, is absolutely false. No Master ever cared a rap for occult powers, for he has no need for them in his daily life.*
(From the Maharshi's Teachings)

Development: These words are so simple and clear, that they do not need any explanation. What I have to do is to memorize and meditate about them, in the spirit of the former, the sixth theme of meditation. But in the following texts of the Master's sayings we find statements of enormous weight for the seeker, so therefore, let us listen to them and think about them.

We should not fix our attention on the phenomena of the surrounding world, on the transient things like life (physical), death, and so on. The only aim which must be pursued, and which will richly repay is: TO THINK ONLY ABOUT THAT WHICH IS RESPONSIBLE FOR ALL MANIFESTATIONS OF LIFE; ABOUT THAT WHICH ALONE *sees* ALL OF THESE. AND THAT IS THE WAY USED BY THE MASTER WHEN ATTAINING HIS HIGH STATE. BRIEFLY, FIX YOUR MIND UNSHAKENLY ON *that which sees*.

If we try to realize the deep meaning of these teachings, we may be attracted by their power and spiritual charm. To look only at THAT, which is in the beginning of the Allness! So where is the unveiled secret of Attainment of such a Path, which has often been called the 'Path of Wisdom', of 'Jnana', and which the Master Maharshi simply called the 'Direct Path'.

Those who have tried this sublime Path, know that it also leads to manifestations of different Siddhis, but to unconscious ones, without any effort on the part of the seeker to develop them.

I see that the words of the Master, as given on page 245 in *capitals* are a direct *initiation* for those who have eyes to see and ears to hear. This is that 'inverted' spiritual sight, which decides about our progress and attainment. Simple as it is, it should be constantly meditated upon, until the Light comes. And It invariably comes, if we act wisely and as the Master taught us.

HE WHO SEES IS INSIDE YOURSELF, he added. Can the object of a search ever be closer than THIS ONE? He waits, in holy Silence, for our inner voice to call for HIM from the depths of our hearts.

8. THEME: *The Master dwells in the perpetual state of spiritual consciousness, beyond mind and feelings (mental and astral realms), that is, beyond the illusion of the world and separate being, with the only difference, that in some way incomprehensible to us, he can use the mind, body and intellect without falling back into the delusion of having separate consciousness.*

(The Maharshi)

Development: The words of the Great Rishi are so clear, that no further explanation is necessary. It therefore remains to meditate about them directly, in order to get illumination.

Perhaps it would be useful to remind those who have not studied some of the former works of the writer (especially *Concentration, Samadhi*, and *Ways to Self-Realization*), that this sublime state of consciousness is called 'SAHAJA SAMADHI' in the East, or the 'Perennial Superconsciousness', which only those can possess, who have concluded their evolution as human beings, and have become united with the *Whole*. It is uninterrupted and natural for them, although some advanced disciples can reach a similar state of consciousness, but only for a limited time and while their bodies are immobilized as in catalepsy.

After having experienced this kind of Superconsciousness, a temporary one called 'KEVALA SAMADHI', a man often feels the ecstasy of mental bliss, as a reflection of the spiritual awareness he has been able to reach.

Then his subsequent actions may be enlightened by the light

of that ecstasy, but not by the direct Spirit, experienced in the SAHAJA SAMADHI, which, as we now know, continues without interruption throughout the whole of the physical life of the Master. Therefore the actions of the Master are infallible, while those of people who can operate only in the reflected Light are not necessarily perfect. This knowledge may explain the absolute confidence and obedience to Spiritual Masters, offered to them in the East by their true and intelligent disciples. Such a man, who has obtained the grace of encountering a true Master in his lifetime, will possess that Faith spoken of by Christ.

9. THEME: *A Master in meditation, though his eyes and ears are opened, fixes his attention so firmly on* THAT WHICH SEES *that he neither sees nor hears, nor has any physical consciousness at all, nor mental either, but only spiritual.*
(The Maharshi)

Development: Here we have the key to true meditation, given to us by the one who possessed this art in full. There can be nothing better for an earnest student of meditation, than to dedicate to this Theme No. 9 as much time and attention as he is capable of doing. Meditation along the lines shown by the Maharshi is unsurpassed for our progress, since it opens the eyes of our spirit, veiled by the shroud-like illusion of the surrounding world. I am now merging in it.

'. . . THAT WHICH SEES. . .' There lies the secret! This should be meditated upon WITHOUT VERBALIZATION, that is, no words, nor sentences should be admitted into our awareness, if we really want to be initiated into the art of meditation. Seek THAT WHICH SEES AND HEARS alone, in full inner silence, acquired by the ability of *passive* concentration, and guarded by its *active* sister (see *Concentration*). The solution of this great mystery lies in the DIRECTED SILENCE IN CONSCIOUSNESS. Do you understand the meaning? Passive concentration alone will not suffice, for it must finally be interrupted by thoughts and clichés, over which you may have no control at the time, if you have not directed your awareness to be opened ONLY TO A CERTAIN INFLUENCE, which in this case will be the ONE WHO SEES AND HEARS THE SIGHT AND SOUND OF THE WHOLE. You know His Name! He is accessible only through the SILENCE, but not a

247

mechanical, mental silence, obtained merely by a certain mental training in concentration. No, it is only an instrument and should not be confused with the conscious action of your Spirit, coming into contact with the Spirit of the ALL. Briefly, what do you have to do? MEMORIZE WITHOUT WORDS, THE THEME OF YOUR MEDITATION AND MERGE INTO THE SILENCE, BASED ON THE SPIRIT OF THAT THEME. Perhaps you will first have to meditate about this sentence before you arrive at the proper action, and that is what I am strongly advising you to do. Thus taught the Master Maharshi, as well as other Great Souls. We can rely on the words of those who KNOW.

10. THEME : *We must take away the world, which causes our doubts, which clouds our mind, and then the Light of God will shine clearly through.*
(The Maharshi's saying)

Development : After our study of the previous material in this book, we should be neither puzzled by, nor unprepared for such a statement. The Maharshi, in his wisdom, compares God to the WHITE LIGHT, undispersed by the prism of the world. Remove the prism and the illusory colours will disappear of themselves, and you will see the LIGHT which is the TRUTH-GOD. What a powerful injunction there is in these simple words for a leap ahead for us !

If we look attentively at the lives of the Saints, mystics, yogis, spiritual Masters and men, who achieved spiritual consciousness, we will find one common factor in their philosophies and teachings. All of them recognize the visible world as an obstacle to spiritual realization, unless the attachment to that world has been controlled, or removed.

The Maharshi's simile comparing the world to a prism, which deflects and decomposes the primordial WHITE LIGHT of the Supreme, is unique. It explains why we do not see things as they really are, for in the coloured rays there is not and cannot be objective, or true perception. But, at the same time, the idea of the unspoiled white Light shows the way out of that impasse : the return to the *true*, to the *unadulterated* vision of the pure white Light.

It is not any coincidence that light is always considered to be a symbol and even an attribute of the Highest, in all schools of philosophy and religion, while darkness—as the *absence* of that Light—is looked on as the symbol for evil and suffering.

The Master Maharshi does not bid us to deny and abandon the visible world as such. The fact itself, that we still have our bodies, clearly belonging to the material world and dependent upon it, tells us that we still have some lessons to learn in this dense realm. What he stresses is the right attitude towards the unreal and perishable, the putting of things into their proper place, and the not setting up of destructible idols on the throne belonging to the Spirit-Life. He equally disapproved of the soul-less man, believing only in his body, like a fanatical fakir, who allegedly uses his bed of nails in order to conquer the enemy—body. He called for true discrimination and common sense, so often lacking in many of us.

11. THEME: *These bodies and minds are only the tools of the Self-I, which is the illimitable spirit, in which alone there is the ultimate freedom of man.*
(The Maharshi)

Development: In this meditation of Series II we find the final teaching of the Master about the true relationship between the physical and spiritual man. No sane person would deny that the physical counterpart of every living being is mortal and impermanent. Maharshi calls it 'a tool of the true Self-Spirit, which uses it for certain purposes, not always clear to men'.

What had a beginning must have an end, and what is limited cannot embrace what is unlimited. How logical these statements seem to be, yet why do men on this earth not put them into practice in their lives? Why do they live as if they were here forever, and why do they try to operate only with the limited resources of the mind, dependent upon such a fragile (and mortal) instrument as is the human brain? Merely a small abrasion of it can instantly turn a genius into an idiot.

Quite definitely humanity is not scientifically minded as regards its most vital problems, which touch on its very existence. Instead, it boasts of its 'science' in second-class matters, connected with variable physical conditions, limited in time to an infinitesimal fraction by comparison with the vastness of the cosmic duration of the visible universe. Man tries to subdue infinite space, but is unable to subdue his own shell, in which he lives for only such a short period. That outward expansion without consolidation of the inner factors (moral, intellectual and spiritual) seems to be like a soap-bubble, which expands for a short time, glistening on the outside with many colours, but empty inside, and finally collapsing into a few drops of inconsequential liquid, when it finally bursts.

My purpose is to establish the true relationship between the perishable and perennial in myself. Nobody can perform it apart from me.

Meditation about the words of the ONE who KNOWS is dedicated to the cognition of his wisdom.

12. THEME: *The Sacred lore (Scriptures) is of value only so long as one does not turn inwards, in the Quest of the Self. As soon as he does so, all that he has learnt of it will be forgotten and lost.*
(The Maharshi, quotation from *Maha Yoga*)

Development: This theme may serve as a final description of the attitude of a Master, who has reached his aim. Now it becomes obvious what is wrong with all those sects throughout the world, who choose one or another part of religious lore (such as the Old Testament, Upanishads, etc., together with all the theoretical philosophies), and stick exclusively to them because they consider them to be the only true and worthwhile material, while having nothing but contempt for everything else.

I see the narrowness of the limited human mind, unenlightened by any Spiritual Inspiration. The Maharshi knew it and from this comes his words as given in the theme. Let me take the Master's point of view, not that of my own mind, which can only lead me astray.

Truth is above and beyond any thinking processes. Meditation should gradually teach me to transfer my consciousness beyond them.

CHAPTER XXVI

Meditation on God – Series III

As you may see, this manual on meditation is not limited to any particular creed, philosophy, or religion. My purpose is to give you full freedom of choice, as to which kind of meditation suits you the best: whatever is closest to your heart. This is because no compulsion can ever be used in order to force you into this or another path.

However, there are certain conditions, which I believe are being fulfilled in this work. Firstly, when you want to leap, you must have ground from which your body can rebound. Secondly, you must have limbs strong enough to overcome the force of gravity for a moment, and so allow you to throw your body into the air. And thirdly, you have to be able to direct the concurring actions of your muscles properly in order to retain balance and so secure a safe landing.

When you look back at the earlier chapters, you will see how these conditions have been handled in the text, and how your *knowledge* of the subject, *techniques* and *material* with which you have to operate were developed before your eyes.

I will not enter into any further deliberations in that regard, for it is your duty to find and follow the synthesis of the three factors, just mentioned. You have to digest them mentally and then refer to your 'heart', that is, to the innermost core of your being. If you have worked through the exercises as intended and advised, you will already have some firm ground under your feet in order to rebound, some force to set your muscles in action and a certain insight to show you where you are going. It is not my job to make up the account and draw conclusions instead of you, as you will undoubtedly realize and accept.

There is also another aspect of meditation to which I would like to draw your attention. Meditation, as you know, is the highest possible function of our consciousness, still based on the mind's experience and powers, although not in any way bound by them.

In this part of the present work, we have not used any concepts connected with another high function of the human consciousness, which is PRAYER. We will have enough time and space in the final chapters for it. In spite of this you can see the delicate thread running, often without definite terms, through the themes as well as the developments. It is the idea of the *Supreme Power*, as the final receiver of the energy from meditation and the fulcrum of the inherent concentration. This is because, on the highest level of human consciousness, the ONE WITHOUT A SECOND appears as of HIMSELF, being the only worthy aim for the supreme effort of the INNER MAN. I am simply stating the fact, without entering into the hopeless and insoluble 'whys'. We do not know! Deep within us, when the Silence starts and the storms of the world and mind subside, there appears a faint light, as delicate as a flower's petal, but firm and inaccessible to any outer shocks. All mystics know about It, but It is not confined solely to those 'specialists' in every spiritual business, as we may jokingly say. The basic core in every man is the same, his spiritual awareness, having its dynamic manifestation in the Hyperconsciousness.

As Spirit is unchangeable, uniform, motionless (in our earthly meaning), limitless (that is why it does not perform any movement, nor underlie any change), all-penetrating and omnipotent because of its unique, true existence (Reality), so there cannot be two or more Spirits: for how, and in what way could they be different? The conception of the Spirit is tantamount to God and many people prefer this term, and not without good reason.

That is what we may think, accept, believe and repose in. This 'inner Light' tells us that '*it is so and not otherwise*'. And our mind can still bear this revelation, for it is in the realm of facts, which are operative for it. But there is no answer to the question 'WHY?'. It is a pity to spend time trying to solve what cannot be solved. To my mystically minded readers I can only quote the answer given to the well-known French mystic, occultist and philosopher—Paul Sédir of Paris, by his spiritual Master, the mysterious Monsieur Andréas, as he called him. In brief it was the reply that: 'Perhaps, some day, when we are ripe enough, the good Father will reveal to us, WHY things are as they are'. No doubt this 'day' may be aeons in length.

*   *   *

So our next Series, No. III of the advanced meditations will cover the conception of the *Supreme Being*, as left to us by leading spiritual Masters, belonging to different schools, races and religions. Of course, they will be only a few selected items, and I am conscious that you may find even more suitable ones for your own use. Try them also, but remember that they must not belong to any sectarian, high-walled gardens, but preferably to men of tolerance and deep experience. They should be short, as those in this book, for otherwise you will not be in a position to cope properly with the core of meditation—its very THEME.

The method will remain the same. Firstly, work through the development, after reading the theme several times. What is the purpose of such a proceeding? To put you on the 'crossing' (the theme) and then, through the development, to mark the paths, which radiate from that central point in any direction. The developments contain the basic ideas and their elaboration, which will assist you and widen your mental horizon. And there will certainly be some new and useful material in them for you. But, I repeat, if you feel yourself so strong that you can pass over the available development and create your own satisfactorily, by all means do so without a second thought. But be warned, that our treacherous mind, which feels that successful meditation will lead us to even greater domination of it, will do everything it can in order to prevent you from being successful.

It may suggest to you that: 'Of course you may have much better ideas than the writer has given to you, and you should reject the latter and use only your own'. Theoretically it sounds fine, but the catch may be that 'your better ideas' may be simply transformed by your mind into its own uncontrolled vibrations, 'floating' aimlessly and far distant from the theme. In other words it will have its victory over your concentration and line of work you wanted to realize. If you are unable to stop the malefactor, it may suggest, after you have been duly exhausted by mind's whimsies, that you are unsuccessful, not because you

253

did not observe the instructions as given in this book, but because this book is probably not good enough for you, and so on. If you accept the malicious whispering, you will lose the battle. Years will pass, and they never return: instead of practising you will only seek different books. You can find the final result for yourself.

My duty was to warn you: yours to accept, or reject that warning.

Before we pass to the meditation proper on God, according to texts taken from leading spiritual and philosophical authorities, it would be useful to elucidate certain lines of our relation to the *Supreme Power*, which can be conceived and accepted by our intellect.

(1) The necessary acceptance of the *omnipresence* of God leads to a very profound conclusion. We cannot be APART from Him, under any circumstances, for otherwise it would mean that there are some places where He is not present, as they are beyond His reach, which naturally, is absurd. Therefore we are 'merged' in Him, and every process in our physical and spiritual structure lies in His full awareness, and nothing can escape from it. If we think deeper about this axiom, we may see the importance of the right attitude towards Him, far beyond those childish, subconscious beliefs, that a man can hide anything from the Supreme, and that there can be something unknown to Him. That is why, for example, in Theurgy, which operates through the direct turning to the Lord by means of prayer, the absolute necessity of *full sincerity* towards Him is so emphasized. Otherwise an insincere prayer would be only a hypocritical action, not bringing the desired results, but rather a just retribution.

Equally, in your meditation, be fully conscious of this, and do not allow your mind to trick you with the false idea, that you can hide something, and still enjoy the blessing of good prayer or meditation. This warning may seem to be superfluous to many of you, as you may have realized earlier the decisive importance of opening man's whole heart before the Lord, without leaving even the smallest and ugliest corner of it in shadow. There is no shadow before His sight!

(2) The inherent *omniscience* of the Lord makes our meditation easier, for we do not need to explain everything to Him, as to another person, who may not know unless told. This is also an

absurdity! Moreover, the highest meditation, as you will know later, is that beyond any words and thoughts, a *mute* meditation, paralleling the highest kind of prayer—the *mute* prayer. Therefore, our elevation of consciousness may well be free from verbalizing, and the wordless attitude will be the purest and hence the most effective of all.

Is it possible, to reflect something of the powers belonging to the Supreme Being in our mentality? Yes, to a certain degree, if you have an alert apparatus, well-developed and acquainted with abstruse thinking. If you have performed the final exercise No. 9 of the Fifth Series of *Concentration*, then you should have no difficulties at all in experiencing these TWO qualities of God —OMNIPRESENCE and OMNISCIENCE, in relation, of course, to your own Self.

For the first (Omnipresence), the idea of infinite SPACE will serve best. Now follow my thought exactly! Can you imagine an end to space? This means a place, or circumstance where there would be no more space. If your mind thoughtlessly says perhaps it may be so, then ask yourself, working all the time with your imagination, as to WHAT *would lie beyond that 'non-existent' space?* You will see that it is impossible, that space cannot be annihilated, at least, in relation to what we are now on this earth. The continuity of space is a common sense axiom for every developed mind. It is exactly the same with the all-penetration of that space. For example, take your room, partially filled with furniture, and so on, can you eliminate the space in it, or change, or limit it? Are the dimensions of that room changed because of the presence of certain objects in it? Of course not! That is why the Great Cosmic Space is not at all affected by any of the innumerable galaxies and universes in it. Think about this, realize it and then try to compare the *omnipresence* of the Lord with that of all-penetrating space and you will not be far from the Truth. He is everywhere, and nothing can escape being in Him. You are merged in Him!

For the second (Omniscience), less exploration will be needed, for it is easy to imagine, that the OMNIPRESENT cannot be unconscious of anything in ITS reach, that is, in any place and under any conditions. So He must know your every thought, feeling, beat of your heart, every movement in you and of you, the circulation of your blood-particles, the currents in your brain and nerves, in brief, all your being, physical as well as non-physical.

To become really aware of all of the foregoing, to practise this awareness every day and every hour belong to one of the highest 'Initiations' a man can ever pass through. It conquers death and explains life, and it is the dearest treasure which the Sages secured throughout aeons of toil.

1. THEME: *I am that I am.*

Development: This brief sentence is of enormous meaning, for it has been taken from the Bible, in which the Almighty, as the Sage Maharshi told us, gave up His true Name and substance. The Name cannot be given as something for us to use, for there is no comparison for the ONE WITHOUT A SECOND. Every earthly name has some meaning, or origin, but where would you seek for the origin of THAT, which is ITSELF THE ORIGIN OF EVERYTHING? Nevertheless, even this definition which Moses transmitted to us from his own relations with the Supreme, has enormous meaning and inspiration for those who are ripe enough to be able to raise their mind beyond its usual limitations, and to 'read' the Unique Name.

In this sentence we can see the element of *unlimited existence*, beyond all the laws and conditions with which, we, as humans, are physically, or mentally acquainted. Therefore no closer definition can be transferred from the Highest Region into the mortal mind. But those who are pure and advanced enough in order to raise their consciousness into the Spiritual Realm, or, as the Eastern Initiates say, into the FOURTH state, or Samadhi, have the actual and unmistakable EXPERIENCE of God. It is not *seeing* Him, because seeing necessarily implies being APART from Him, which is, as you already know an absolute fallacy.

I came across another expression, used by some Saints, who were able to become conscious of the Almighty. They speak about 'living' in the Lord. I find this term a very deep and inspiring one.

The purest clichés, on the highest planes, closest to the *Absolute Being* are probably inaccessible, until 'The dewdrop slips into the Shining Sea!', losing its identity in the OCEAN OF GOD, as the Sage Maharshi said. There are people who feel the truth of this statement, if not through their mind, then through their *heart*. They are fortunate, for they have an ineffable, final consolation and hope while still alive in their physical bodies.

This great sentence has the property to still the wandering mind, and allow us to approach even closer to its realization.

Before you finish with the development, try to weld together the theme and Sir Edwin Anold's words, so as to achieve the experience, which cannot be expressed in any words.

2. THEME : *Be still and know that* I AM THE LORD.

Development: This is another great saying from the Bible, dynamic 'par excellence'. Meditation about it leads to realization of the decisive importance of stilling one's mind, before any spiritual experience can be achieved. You already know, from your study of *concentration*, that the mind must be silenced by the will-power of a man himself, and at the time desired. Here we see an even more important use of the domination of the mind : ONLY IN ITS STILLNESS CAN WE HAVE COGNITION OF THE LORD'S EXISTENCE. Under 'existence' I naturally mean the EXPERIENCE, but not any guesswork or theories, which are valueless. Unfortunately, innumerable works, pretending to be 'spiritual' and 'inspired' are unable to do anything better than just verbalize and theorize, when only a living experience will do! Most certainly you have encountered them several times in your life. Now, do not be deceived, and courageously separate the wheat from the chaff.

The Lord is not outside, and we should eradicate such a conception, which may be deeply rooted in us, from our previous incarnations, when we were less developed and unable to obtain a clearer and closer vision of Truth. He pentrates you wholly, but the full meaning of this fact arises in us when we BECOME CONSCIOUS of it! And one of the aims of the School of Life is to *teach us this becoming.*

The utterances of those, who attained this great Achievement may serve us as a bright beacon. In certain chapters of *The Imitation of Christ* you will find recorded experiences of this kind.

The KNOWLEDGE about which our theme speaks is the highest of all possible knowledge. We will do better to call it WISDOM, not knowledge, for in the latter term the idea of the KNOWER and the OBJECT of knowledge is included.

But the Lord can never be an *object*, for He is—the ALLNESS itself. Again, the hopeful condition of *stillness* tells us that through it we may successfully approach Him.

3. THEME: *Having penetrated the whole Universe by a part of Me, I persist.*
(Vedanta)

Development: This theme, taken from the Vedantic Tradition, equals in greatness the other two at the beginning of this chapter. We see the effort of the finite human mind to express the Truth, otherwise inexpressible in any words, in such a manner that they may kindle in the consciousness of the student the fire of the true intuition, leading to the realization of the theme. Here the Lord confirms two axioms:

(a) That He is present in every particle of the manifested Cosmos. This idea is not new for us, as full emphasis has been placed on this truth in almost all religions of the world. But it was important for our Eastern brethren, because of the many cults of much minor range and fineness, which prevailed in their lower classes, for whom the lofty idea of the ONE WITHOUT A SECOND was too abstract and hardly conceivable. Anyway, when Christianity entered India, its teaching about ONE God, even in the form of three Persons, was not something revolutionary in that country full of temples with their thousands of figures of different gods in the vast, national Hindu Pantheon. The more educated and enlightened circles, acquainted with the philosophy of Vedanta were well prepared to confirm this doctrine as being familiar to them.

The sole Central Spiritual Consciousness of the COSMIC SELF is to them only another term for the UNIQUE LORD.

The writer himself was especially charmed by the beautiful hymn 'To the Glory of the Lord of the Universe' sung after evening meditation at the feet of the Master Maharshi, by a selected choir of Brahmin devotees of the Great Rishi.

When realizing this part of the theme, you have to try to feel the Great Truth of *Him* in yourself, as a living experience. IT IS POSSIBLE, for even at this time there are men who are doing it, and all of us are children of the same Father, Who is only glad

when they approach closer to HIM, of their own will and understanding. May these words be your encouragement and inspiration. He is in you now, at this moment, He is listening to your
soul's silent voice, and He KNOWS that one glorious day you will
join His eternal JOY of UNION in the TRUTH OF THE SPIRIT.

His welcome was the hope and inspiration of so many ripe souls
long before you came into this world to learn.

(b) This second part of our theme teaches us that the Lord
exists not only in and through His Creation, but that He has
independent being, beyond all Manifestation, as He was before
Creation started in Time and Space. We may be unable to conceive this, as well as the initiatory and mysterious words of St
John, when he reveals that: *There will be no time any
more.*

It would be good to remember the beautiful and meaningful
Vedantic conception of Manvantaras and Days and Nights of
Brahma when meditating now. The idea in them is that the
Supreme creates the CYCLES OF LIFE, that is, at certain periods
IT exhales the Manifestation, and then annihilates it, as in the
process of the cosmic inhale. The periods between being called
'Pralaya', or universal Rest.

For as long as we cannot transcend our relative thinking, the
periods of non-existence of the universe may well be inconceivable to us, but it is not required for our meditation. We have to
face this truth and let the inner voice of intuition do the rest.

Lord Buddha also taught, that there will be the final end of
conditioned existence in Nirvana, when all the illusions of
separate existence in forms will be extinguished forever.

It is HE in Whom we find the eternal Peace after having passed
through the aeons of wandering in matter of all kinds.

* * *

We will now continue our meditations according to the following themes, selected from appropriate texts, related to the
purpose of this chapter, that is, on GOD. In all further meditations, the student is strongly advised not to forget the previous
ones, which furnish conceptions on the same subject. In this way
every succeeding meditation will be deeper and more knowledgeable than the former, and he will progress in quite a perceptible
way on such a path.

It is astonishing how the most advanced spirits among the human race have been concerned with the idea of the Supreme Power throughout the innumerable ages, and the same is valid for our own epoch. Many students of this work will find this chapter more enlightening than the others just because of the importance of its themes.

4. THEME : *That one point where all religions meet is the realization in no mystical sense, but in the most worldly and everyday sense, that* GOD IS EVERYTHING, AND EVERYTHING IS GOD.
(The Maharshi)

Development: Apart from the nominal value of a statement, we have to accept that this value may also be positively influenced by the person, who issued it. Words of a recognized authority in a certain matter have quite a different weight to utterances of a so far unknown person. This is only natural. The Maharshi, the modern and last Indian Rishi, who represented the best and highest tradition of the ancient Vedantic Sages, was at the same time a contemporary man, who neither shunned, nor was ignorant of the conditions of life in our own epoch, this dazzling twentieth century.

He represented a happy union of the spiritual peak of development and sanctity, with a powerful and lucid intellect, able to realize every side of human life, and consequently to offer a realistic and realizable teaching to modern men (see *In Days of Great Peace*).[1]

That is why the statement of such a man has quite a different value to the mental theories, guesswork and verbalizations of the representatives of formalistic philosophy, who never lived what they try to propagate. Such people hide their lack of spiritual experience behind cleverly selected sentences of exquisite outer form. Involuntarily the simile of Jesus about 'painted coffins' comes to mind.

But when a man gives support to every word he utters by a crystal-clear life, free from sin, erring and egoism, and full of holiness and wisdom, we have to give different consideration to his teachings.

Theme 4 seems to be hard material for meditation, for its

[1]London, 1957, Allen & Unwin.

statements are rather unusual. Therefore, let us analyse them in the spirit in which they were uttered.

The Sage was by no means guilty of the error, committed by the pantheists, since he did not deify any force, or manifestation of Nature, and did not ascribe any higher meaning and value to them other than in their own limited realm of matter. And still we find that: '*God is everything and everything is God*'.

In theme 3 of this chapter we said enough about the omnipresence and omniscience of the Supreme Being in order to be able to understand what the statement of the Sage really means. As we all exist in the *Ocean of God*, so He is in us and everywhere, in every thing, for nothing can be apart from Him. That is why, in our theme, the meaning is not that literally 'every thing' (like a stone, a plant, or any other material object) IS God, which would be absurd, but that He is in every thing just as Space penetrates the whole universe.

But for our purpose, we are seeking another solution, which affects us in our deepest consciousness. Men usually feel themselves to be 'apart' from the Lord, and in his statement, the Maharshi fought against just this fallacy, which makes it impossible for them to approach the Supreme in their meditations as well as in everyday life.

Furthermore, in teaching us to realize the existence of God as an utterly real truth, just as we consider our personal life and its environment to be, the Maharshi destroyed the myth of the 'distant' ruler of the universe, the idea which could (and did) lead men to the childish and wrong conception, that they can hide something from the Almighty.

We are seldom able to deepen and investigate the highest aspects of religious teachings (I am speaking here of those few great religions, founded by the true Spiritual Giants), and even then we may lack the ability to rightly understand them. That is why only a few know about the ultimate aims of those religions. The Maharshi reminds us about this fact.

Finally, the true meaning of the theme will come, when we try to contemplate it in the spirit of the idea it embraces, then face it, and let it *penetrate our awareness and the life in us*. In this way we return to the theme, armed with the explanations and ideas of the development, and then we have a chance to really understand it.

The realization, which comes from successful meditation as mentioned previously, allows us to live our days in HIM, Who then becomes the only reality worthy of the name, and this achievement follows us during all our subsequent wanderings through other states of consciousness, as well as through the different worlds between incarnations.

5. THEME : *God is infinite, and therefore existence and non-existence are merely His counterparts. Not that I wish to say that God is made up of* DEFINITE *component parts. It is hard to be comprehensive when talking of God. True knowledge comes from within and not from without. And true knowledge is not 'Knowing' but 'seeing'.*

(From the Maharshi's Teachings)

Development: It would be only logical, if I say that the more a man is closer to God, the more and better he may be able to speak about Him. If the man, like the Maharshi—who dedicated his whole life to seeking and to finding the Supreme—, agrees to tell us something about IT, then this must be closer and clearer than what the average person, lacking the experience of the Indian Sage, could ever imagine. And still human language is unable to express what the Maharshi called the 'Infinite', for even our mind stops in awe before the realistic conception of *infinity*.

Nevertheless, we can take the best we can from this theme.

We learn, that our definition of both of the terms, 'existence' and 'non-existence', so often used in our 'formal' philosophy, are void and useless when applied to the Supreme, Which is absolutely beyond them. Under the term 'counterparts' we can realize certain aspects of His manifestation, capable of being reflected in our minds.

But they are NOT 'parts' or 'components' of God, and the Sage warns us about such a misunderstanding, stressing that speaking of God is hard and therefore must be inadequate.

The only approach to Him is from the INSIDE of a man, never from the OUTSIDE. This can be better understood after we have had some experience of the INNER LIFE IN US, from our former work on meditation, in the previous chapters.

Only the standards of this inner life—*silent* from the point of view of our restless mind—can be applied to the search for Him, as was done by all the Saints, true Yogis and advanced White Occultists, during their lifelong experiences, and who succeeded in reaching the final PEACE, *beyond all human understanding.*

This meditation shows me the true Path to Him. But nobody can walk this Path instead of me, if I have to reach the Aim.

The Master says finally, that this '*knowledge*' of God, which he himself possessed, is not like any of our 'knowledge', which implies a subject and object in the knowing, but is rather like 'SEEING'. How can we 'SEE' God. Certainly not as an external vision or impression, and the words of Maharshi about the 'knowledge from within', tells us of this.

Perhaps only a simile will give us a picture of this hard concept. Let us return to the 'Drop, slipping into the Shining Sea'. What experience can such a drop have? Most probably, it will be conscious of the infinite Light, penetrating that *Sea*. I can accept, that this may give the best reflection of the idea.

In the next excerpt from his Teachings, the Maharshi will tell us more about this.

6. THEME : *Realization is nothing but seeing God literally. Our greatest mistake is that we think of God as acting symbolically and allegorically, instead of practically and literally.*
(The Maharshi)

Development: Here we have another great injunction, as to how we should realize the Supreme. Seeing God literally is nothing less than a full culmination of the power of Faith in us. Faith has nothing in common with that which men call 'believing', and which belongs to only one of the functions of of our mortal mind. It is powerless, while Faith *can move mountains*. There are few who really know what FAITH is! But it necessarily brings about the 'seeing' of God. Jesus spoke about the possibility of such a 'seeing' (see Theme No. 6, *The Sermon on the Mount*), and it is no wonder, for, as Maharshi said, ALL MASTERS ARE ONE THEY NEVER CONTRADICT ONE ANOTHER.

Being unable to transcend our limited minds and operating only between certain states in our consciousness, we may commit just the mistake, spoken of in the next sentence of this theme:

that of thinking of God as something unreal, symbolical. This is the proof that we do not possess any true Faith. Do you think that the Martyrs and Saints, who were eminent men by any standards or from any point of view, would commit something like the sacrificing of their lives, for a dimmed, imaginary idea or 'belief'? Dig into your own awareness! Would you sacrifice your life for a doubtful, minor purpose? Of course, I am speaking here about men in possession of full sanity and mental balance, for many unbalanced people of inferior mental abilities were and are able to commit suicide in their folly. It is hardly to be doubted that, if men who are mentally and physically sound, sacrifice their lives for an idea, it must be a powerful one, and if this means action motivated by the attraction of the Supreme Power, that Power must be utterly real and not allegorical or problematic. Therefore, the words of the Sage Ramana have been justified again and again, and his own life was the ultimate proof of it. He had no fear of death, for he considered it only as a transition to the higher, real life, by comparison with which the material life in the physical body is only a dream, full of unreality. He was often asked about the way in which he saw this world, where we all live, as if in realistic surroundings. As a rule the Sage mildly declined to answer such questions for he was probably quite aware of the uselessness of telling people something, which they could not experience for themselves and therefore, could not accept as a truth.

But once, pressed on many sides, he interrupted his long silence and gave a brief answer to the question as to how he saw the world and the people around him. '*You are unreal for me, like shadows*', were his words.

If we think deeply about this apparently cryptic remark, we may find the right key to it. Even Krishnamurti in answering a similar query during his visit to South America many years ago said: '*Your "I's"* (that is, egos) *are non-existent even now!*'

Are we, being as we are, without any deeper inner knowledge based on spiritual (not perishable) experience, and fully engrossed in the physical life, as the only accessible reality for us, *really existing*?

As we know from our study of the previous chapters, the short period of a few dozen years spent in our physical bodies, which later disintegrate into dust and nothingness, cannot be said to have a real existence.

A profound conclusion can be drawn from this meditation. If we possess REALIZATION, which means the conscious existing in God, then we are real beings, not subdued by the destruction of death. If not, that is, *if God is not real to us*, then we ourselves are only temporary shadows, waiting for some future confirmation of life.

'Practical' relations with the Supreme imply, of course, full *faith* and the experience of His presence and influence on a man. We had meditation about this in the previous themes.

The Maharshi spoke mostly about the realization of the true Self (or Spirit) in man, but, because he constantly taught that the true SELF is at the same time—God, his Realization meant just the realization of the Supreme in man.

We can see how closely the two are bound together. In knowing our true nature we come, at the same time, closer to the CENTRAL SPIRIT-CONSCIOUSNESS, which is what we call—God.

Undoubtedly, it is a great achievement, to able to feel God 'practically and literally', as the Maharshi advises. And it can be achieved, for others have done it.

Only a real approach to the Lord will give a man that ultimate confidence, peace and happiness, here and beyond his grave, but theories and guessing will not do anything permanent for him. Even physical suffering, if not counteracted by inner, spiritual certainty, may easily break a man's resistance and balance.

If we read the lives of the Saints, we can see for ourselves how sure they were of their faith, and how real for them was the Eternal Presence of the Lord. They knew about it practically.

Although this Presence is immutable and unceasing, millions (actually, the majority) of men do not feel it and do not know anything about it. For them it is as if non-existent. From this we can see, that IT IS THE INNER ATTITUDE OF A MAN WHICH DECIDES EVERYTHING, just as good sight allows him to see an exact picture of his surroundings. A blind person does not know anything about the sun, although this life-giving star exists and exercises its influence on him just as it does on those who see it.

As one of its cardinal aims, meditation has to develop in us the correct 'seeing' attitude towards the realities of the inner, non-perishable and material life.

It is in this spirit that we should study and practise it.

7. THEME: *We must take away the world, which causes, our doubts, which clouds our mind, and the Light of God will shine clearly through. It can be done if, for example, on seeing a man we think: 'this is God animating a body', which body answers, more or less perfectly, to the direction of God, as a ship answers more or less perfectly to her helm.*
(From the Maharshi's Teachings)

Development: The reason why we cannot 'see' God is given in this meditation and is already known to us, it is the world, or, more exactly, our attachment to its perishable values and conditions, which splits the WHITE LIGHT OF THE LORD, just as a prism splits the basic white colour into several different ones. Putting another prism in the way of the spectrum, we are again able to obtain the primordial, unsplit Light, by the process of *synthetic reintegration*. As thoughtlessness, emotionalism, lower physical life and ignorance, joined by attachment to the worldly existence, were there first, disintegrating and obscuring the prism, the second, reintegrating one is composed of the opposite factors. These are *control of the mind and emotions, the wisdom of the true life* and *non-attachment* to that, which must inevitably be lost in time and space. Another mystical but how realistic piece of advice is given in the next statement of the theme. We should not be deceived by living forms, by their outer appearance, which is only illusory, but we must look deeper, into the genuine fulcrum of their true Life. On looking at a man we should not see his perishable personality, enwrapped in the gross material body, as well as in his *astral* and *mental* (feelings and thoughts) counterparts, but ONLY THAT WHICH REALLY ANIMATES him, that Light of the Supreme, without which there is no life at all, merely decaying matter.

In the previous meditations you have already been told that man is basically the INNER LIGHT WITHIN HIM (as St John told us), so this statement agreed to by both an Indian sage and an inspired mouthpiece of Christ, should be beyond any doubt for you now.

You know that there are 'good' and not so good people. How does this happen? The last sentence of our theme gives an unmistakable answer: every body does not obey its INNER LIGHT perfectly, just as every ship does not respond to its helm.

I know that you would immediately like to pose another question. Why is that the case with the body and the ship? The direct, absolute answer, is known only to the ONE, who once started the universe and you along with it. It is useless to enquire into matters which lie far beyond the mind's powers and ability to reflect the Truth.

Nevertheless, there is a means for getting a *personal*, that is, most convincing answer, and it will come from your own depths, which are little known to you.

Ask yourself, WHY DO YOU OFTEN BEHAVE IN A WAY, THAT LATER CAUSES YOU TO REGRET SUCH BEHAVIOUR AND ACTIONS? Enquire with full energy and sincerity and you may obtain the answer even if without words. Others have done so and thus learned their own truth. But Truth is reflected in every living being and so it is also in you. In you lies the SOURCE OF WISDOM and it depends only upon you, whether or not you look into it. And on these alternatives also depends whether or not you possess the Knowledge!

Circumstances, as your mind may suggest, do not belong to the realm of CAUSES, which make you live in such or another way. They are merely like a screen on which your activities and life are reflected, just like the pictures in a cinema. The action belongs to us—men, and so does the responsibility.

If you form the habit of looking on every living being, men foremostly of course, in the way previously described, then a strange, mysterious, but beneficient change beyond all imagination will occur in you, and you will see the world with a much clearer view than ever before. One of the chief gains will be the annihilation of any inner bitterness in you, despite the always possible reverses and 'injustice' from the outer world. There is no doubt that under similar circumstances, either adverse or propitious, two different human beings will behave differently. One will suffer more, another less, and one will be more enchanted by temporary relief than another.

Nobody can live our lives instead of us, and it is we alone who are responsible for our reactions to the circumstances and shocks from the side of the world. They have been earned by us in our distant past and are our Karma, as some like to say. While they cannot be changed, our attitude can be changed from a foolish to a wise one.

8. THEME: *After all, what is God? An eternal Child, playing an eternal game in an eternal Garden. . .*
(Aurobindo Ghose)

Development: One may find this aphorism of the famous philosopher a bit controversial. But only at first glance. Do not ascribe to this Divine Child the qualities of a human infant, that is, undeveloped intellect, lack of experience and weakness. It is not in this meaning that Sri Aurobindo used the term 'Child'.

Let us analyse it more closely. A child is essentially free to play what it wants: so who would limit the Infinite Power, which produces the universe without toil and effort, but just in the illimitable Joy of Creation?

Not all my students will accept this aphorism of the Indian philosopher and occultist, but for those who will, I shall continue to develop its theme.

We do not need any special proof, that the element of JOY exists in every spiritual experience. The ecstasies of Saints, the elation in Samadhi, the bliss in the admiration and communion with Christ, all these are filled with supreme Joy and happiness. But it is only a reflection of something illimitable, eternal in as yet limited and mortal beings. Imagination stops in awe before the conception of how great and powerful the Joy must be in its own SOURCE, that is, in the Lord Himself. The Great Teacher used the expression (directed to the righteous): 'ENTER INTO THE JOY OF THY LORD!'

We should not think, that Saints, true Yogis and other ascetics exchanged their earthly pleasures for something lesser, perhaps even suffering. It would be cruel nonsense and an untruth, closing the Path for all intelligent and inspired sons of man.

Only read their lives and experiences, and you will see where the actual Truth lies. These advanced men were and are happy beyond any earthly measure, and their bliss is not limited to their earthly incarnations alone, for they take it with them into the higher and more real spheres of life.

In this light, the drama of the universe takes the form of an eternal Game and its final cliché is Bliss and Perfection for all its participants. The Garden in which the Great Game takes place, is also eternal; eternal as are the Player and the Game themselves. This meditation has a subtle aroma of spiritual optimism, and many of you will find inspiration and joy in it.

9. THEME: *O Thou being infinite in space,*
Alive in all the movements of matter,
Eternal beyond all time and space,
One, yet three manifestations of Divinity!
O Unique and Omnipresent Spirit!
Transcending every place and cause,
Who could never be cognized,
And Whom we dare to call—God!
To fathom the depths of the oceans,
To count the rays of stars and grains of sand,
Even if some high mind could,
Still for Thee there would be no number or measure.
(Denis Derzshavin)

This long theme needs some special explanation. It is now about 200 years old and taken from the *Ode to God*, written by an eminent Russian poet and philosopher—Denis Derzshavin, who lived in the time of the Empress Catherine II, often called 'The Great'. In translating, it was impossible to render the original beauty of the verse and music of a language, so distant from English. So I limited myself to the most exact and ideologically true translation, which forms the present theme for meditation. In the lives of many eminent people there are moments of highest inspiration, when it seems as if the transcendent TRUTH becomes perceptible to the human mind. Derzshavin's ode was undoubtedly written during just such ecstatic hours in his life. You already know a lot about the Lord, from your former meditations and are aware that He may grant us Grace and send upon us a ray of His Wisdom.

Then the human soul reflects IT and is inspired by IT. This reflection survives us and sometimes it is resurrected from its long oblivion by another soul, posing to itself a similar great inquiry. And a mystical, but true affinity of human spirits then again appears in all its splendour.

Think about this, realize it and memorize the theme. For my part, I shall do my best in the following development of the Ode.

Development: We see that in spiritually inspired moments human conceptions about the Supreme often take a similar outer form. And thus it is with the present theme of meditation. We have already learned to use the simile of the infinity of Space in order to allow and facilitate the basic idea of the omnipresence and *infinity* of God to germinate in our minds. The Maharshi placed his emphasis on this subject (see Chapter XXVI, Theme 5), explaining that this *infinity* makes it hard to find any expression for the *Supreme* in human language. But omnipresence and continuity of Space is somewhat accessible to our mind. From this comes the present simile.

God can be perceived as acting in the movements of matter in His manifested universe. This understanding also allows us to make the next approach to Him: for He is eternal and beyond all time and space, being present in both (compare Theme 3 of this chapter). We already know something about this from our former meditations.

Now come the three mysterious manifestations of the Absolute Divinity, in Its three forms, known to us from the Christian initiation as God the Father, the Son and the Holy Spirit. There is not much to add to this in words, but meditation about the Holy Trinity, after having read Christ's teachings in that regard, may assist you to get a true, spiritual conception.

Derzshavin tells us, that the omnipresent, unique Spirit, which transcends every condition known to men, 'could never be cognized'. It is only natural and logical. A drop cannot reflect the whole immense ocean in itself, since it is a part of that ocean.

Now we arrive at a wise comparison of mind's powers in relation to the Infinite Lord. Derzshavin gives the example of enormous, almost unimaginable powers, which might be possessed (in theory, for him) by the human mind. Powers such as that of counting the innumerable rays of the multitudinous stars (and we now know about billions of them), or similarly inconceivable figures, expressing the number of grains of sand on our planet, and then states that God infinitely transcends all these hard to imagine things: '. . .*there would be no number or measure*' for Him!

The words of the Ode are so simple and straightforward, that there is no need of any further special explanation. Find the true reflection in your own heart.

10. THEME: *The omnipresent Lord is in me, no matter whether or not I am aware of this fact.*

Development: It is inconceivable to a sane mind that there could be something *apart* from God, or beyond His reach. But from an intellectual conception to realization is a long, long way. And that is just the difference between those who do not know, and those who KNOW. This was underlined by the Maharshi. The Great Teacher told us briefly: 'KNOW THE TRUTH AND IT WILL MAKE YOU FREE!' There is not and cannot be any Truth greater than the realization of God. Everything else is only relative, temporal and mortal. Can we rely on such evanescent manifestations of life as we see around us every moment and every day of our physical lives?

There is a way, a blessed one, which allows man to become conscious of the omnipresence of the Supreme, through the realization of His presence in him. It is possible to 'feel' this presence, to be sure of it and of its infinite superiority over every other awareness, which is the best proof of its truth.

The surest path leads through a good, honest and pure life, accompanied by intense meditations, having their foundation in the inner desire to be united with the Source, with the Father, in brief, with the ONE WITHOUT A SECOND.

Here, if you feel so inclined, you may substitute the word 'prayer' for that of 'meditation': for both are synonymous in the spiritual realm. You will notice this in the 'Epilogue' of the present book.

The transformation of true meditation into true, spiritual prayer, comes imperceptibly in a natural, and therefore effective process. As you start to discard words and any other variety of verbalizing in your consciousness, and learn to perceive without the gross participation of your mind, then you find—as the Sage

Maharshi predicted—that everything comes together in one point, which is REALIZATION, or—awareness of God.

Thus spoke the Indian Rishi, who was considered to be a leading representative of the SCHOOL OF WISDOM, or Jnana, in Vedanta terminology. And his Wisdom melted into God.

Towards the end of that last night, during the closing hours of his terrible physical suffering (the Cross, which he accepted for us), and shortly before he left his body, his words were: 'Father, Father!'

11. THEME: *The starry sky is above me, the Eternal Moral Law is in me.*
(Immanuel Kant)

Development: Seldom can we encounter a sentence, so brief outwardly yet so deep and beautiful in its true meaning.

The great philosopher of Königsberg knew of the innumerable universes existing in illimitable space. He was conscious of the enormity of the Creation, but it did not oppress him by comparison with man's apparent smallness, because he was also aware of another greatness, this time within himself, as in every man. He called it the 'Eternal Moral Law', thus avoiding the so often misused and misunderstood term of 'God'.

When on some clear and quiet night, we look into the dark-blue sky, strewn with innumerable stars, which our eyes can still perceive, and when we realize that these luminous points are worlds in themselves, mostly much larger than our little planet, it allows us to approach closer to a right appreciation of our own possibilities of perception and understanding.

We know that practically, the fastest known movement, is that of a light ray in space. For some distant worlds this light needs millions of light-years before it reaches our eyes, so that we may be able to see that little luminous point in the dark sky.

At the same time there is a power in us, far superior in speed to that light ray. With the eye of our thought, of our mind, of imagination, we are able to transfer ourselves to the farthest planet or star in a moment, in an almost incalculable short space of time. In a Vedantic treatise there is a statement to the effect, that 'A Rishi (that is, a perfect Sage) can see, from his all-embracing consciousness, the whole universe as if in a drop of water before his sight'. It is worth giving due consideration to this statement.

Those, who have passed successfully through a course of *concentration* and have attained the stage of enlightenment, allowing them to 'burst' into Space (see *Concentration*, Chapter XX, exercises Nos. 9 and 9A), will have the opportunity of proving it through their own personal experience. And it is not so 'impossible' as many would believe. Therefore, the starry sky is a suitable ground for us to rebound into the Infinite, and thus to enlarge our abilities of perception enormously. That is why that picture brought so much inspiration to Immanuel Kant. It can do the same for us, if we try with clarity of mind and the ability to concentrate it on a lofty subject.

But, the great philosopher did not stop solely at this point. He found something higher, and it was in his own soul. He called it the 'ETERNAL MORAL LAW'. By Law he understood the innate rule reigning in an advanced consciousness, and manifesting in the moral value of a man. It means, that such a man lives according to this law, and not like an emotionally and mentally uncontrolled unit. And this Law is higher than all the material laws, which rule the physical manifestation of the whole immense universe.

This is the Light, which enlightens every man, who comes into this world, but few are aware of it, and for the majority it is as if non-existent. But ignorance does not destroy Reality. Even on the lowest, called the 'physical' plane of existence, we do not know much more than a fragment of these physical laws, according to which our bodies are built and live. And yet, a primitive savage, along with a 'cultured man', will use these laws subconsciously, and this allows them both to live and enjoy living.

But different moral laws direct, say, a philosopher like Kant, and different ones again an uncultured dweller of Central Africa, and so on.

The awareness of the higher law of morality and the prevailing of it in one's life makes the whole difference. This law allows us to control the stormy sea of our emotional and mental life, when others are tossed among the waves, like helmless boats.

Now we come to the final conclusion of this theme of meditation. The INNER LIGHT, equal to Kant's Law, is a reflection of the ONE WITHOUT A SECOND in us, briefly, we call it—GOD. The Lord is not jealous of the names we may give to Him, nor of the theories we may build around conceptions of Him in our minds. He IS PRESENT FOREVER, and it counts for little as to how men would like to call Him. We know that one of the 'attributes' ascribed to the Almighty is His INFINITY, that is, being above all the attributes, which our limited mind can imagine in Him.

It embraces the wholeness of attributes, while being free from all their limitations.

12. THEME: *I yet live, said the Lord, and am ready to help thee, and to give thee greater comfort than ever, if thou put thy trust in Me, and call devoutly upon Me.*
(From *The Imitation of Christ*
by Thomas a Kempis)

Development: Our set of meditations about God would be incomplete without this text from the last book of *The Imitation of Christ*, inspired in all its simplicity. It is as if we hear the Lord speaking and revealing to us what we so badly need in our struggles during our incarnations. In this comparatively short meditation we have at least five points on which to work, while journeying through its text.

Firstly, there is the statement that the Lord LIVES. Is it so for all of us, and does humanity really need this reminder? Clearly, in the overwhelming majority, men forget, or even do not want to know anything about the Supreme Power, in whose hand lies every life and existence. They spend their incarnations, pursuing every ephemeral aim, doing everything except that of coming closer to the Absolute from which they were emanated before time began.

That is why here we have a categorical confirmation of the truth of the existence of Him, Who is above and beyond every existence, as the Indian Sage Ramana Maharshi told us, thus fully concurring with the Christian mysticism of the highest kind.

If the mysterious knowledge of the reality of God penetrates us, we then participate in His Grace, without which there is no spiritual achievement at all, and without which our meditations would never reach the highest, and only effective peaks for merging in Him. I now have to think deeply about this before I join the next cross-road. The final illumination will come in deep Silence.

Secondly, the Lord is ready to help us! What a hopeful and munificent truth is enclosed in those simple words for me. I know that the greater my troubles, the higher the Power which is needed to overcome them. Can I count only on my own poor little personality, which cannot even be sure of what the next hour will bring? I can only guess, and guessing is inconsistent and devoid of happiness. If, according to the Lord's words, I turn to Him, could I find any better, more gracious and omnipotent protector, Whom Christ taught us to call 'OUR FATHER IN HEAVEN'? By meditating on these great words, I am opening the secret door, through which He may come and enlighten the whole of my life, removing my fears and troubles, showing me the unique Aim worth striving for, and sanctifying my consciousness-spirit, which is still here while I am fighting my battles in the fleshy cage of temporal existence in matter.

I will not beg him for assistance in my particular needs, for there is nobody who would know better what I really need, than that Central Light of Being, which is the Lord. In Him there is no shadow nor imperfection and that is what He expects to be awakened in my own soul.

Therefore, let Him decide what, when and in which way His help may descend upon me, not as a temporary consolation, but like the eternal Grace of the *Good Father*. I know that Saints turned themselves to the Lord in just this way. I wish to follow their Wisdom in humility and admiration.

Thirdly, He alone can give the greatest comfort, for the Omniscience does not commit any error, nor is it affected by our human failing of ignorance. That is why He tells me, that He may grant me that supreme comfort, after which there will be no darkness nor suffering in me. The condition? I can see it clearly now: IT IS THE ABSOLUTELY SINCERE AND FAITHFUL TURNING TO HIM, WITH FULL AWARENESS OF HIS INFALLIBILITY AND OMNISCIENCE, WHICH CANNOT BE DECEIVED, NOR DIMMED BY ANY HUMAN INFIRMITY.

This comfort will come not from outside, but from inside myself, for it is in the deepest recesses of the human heart-awareness, where He dwells and from where He speaks. This means that my attitude will be corrected and the same outer and inner troubles will be disarmed and rendered harmless, because of His voice speaking in me. This is the way in which I have to realize and I have to approach Him in this attitude.

Fourthly, all of this will happen only if I put my full and unconditional trust in the Lord. This is only natural after I have meditated through the first three parts of the present theme. Spiritual surrender because of absolute faith in the Highest must have a peculiar power in itself, for I can remember the powerful words of the Maharshi, uttered to those around him, who complained about difficulty connected with domination of their minds and of reaching the inner peace: '*Surrender to me, and I will strike down the mind.*'

In the East a great spiritual leader, as was the Rishi, is considered as an emanation of the Divinity Itself. In any case, such a man stands much closer to the Lord than ordinary, weak and sinful people, and there is no doubt about this for me. Even a logically operating and not utterly perverted mind will confirm this truth.

A human being is unable to obtain or to bear any unveiled vision of the Lord Himself. No imagination would assist in this problem, only direct SPIRITUAL EXPERIENCE. But to obtain such experience a man himself must be far above the average level and it may require many incarnations to reach this state. Therefore, are there no means by which to get close to the Aim, while still in this body and under these conditions? There are, if we are able to see and recognize *one of the great souls* during his earthly incarnation, for he is the REFLECTION of the Infinite Lord, made visible even to our mortal eyes. Surrender to such a Being, and we surrender ourselves to the Lord Himself, Who then graciously accepts our devotion and zeal.

Fifthly, there still remains the last effort on the Path: it is to CALL ACTIVELY TO THE LORD FOR HELP. I feel that this must be accepted literally and not just symbolically, as the Great Rishi Ramana taught us (see Theme 6 of this chapter), that is, one has to call, as one would call for assistance for anyone in need. There are many obstacles for this deciding step: our nonsensical egoism, expressing itself in false pride and self-confidence, wrongly directed and therefore making void any true approach to the

Supreme; next comes our lack of faith, followed by unceasing
DOUBTS as to whether the Lord exists and can be reached by
human prayer, and whether there might be some other means
to pull us out of our troubles. There is no reason to enumerate
all of these fallacies, dictated by our ego-mind, that mortal
phantom, which would like us to die together with it! Let us
not succumb to the voice of the *Darkness*, but follow the LIGHT,
which never errs or misguides.

13. THEME :   *May God be risen and His foes vanish,*
              As wax melts before fire,
              As smoke is dispersed by the wind!
              So may all who hate the Lord, flee from His sight,
              And the just rejoice!

As the concluding theme for meditation on God I am giving
here an ancient and most powerful EXORCISM, dating from the
early Christian era, and used as an effective means of resistance
to evil forces, which attack those who try to dedicate their lives
to the Lord. It is known to contemporary Theurgic circles, and
was mentioned briefly in my *Concentration*.

Here it will be fully explained and appropriated for meditative
purposes.

Development : The first sentence of the *Exorcism* should not be
wrongly understood. God exists forever and beyond any time and
space, so there cannot be any moment when He is absent from
His Creation. This is the basic truth about Him, but there is
another, a relative truth, which concerns us as men. We are
not always, and in every place conscious of His Presence, nor
have we sufficient *Faith* in him. There are periods (unfortunately,
too long) in our lives, when we simply do not think about Him,
and He is as if non-existent for us. These are just the moments
when Evil makes its attacks against us, sending us troubles,
disasters, fear and passions to lead us to spiritual eclipses, and so
on. In such moment we need Him, and then, if we call Him
sincerely and with faith, He as if RISES IN US AND FOR US, FOR
OUR DEFENCE. This is the way in which we should meditate on
this part of our theme.

We can see in this world through our own eyes, that Evil
does exist, that it fights against Good and causes troubles of all

kinds, from personal suffering and crime to enormous conflagrations of multi-million nations, which try to annihilate one another, for materialistic and egoistic purposes. We know there is Light, but that there is also Shadow, of which St John the Evangelist said: 'Darkness is unable to swallow the Light.' God is the Light and Truth, and Evil is darkness and deceit. The personification of Evil was justly called in the Scriptures the 'Father of Lies'.

Finally, we realize that where there is a fight, there must also be animosity. In this part of our meditation we call for the vanishing, for the annihilation of the Lord's enemies. This may seem a bit strange for those who followed our former meditations, who are convinced of the omnipotence of God, and who consider that this attribute should exclude any probability of the existence of His enemies.

Here we are intruding into the WORLD OF CAUSES, which is absolutely beyond the ability of understanding of our mortal mind. As has already been mentioned in one of the former chapters, we cannot penetrate into the ABSOLUTE, UNCONDITIONED CONSCIOUSNESS OF THE SUPREME, just as say, a red corpuscle in our bloodstream cannot ever cognize WHY AND WHAT THE MAN IS THINKING, in whose body this corpuscle lives and moves. There is a *blank wall* for human mental cognition, and this wall efficiently prevents our penetration into the realm, which does not belong to the mind. Otherwise, it does not mean that we will remain eternally in ignorance! For what is inaccessible to a human being's mind, is clear to his Spirit, once he becomes able to raise his consciousness to the height of the UNIQUE SPIRIT. In this lofty state there are no queries, problems, binaries to be solved, and similar attributes of the mind. The higher consciousness, no matter whether we will call it 'Spiritual Ecstasy' or 'Samadhi' (as our Eastern brothers do) is beyond all problems and questions, for in it there are no Shadows, but only the LIGHT. You will find the most beautiful atempts to convey the inaccessible in the Revelation of St John, describing the love and kindness of the Lord towards His children—men.

But here, on earth, we are in the realm of facts, and in conforming with them, we ask about the removal of Evil, or the Lord's enemies from our sight. Now we can pass on to the next line of the theme.

This defeat of the Enemies may be like the disappearance of hard wax when confronted by fire, inexorably ending any shape it may have had. Think deeply about this symbol, and you will see the way in which Evil should be defeated by Good. The second simile concerning defeat presents us with a picture of smoke disappearing, when dispersed by the movements of the air which we call wind. In both cases the way of annihilation is similar and yet unique in their hidden reality. Nothing more can be said about this, but try to think deeply about both of these ways of defeating Evil and you may arrive at the right conclusion, although inexpressible in words.

The next line speaks of those 'who hate the Lord'. It is a sad and revolting truth, but still a truth, which cannot be denied. It would be playing right into the hands of those 'haters of the Lord', if we succumb to the treacherous efforts of the Enemy to confuse as many men as possible and in an unwise way to refuse to recognize the real state of things. I know of a case, where an old man, a 'minister' of an obscure sect, who, while trying to pass it off as a 'Christian' one, boldly attempts to convince young people of the 'non-existence and historical nonsense of Christ's person'.

This has been observed in the place where I am writing these lines and every Sunday, this 'minister' dons a kind of chasuble with Christ's Cross embroidered on it.

This may suffice to give an example of how Evil can find its treacherous ways in, even under the cover of the sign of Light. This exorcism calls for such enemies to fly from the SIGHT OF THE LORD, just as darkness must fly before the Light.

We know of large nations, dominated by the 'haters of the Lord', who try in every way possible to eradicate all ideas about God from their hapless and tyrannically ruled subjects. But we also know, that the Great Teacher foresaw everything and advised us to persist in Truth and Light, saying that: 'Those who will endure to the end will be saved'.

The end of the theme tells us that the 'JUST WILL REJOICE'. It is the final triumph of Good over Evil. Those of us who, during our lives, have actually had to fight the evil in ourselves, know about the bliss of that spiritual victory, when impurity has been substituted by purity, and darkness by Light. Would this bliss be possible if there were no fighting and everything just came 'of itself', without our participation? If such were the case it would only be a degrading of our being to the role of a dead automaton, and the gift of LIFE was not given to us for such a fate.

CHAPTER XXVII

Meditation *on* The Imitation of Christ *by* *Thomas a Kempis* – Series IV

In this chapter I will give you some fragments from a very old spiritual book, which is extremely suitable for deepest meditation, being written by one who really lived all that he said in his immortal work. The aim of my book is to furnish you with certain knowledge and the techniques of the art of meditation, which can be practised during your everyday life, without requiring any monastic vows, or surroundings. Likewise, I am not trying to 'convert' you to any of the existing religious currents, for the choice belongs exclusively to the student himself, and must be made in a natural and free way. I am also giving material to which you may apply your acquired theoretical knowledge of the first two parts of this book.

The size of a publishable book does not allow too much material for meditation to be given, but such is not necessary. The value of a practical study of meditation is *not in the number, or variety of themes* the student is supposed to work with, but in the QUALITY of his work, that is, in the degree of elevation which he is able to attain in his consciousness, during that mental work.

Here you will find about two hundred exercises and themes for meditation, but do not believe that you MUST attain perfection in ALL OF THEM, especially if some disagree with your heart and convictions. The writer has worked with meditation throughout his life and consequently knows from experience what is possible (hence recommendable) and what is not (therefore unsuitable). Everything depends upon your inner line and your tuning to certain spiritual currents, all of which are represented in this book. Take what you feel '*belongs to you*' (I mean Parts III to V) and do your best. But Parts I to II MUST be studied attentively : for *from this depends the success with the next parts.* Nobody can read or write unless he knows the alphabet of the language concerned, and in this case it is just the PREPARATORY CHAPTERS I to XIX which are the alphabet of meditation. My advice remains as always—before starting the actual work (exercises and meditation) you should read the *whole manual* at least SEVEN times. Only then will the mind be well acquainted with the matter and you will have no technical obstacles, or memorizing difficulties from its side. As my other manual— *Concentration* was published several years ago, I quite naturally receive a lot of letters from students of it. *Those who followed my advice*—to read the text several times first—have put reasonable questions to me, stemming from their current experiences with exercises and certain phenomena, which can appear for a certain type of person. But there are also many letters containing inquiries and problems, *which have been fully explained in the text of the book,* as I always try to see my work *from the point of view of the student,* who may have the same questions as myself, when I too started on the same path, many years ago. So I am not writing '*from my own point of view*', which quite easily could still be unacceptable for inexperienced beginners. And I think I am right in this.

In the case of the *second type* of inquirer, it is evident that they simply 'touched' lightly on the book, without memorizing any basic material in it. And since it is utterly impracticable to retype whole chapters of a book in a letter for such people, I am often compelled to draw their attention to the text, which deals with their queries at full length. This simply results in consider- able loss of precious time for both my reader-students and myself, which could easily be avoided.

The success of any deep psychological and practical study like concentration, meditation, contemplation and development of the higher consciousness in a man, depends upon the reasonable and rather scientific attitude of the student, exactly as he or she had during their 'official' learning in schools and universities. If they missed some part of their study, they jeopardised their examination results and created a certain amount of disappoint- their missed knowledge, otherwise they could be refused their bread-winning diplomas. With our kind of study, this bread- winning element is absent, but otherwise, everything remains the same: negligence must bring disappointment and lack of success. Only in cheap and worthless booklets can one find assurances that someone 'can do all the work for us' and that the reading of such a book can bring the most 'marvellous results'. No intelligent person would ever accept such nonsense.

1. THEME: *The more thou knowest, and the better thou understandest, the more strictly shalt thou be judged, unless thy life be also the more holy.*

Development: Here we have a great spiritual Law expressed in full. Even human justice has some consideration for the measure of responsibility for an offence that has been committed, if the culprit is not in the best position to understand what evil he was doing. Although Thomas a Kempis was probably not instructed in Hermetic philosophy, which teaches that: *'as above so below, and as below so above'*, his words tell us the same. Here human justice clearly, although unconsciously, follows the Hermetic doctrine. Knowledge places certain obligations on the man possessing it. In our own conscience, which is a reflection of the Lord's Law in us, we will find full support for the statement, that those who are more enlightened bear more responsibility, and what could be forgiven in an ignorant person, will not be forgiven in a learned one.

Then what sort of solution exists for this problem? Should we then avoid knowledge? Not at all, but we are obilged to shape our lives, our deeds, feelings and thoughts according to the higher standard of our intelligence.

The inspired author of *The Imitation* tells us that, the judgement will be more severe for a learned man, unless he tunes his incarnation according to what he knows.

If we really strive for the perennial and are not blinded by the perishable visible world, the lesson for us will be that our actions have to parallel our mental development. In brief, MORALITY MUST EQUAL KNOWLEDGE. This is an axiom.

What happens if this is not the case? The present fate of the world is the best answer. Knowledge is racing ahead with enormous speed, never before encountered in human history. But is this planet happier because of it? In no other epoch has there been such animosity between nations and ideas, such suffering, so enormous in extent, such blind egoism to poison everything, from individual, family and social life to that of whole nations.

We know too much, but morally, we have advanced too little. That is why the most wonderful discoveries of this epoch are turned to the dangers of destruction, instead of constructive work. This refers, naturally, not only to one nation or political group of states, but to all, although some are evidently much more aggressive and eager to improve their material status by armed robbery.

But large conglomerations of human beings are only a reflection and result of the value of the individuals, which form whole nations. And therefore, the problem of the world can be solved ONLY BY THE INDIVIDUAL SOLUTION OF EACH MAN. Multiplying a match we will obtain only matches, no matter how many millions of them there are. In multiplying ignorant and egoistic man by millions, what can we get as the end result? It seems that men are not conscious of this absolute and unassailable truth. In this fact lies the tragedy of mankind on this planet.

When forming a society, unhappy individuals will only create a similarly unhappy social unit, for there is no 'salvation' in numbers alone.

From this meditation we may establish a new, more realistic outlook, instead of general confusion. The next texts from *The Imitation* will bring us more light.

2. THEME: *If I understood all things in the world, and had no charity, what would it avail me in the sight of God, Who will judge me according to my deeds?*

Development: This meditation is as if a continuation and development of the former one. The factor of *charity* (or love) is shown as the deciding one in the life of the individual. It is this quality, which makes the greatest knowledge harmless and useful. Charity cannot destroy, it can only build! And our deeds are the direct reflection of our inner, *moral* world. I say—MORAL, not intellectual. The mind can justify almost anything if it suits it and the '*dialectical philosophy*' still ruling a large part of this planet is only another proof of this. It is NOT THE MIND which will be the saviour, and it is not the mind which will inspire the creation of a better society and conditions among us. Yet that mind-intellect may be an invaluable tool, or instrument for the plans born in the HEART. For it is in the HEART, where WISDOM dwells, it being our only aim, which when achieved, all becomes achieved.

3. THEME: *Surely great words do not make a man holy and just; but a virtuous life maketh him dear to God.*

Development: Although these words were written several centuries ago, their deep meaning is perhaps still more alive than ever in our own period. We can read and hear of innumerable apparently wise and good words, but we can also see rather disgusting deeds around us. Brutal killings and wars accompany high-worded declarations and ideas.

Which would be more important for a sane man, if, for example, a primitive native in a desert saves his life, endangered by thirst, by offering him water or leading him to a well without any refined speech and gesture, or if a scholarly looking, heartless egoist passes beside him and pronounces a 'wise sentence' about the justice contained in all tragedy and suffering, as repayment for his former 'errors' and so lets him perish?

We should be careful not to fall into the trap of the Enemy, who often assumes the mask of false wisdom. Also, it is the product of egoistic (as it always is) mind, not ennobled by the light and warmth of the Heart.

We already know the true meaning of this term in our philosophy, so there is no need to repeat it again.

What we really need is to sit quietly and meditate again and again upon this worthy theme, as given to us by the great ascetic and wise man, whose heart burned within him.

He says that the Supreme Justice, which is the Lord Himself will make the right choice. You know WHAT that will be. What ALONE matters is that WE WILL BE INCLUDED IN THAT CHOICE.

And this will not happen to us 'of itself' and without any action by us. As you know, in the normal spiritual development of man, meditation precedes the action, and that is why we are learning to meditate. Of course, there are also 'spontaneous and inspired actions', but they are unpredictable and we cannot wait until intuition comes and in the meantime remain spiritually and physcally idle. It is true, that Great Souls act exclusively through intuition, that is, wisdom without thinking. But we are not yet as they are, so their rules are premature for us, although we too will most certainly have the blessed moment of true intuition, when we become riper.

4. THEME: *If thou knowest the whole Bible by heart, and the sayings of all the philosophers, what would it profit thee without the love of God and without Grace?*

Development: The first part of this theme has already been explained, as it is similar to the spirit in which the former themes (Nos. 1 to 3) were written. But another lesson is given here: the problem of the love of God and His Grace. The way in which one comes to that love is a deep mystery. Therefore, it is extremely hard to discuss, for all talk will only be from an individual point of view, which has infinite variations underlying it for every other human being. The best that can be advised here would be to place special attention on meditations, in which God is approached and an attempt made to realize His attributes. Find this in one of the previous chapters.

But the Grace, although equally an interior experience, has been more explored by those, who were and are fortunate enough to participate in it. The basic material can be found in the chapters treating of meditations about the Presence of the Lord (see Chapters XXIV and XXVI). It seems that our experiences of the PRESENCE and GRACE of God are very similar. In any case, it is hard to draw a dividing line between them. And it is unnecessary if we realize that all these attempts to 'classify' what is beyond any classification, is only another trick of our mind, which cannot participate either in the awareness of the Lord's presence, or in His Grace. You know, of course, that in both blessed states there is not and cannot be any thoughts, because they spoil the concentration of our spirit with their vibrations.

However, one thing is certain: in the State of Grace you LOVE GOD BEYOND EVERYTHING. If it is otherwise, you are not enjoying His Grace.

The doctrine of the Saints fully emphasizes the deciding importance of Grace in a man's life. And Theurgy teaches us similarly, that all its operations, prayers and exorcisms (see my *Theurgy, the Art of Effective Worship*, published by George Allen & Unwin Ltd. of London) have one and the same purpose: to implore and secure Grace for the operator, or those for whom he acts. This Grace may take the form of healing, consolation, or spiritual enlightenment and bliss.

5. THEME: *It is vanity to follow the desires of the flesh, and to labour for that for which thou must afterwards suffer grievous punishment.*

Development: A man who dedicates his incarnation (or even part of it) to the pursuit of physical pleasures does not care about his more permanent bodies, like that of emotions (astral) and thoughts (mental). In this way he acquires a lot of negative karma, involves himself in dangerous and costly karmic ties and does not advance spiritually, for he simply has neither the time, nor the desire to place any attention on the things to come after his body is inevitably struck down by death. Therefore, he contracts new debts and must pay them, while, at the same time, he is not prepared for the interincarnation life, and enters into the unknown and hostile worlds alone and in fear.

The astro-mental realm is hostile to him because, in his physical life, he created many negative (evil) clichés, which are visible to the dwellers of those subtler worlds. These clichés attract a similar kind of astral being, and because, in that world, feelings and thoughts are both visible, these dwellers and their emanations so often look horrible and repulsive. And so the sensual and nonsensical man is a victim of these 'devils', who frighten him and make him suffer, although, of course, there cannot be any more physical pain. That is where lie the roots of certain religious and other tales about the horrors of hell and purgatory after death.

There is a strange recollection in man, which comes from his former incarnations and reflecting his suffering between his physical lives. It is one of the causes of that subconscious fear of death. At the same time, it is the reason for the fearlessness of the Saints, true yogis and other spiritually advanced people, who do not take dangerous clichés with them after death, but only positive ones, composed of their good and noble feelings and thoughts and the strength developed during the subduing of all lower passions. Therefore, no monstrous or evil being in the astral world has any power over, or even access to them.

That is how the 'punishment' looks of which Thomas a Kempis speaks. Man himself creates his 'hell' and his 'paradise'. Now we can see the meaning and purpose of the physical life, which is the LIFE OF CAUSES, CREATED IN ITS TIME AND DECISIVELY AFFECTING THE FURTHER WANDERINGS OF MAN. The life after death is therefore, rather an *existence of results*, during which little can be changed in our destiny, so well earned on the earth.

Hence, the evident pessimism of the author of *The Imitation* is justified up to a point. We know very well that the overwhelming majority of people in this epoch do not care much about life after physical death, and many do not even believe in such a thing at all. So they behave accordingly, and consequently earn their 'punishment', which is not imposed by a cruel God, but by themselves, just as a stone thrown upwards will fall back to hit the unwise thrower.

For those acquainted with occult philosophy, the problem is even more obvious, for they know that no energy put into action ever perishes, and that every force is confronted by an equal but diametrically opposite one.

It is strange to see, how often intelligent people, even scientists, who, while fully recognizing the unchangeable and fixed laws of Nature (that is, of the physical world), cannot logically extend this knowledge and so realize that, in a similar way, moral and mental forces may have their immutable laws and rules.

They think that emotions and thoughts are not subject to any laws and foremostly to that of CAUSE AND EFFECT, so inexorable in earthly life.

This is one of the cardinal mistakes which humanity is liable to commit in this period of its development and consequently, to pay a dear price for it.

*　　*　　*

I recommend that every earnest student of this work divides this 'development' into certain parts, thus making the meditation easier and more exact, because these comments are too long to be worked with at once. Even memory may suffer some lapses if overburdened by an excess of material.

This meditation will be useful for further work on the following themes taken from *The Imitation*.

6. THEME : *It is vanity to desire to live long, and not to care to live well.*

Development: The problem put to us here is: WHAT IS OUR LIFE AND WHAT IS ITS PURPOSE? Is it only a certain sum of food eaten, drinks taken, pleasures, ambitions, suffering and reverses? All great Souls recognized that life has much higher values, and the realization of them is its sole purpose. During our lives we can experience many different things, but they will all fall into one of the categories just mentioned. To live for physical and mental, or sensual pleasures is like building a home on quicksand, or to cross a stream on the back of a crocodile, believing it to be a tree trunk, as the Sage Sankaracharya so wisely says. Such a life is futureless and ends in the nightmare of physical death, with all its suffering and frustration.

To desire to live long for such flimsy purposes is madness. Living well means to realize the evolutionary purpose of life and to understand that every day and year of it are valuable and irrevocable lessons, which we have to learn. How do we learn? It will either be willingly and intelligently, or stupidly and hesitantly, depending upon our ripeness and intelligence, as well as of our spiritual advancement. To die with the satisfaction of duty well performed during the incarnation, with the certainty that the Lord will call us 'His good servants' and not reject us as useless chaff, means to conclude a valuable existence and to rightly expect a suitable reward of peace and happiness.

Thomas a Kempis, a good knower of the human psyche, speaks from his own experience. He was a prior in a monastery and had to deal with many erring, as well as many happy souls and thus acquired his knowledge and authority. That is why his writings are still alive for men of the twentieth century and many of us are spiritually instructed by them.

Now meditate about the theme itself, as it is so simple and clear for every intelligent son of man.

Refer to that INNER LIGHT in you, and you will see the approach of inspiration and peace.

Then you will lose the desire to live long for minor and futile purposes, simply ceasing to think about this at all.

7. THEME: *It is vanity to mind only this present life, and* NOT TO MAKE PROVISION *for those things which are to come later.*

Development: From the former meditation the meaning of the present physical life has been firmly established, in the spirit of the author of *The Imitation*. This life should be considered as an inevitable preparation for another, more real and important existence.

Although there still are souls undeveloped enough to deny every idea of a future life after death, we do not have to follow these retarded individuals, but rather those who give proof of higher qualities in themselves. More developed men invariably have intuitional certainty of their immortality and they live their physical life only as an intermediary stage for something more important and sublime. They also see clearly the imperfections of the material existence alone, with its worries, suffering and frustration, which by far outweigh the pleasures and momentary short happiness.

Christ's parable of the twelve wise and the twelve foolish virgins is the best illustration of this.

When we are not prepared for a sudden change in our circumstances, it comes as a bitter blow for us. When we do not make provision for our existence, once the physical body is taken away from us, we are as if stranded in a desert. Someone rightly said that: 'the best preparation for death is a well-spent life'.

Now we may see what kind of 'provision' for the future existence is required of us. Even if, on this imperfect plane of the physical life, humanity still tries to establish its primitive rules of justice, we cannot believe that, on a higher level, in less materialistic conditions, when we live without the body and only through our emotions and thoughts, there should be no justice and inviolable laws.

We may meditate about it and then some more inner light may be our reward. Without any effort to deepen our understanding of the perennial problems of our life, there cannot be any solution for the future for us. As we sow, so we reap! Let this meditation conclude our present lesson.

8. THEME : *It is vanity to love that which speedily passeth away, and not to hasten thither where everlasting joy awaiteth thee.*

Development: In the light of the foregoing meditation, this verse becomes an additional explanation and inspiration for us.

Nobody can deny, that everything in this world passes away and is lost in the eternity behind us. With every day, every human being becomes older and approaches closer to his grave, no matter how young, strong and attractive he may seem to be now. It is all as in a theatre, where once the entertainment is finished we leave the hall, from which we were viewing the drama of our life.

Where are the famous beauties, the glamorous actresses and admired actors, the powerful leaders, the prominent philosophers from just the last century? Their days have passed away, and only their memory still lives in some minds of the present generations. But this cannot revive them, for there is no return from the grave.

Thomas a Kempis says that everlasting joy awaits us after our earthly pilgrimage is over, but it is valid only for those, who knew the purpose of their travels and saw their aim.

Attachment to the vanishing and impermanent is vanity, and its cost is really high for the foolish men, who dedicated their lives to the pursuit of that, which must and will be lost.

The temporary enchantment of life has undoubtedly its intoxicating influence on the majority of people, but it is possible only because of their limited minds and instability, as well as shortsightedness about the future. We know that unchangeable happiness and permanent satisfaction in life do not exist at all among us here, on the earth. We may have some periods when we imagine we are happy, but all too soon there come the next scenes from the film of our ever-developing lives and other, more dramatic pictures come to the fore.

Even the most vigorous health must be destroyed and the sturdiest body must find its final rest in the dust of the grave.

Those who look forward to a different form of life will never be desperate at the losing of their earthly counterpart, for they know that there is no annihilation of life, and a well-spent one is the best assurance for the future.

9. THEME: *It is also a vanity to strive after honours, and to climb to a high degree.*

Development: Actually, who grants honours based on the real virtues in man? And are these virtues any true reason for the granting of worldly distinctions? We know that generally it is not so.

Real virtue, that is, spiritual advancement does not find any ready recognition among ordinary men, who are not engaged in a similar search and who are interested solely in the material side of things. This is because adequate experience is necessary for it and such is not present in the worldly masses. So, we should not strive after things which are inconsistent and therefore not worth having. That is why Thomas a Kempis so rightly called these strivings nothing better than *vanity*.

While meditating about this development, with due attention and clear insight, we will realize why all spiritually minded men on this earth were never interested in, but rather despised all worldly honours and other signs of recognition. What value may something have, which is granted by the ignorant and what loss would a truly wise man incur, when he is deprived of such a doubtful kind of 'satisfaction'.

Having all of that in our mind during our lifetime, we will be able to greatly reduce our worldly disappointments and frustration, which so bitterly affect those who are ignorant.

What kind of 'degrees' are worth striving for? Are they too those granted by the ignorant, or are they just worldly positions of power and popularity? If the world were guided by true moral and spiritual standards, it might be so, but, unfortunately, we know with full certainty that things are just the opposite.

It is sufficient to look attentively at the worldly affairs around us. Involuntarily the old truth that, 'THE WHOLE IS UTTERLY DEPENDENT UPON ITS COMPONENTS' comes to mind. A society of spiritually minded and saintly human beings would most certainly create better and brighter conditions for living and a better ruled population. But a society of egoists, as we are, in the overwhelming majority, produces just the results we can see: the dangers around us, the uncertainty of existence, maliciousness, moral lowness and treachery, which range from individual to national levels.

10. THEME: *It is therefore vanity to seek after perishing riches, and to trust in them.*

Development: This is another extension of the former meditation, this time directed to the vanity of material gain. Actually, there is nothing wrong in having some necessary accessories in our physical life, but humanity goes too far with them, forgetting real values and setting them on the throne, which belongs to inner, deeper and imperishable values in and of man. And this is the true cause of all afflictions, affecting individuals as well as whole nations. This should be avoided by a truly intelligent and spiritually minded man, as it is pure vanity.

, We must think about men, who die when they are rich: would they not offer all their wealth in order to delay that inexorable moment, when they have to leave everything they collected and were attached to during their lifetime. Finally, put yourself in a similar position, and you will realize where lies the truth.

'LIVE IN THE WORLD, BUT DO NOT BE OF IT' these words will remain forever as the solution for all those, who really seek and want to find the solution to their lives.

The second part of this meditation is equally enlightening. How can we trust in something, which must be unconditionally lost and never preserved, or be of any help to us against the final frustration brought about by earthly riches? There is no need to imagine, that while being only beggars we can avoid that frustration and the suffering connected with it. It is interesting to note how the Maharshi explained this problem. He did not advocate any compulsory poverty or asceticism, for he knew how wrong those people are, who simplify this question too much. In Christ's famous simile regarding worldly and spiritual duties (Caesar and God) we find further support for the statements of the Sage Ramana, who taught that real asceticism and renunciation must be in our mind, not on the outer side of life. He told us that *attachment* is the main evil, not the fact of possessing more than one garment, and so on. This is beautifully explained in the famous Indian legend about the king and the yogi. The rich king was not affected by losing all his treasures, but the poor 'yogi' was desperate when he lost his only change of clothing, his yellow monk's robe. He was still ruled by attachment.

11. THEME : *They who follow their lusts stain their own conscience, and lose the Grace of God.*

Development : What actually are lusts and passions? Only the desire to experience certain carnal pleasures and emotions.

Can you retain your body forever, or will it always remain ready for the satisfaction of your lusts? And is the time and energy dedicated to passions adding anything to your inner values, and will these not produce deadly frustration and bitterness at the time, when their main instrument—the physical body faces destruction? Addiction to lust only shows the shallowness of a human being, which allows itself to become a prey to its passions.

There are certain forms of emotional life, connected with physical satisfaction, which are embedded in the overwhelming majority of present humanity by Nature itself. Sexual lust is one of the foremost. However, there is certain justification in this case, for here Nature is following its own aims, and the main one is the continuation of the human species. Our race still needs physical incarnations for its further evolution, and human egos are still unable to progress in a purely spiritual realm without passing through the experiences of the material life. So, bodies are needed and the laws of Nature compel men and women to physical union, in order to produce those bodies for their descendants. It is basically and exactly what all animals do, led by a similar instinct, but minus our human elaboration of sexual 'love' with all its complications and often wickedness. Likewise, the same law leads to the formation of families, which acts favourably for the limitation of the primordial reckless egoism of a savage: this is his care for his wife and progeny.

But the setting of lust and passion on an undeserved throne, as we may easily see in this period, leads to loss of the Supreme's Grace, for it is unnatural and degrading, being a deformation of natural functions, which are intended to be evolutionary for average people. Those who are advanced, of course, transcend this lower realm and realize the great Law of Love in a much more dignified and elevated way, widening it from the physical to the universal, spiritual realm. Meditate deeply about this development, until full understanding enlightens your awareness.

12. THEME: *Vanity of vanities, and all is vanity, except to love God, and Him only to serve.*

Development: This final meditation taken from *The Imitation of Christ* completes the circle of ideas which are contained in the foregoing eleven excerpts perfectly. After denouncing lust, as a falsified and depraved idea of true Love, you are now given fully positive instructions about the truth of it.

Every form of 'love', if not directed towards the WHOLE, which is God, will finally show itself as vanity, that is, something wrong and unreal, which will be lost, because of the limited and perishable attributes belonging to such 'love'.

Does this then mean that 'loving God alone' is to be indifferent 'towards our fellow men and the whole kingdom of Nature, in which, so far, we are spending the lessons of our incarnations? No! The examples of all spiritually advanced men, who long ago abandoned all traces of the vanity of lust and false loves in their evolution, show that they developed just an incomparable charity towards everything living in this world with, of course, men in first place.

The love of Buddha, his compassion; the supreme sacrifice of love for all humanity, as shown by Christ; the examples of all those Saints and Eastern Sages, full of charity and compassion, speak for themselves. Christ taught us to serve our fellow men, saying that in this way we are serving Him best.

And in such love there are no ugly factors, like egoism, jealousy, possessiveness and limitations, all of which belong to the lower manifestations of the same Great Power.

But having the inestimable Grace of such a Love, we serve our neighbours. A great mystic of this century said, that for such service, men will be rewarded by being served by angels.

*　　*　　*

We are now at the end of our twelve meditations, based on the inspired *Imitation of Christ*. They are supreme in all their simplicity and direct language, and yet perhaps not all of you will be attracted to them: for they are uncompromising and strong in definition and have a clearly religious colouring.

Through these qualities Thomas a Kempis will speak chiefly to those, who are able to overcome their often present disinclination towards the religious attitude, and this will help them to take full profit from the spiritual treasures of *The Imitation*.

But others may prefer the chapters of a somewhat different character, and that is why, in this book, I have provided a large variety of themes for meditation, worthy of that name. The general rule for your selection and practice always remains the same: *take what your heart tells you* and know that it is the way in which you meditate, and not merely the numbers of themes, which will decide about the attainment you expect to reach in this course.

Nevertheless, it would be very profitable here for every earnest student if he goes through as many themes as he feels are inspiring for him and, in any case, at least reads all the chapters without exception, as he may easily find something for himself even in certain material, with which he was so far unfamiliar. *For, who seeks will find and who knocks will have it opened to him.* The worst thing is to 'leap' over pages of the book without concentration and due consideration for the contents. Also, another danger lurks for the addicts of incessant and indiscriminate reading. I would say, that when you start to study such a serious matter as is meditation earnestly, you should abandon other books for that time. Otherwise your concentration will become dissipated and, as you know, without due concentration, no meditation can ever be successful.

Now we will come to a very interesting and for some students, a most attractive kind of meditation, taken from the best Vedantic tradition, which consists of *Twelve Axioms of Truth*. Their transcendent beauty and deep meaning are unique. Because of their axiomatic character, as well as the enormous range of their contents contained in only a few words, the true *development* of them belongs rather to the consciousness of the meditating student than to an explanatory text.

These verses are also excellent for the contemplative work to which Part V of this book is dedicated. All the training and persistence in meditation, which you have so far achieved will be needed to cope with these *axioms*. If you pay due attention to them in the prescribed way, your consciousness will be greatly widened.

CHAPTER XXVIII

Axioms of Truth and the Bhagavad-Gita – Series V

THE Maharshi, who liked simple but precise statements and definitions, once explained *meditation* as a passive process, consisting of holding to only one thought, which thereby eliminates all others. When we meditate we first explore the development added to each theme and then, with the mind tuned to the theme by this development, we confront it and remain thus for the time being.

In other words, WE ARE FACING THE MENTAL CLICHÉS OF THE SUBJECT OF MEDITATION. Do not forget that it is the MENTAL CLICHÉ and nothing else. We know clichés extend far beyond our three planes of existence (physical, astral and mental) thereby transcending what we call *time* and *space*, but yet having their reflections in all these worlds. As a human being, I am also a reflection of a certain cliché, in its physical manifestation called —'me', as you can readily see. Meditation in its higher forms aims at discrimination among the infinite number of clichés around us and to the fixation of our attention on the chosen one and so to profit by this confrontation. But meditation does not reach the very substance of clichés, that is, their real essence, or, if you prefer, THE STATE IN WHICH THEY WERE CREATED BY THE SUPERCONSCIOUSNESS OF THE ONE WITHOUT A SECOND. For the approach to clichés, *as they are,* a higher process is needed and we call it—contemplation. It will be the subject of the next, Part V of this study.

In the meantime, we have to finalize our work on meditation by passing on to very inspiring and subtle themes, taken from the Vedanta and composed by the ancient Rishis (Sages) for the use of their advanced disciples. This inheritance now lies before our eyes. The following twelve themes for meditation will give us the final polishing before attempting to contemplate, and here

I mean meditation in full, without any interruptions or deviations. Nothing should exist for us when we meditate, except the THEME alone, after we have worked through it by studying the accompanying DEVELOPMENTS.

1. THEME: *The Truth is one—men call it by many names.*

Development: In the first verse of the *Axioms of Truth* I have its main attribute, which is its UNITY. There cannot be TWO truths, if understood as absolute ones, that is, the very concept of Truth necessitates the exclusion of any similar concept. If there were TWO, one of them would have to be an Untruth. This is like Life and Death, they cannot be together. What lives is apart from Death, and what has died does not live. The manifestations of both are the opposite poles of the same magnet, but they can never be united.

This theme, as well as the following eleven, is magnificent material for CONTEMPLATION and will be used as such after your training in meditation has been successfully concluded.

2. THEME: *Truth is all there is—all else is untruth.*

Development: Truth is all-embracing and in our highest mental flights we may be able to SEE this fact. Truth is a manifestation of God, and as such, it is omnipresent and all-penetrating. What then can be apart from, or beyond Truth? Only Untruth, that which does not exist at all, a flimsy mirage, imagination without any substratum, or, as the Hindus say—*Maya*. From this point of view Maya, being similar to matter with its endless transformations and dependance upon the Energy-Spirit, has no separate or real existence. What is not permanent is only a temporary picture on the immovable screen of Spirit. There was a time when it did not exist, and therefore, unavoidably, it will return to the state of non-existence.

3. THEME: *Truth is all-substance; all-power; all-being; and outside of Truth there can be and is no substance; no power; no being.*

Development: These attributes are derivatives of the former development (Verse 2). Words will be of little use here for the meditating person. The best that can be done is to meditate directly upon the theme, as it is so clear and simple, until our mind becomes acquainted with it and will be able to digest it.

4. THEME: *Truth is all-creative energy; the all-wisdom; the all-good; and outside of Truth there can be and is no creative energy, or intelligence; no good.*

Development: Perhaps the best way for the development of this verse would be to create a cliché in our mind, depicting these attributes. Creative energy contains Truth in it, directed by the all-wisdom, which alone can perform such leadership. What is GOOD? Every being *knows* it, but this knowledge is beyond words and thoughts. It can only be LIVED, not observed from outside, as this problematic *outside* must necessarily be OUTSIDE of Truth-Wisdom and therefore, non-existent.

As with the creative energy, intelligence and good can only be in Truth, there is nothingness apart from It.

5. THEME: *Truth is all-Love; Truth is all-Life; outside of Truth there can be no Love; no Life. All-Love and all-Life proceed from Truth, and are aspects and symbols of its allness.*

Development: Gradually we can see that Truth embraces everything we consider to be the loftiest and most worthwhile in the world. In the knowledge that Love and Life are manifestations of the same Truth, we feel ourselves closer to It, for It is the source of both.

6. THEME: *Truth is that which IS; Spirit is that which Truth IS; Truth is Spirit, Spirit is Truth; Truth-Spirit is all there is, all else is untruth.*

Development: As Spirit is the only real thing which exists, its identity with Truth is evident. They are mutually identical, and it is only in the language of words that we find different terms for it. The all-being is another attribute of Truth and Truth-Spirit is the core of every existence. Everything apart from It does not possess any life, or being.

7. THEME: *The Truth is to be sought everywhere, for everywhere abideth it.*

Development: The omnipresence of Truth makes this verse understandable. There is no place where there would be less or more, or even no Truth. That is why Spiritual Masters always teach, that there is no need to go anywhere in order to find Truth. From this point of view there is no reason to suppose that in certain places Truth is closer, or further from us.

8. THEME: *Truth is ever-abiding within. He who realizes this Truth becomes master of his life.*

Development: An important injunction is in these words: as Truth has no definite place of abiding, but at the same time it is everywhere, the most suitable would be to seek for it in a place which is always with us. It is our own spiritual 'within'. In the silent magnificence of our deepest spiritual recesses we find the Truth, which actually was always with us, but we simply could not perceive its presence. Realization of our inner imperishable Light which is the Truth enables us to become masters of our life, directing that life to the unique, and real aim the abidance in Truth.

9. THEME: *Rejoice and be glad, for within you is the Light of the world.*

Development: We know that spiritual consciousness brings immeasurable joy. Those who have lived this spiritual ecstasy confirm this fact, as being beyond every conceivable joy. So the words of Christ, identical with those of Theme No. 9, are another inducement to find this everlasting JOY. These words tell us, that we are bearers of the Light which enlightens every man, who comes into this world. Could we find something more encouraging and uplifting for every sincere seeker?

10. THEME: *In the perception of the ever-effulgent* ONE *alone there is freedom, wisdom and bliss.*

Development: The Master Maharshi often spoke about the effulgence of the Spirit-Self, in which there is final freedom and liberation for us. What is necessary for this Attainment? Nothing apart from the ability to perceive IT. This gives us wisdom and bliss, based on the eternal freedom of Spirit.

11. THEME: *The Wise ones ever seek that which once known all is known.*

Development: The immense value of this statement for a true seeker cannot be over-estimated. Look at the world both past and present: does it seek the Real, or rather ephemeral, perishable aims? The finding of That, which enlightens every thing, alone gives peace and the realization of Life. And then all other less worthwhile aims are conquered at the same time. When looking first for details we lose the Whole. Discrimination, elevated to the peak, leads us to this achievement. Is it worth trying to cognize anything except the ONE UNIQUE, REAL THING? But for that we must intuitionally know about ITS existence and meaning.

12. THEME: *There is but one Truth, men call it by many names. Above time and beyond space, and free from causation, ever dwelleth the ONE THAT IS ALL.*

Development: The magic circle of this meditation is closed with the same statement, as was at its beginning. It is the many-named Truth. We have already meditated about it. But here is added the final idea about God, already known to us from other texts in the preceding chapters, but imperishable in its beauty and purity of the expressed Truth. The tragic question, put (perhaps, in the name of the whole of seeking mankind) by Pilate to the Great Teacher: 'WHAT IS THE TRUTH?' can be solved, but not from the outside, in words, but in the most sacred, inner temple of the human soul, asking for final enlightenment from Its Father, Who is in Heaven. Christ told us positively that we can find the Truth. Not in the luckless Pilate's way, but in our own depths, in which there is the 'Light of the world'. How many pass by this Light and never see IT?

The realm of Truth is beyond time and space, as well as beyond and independent of the apparently immutable Law of Causation. The mind can hardly imagine the absence of this basic law of the manifested universe. But can such a law bind the ONE, who 'has penetrated the whole universe with a particle of Himself, and Who still persists'?

We are living in a strange world and the most materialistic tendencies dominate the mass of people in it, but, at the same time, there are many living souls, who, as never before, are able to raise their awareness far beyond all limitations, as described in this Theme No. 12 of meditation. Is there a condition? Yes, it is the one which opens the door, which has been closed to us for so many centuries, hidden behind the noisy voices of the world and our own consciousness. Now the secret of establishing this is as if lying open before us. Would we like to accept it? Its true name is: the *Spiritual silence, achieved by man's own effort, accompanied by the Grace of the* ONE, *Who waits for that moment,* in order to let us approach Him, as the lost sheep finds its true owner.

Meditation is one of the foremost means to obtain our freedom from noisy thoughts and to establish the purity of the Silence.

EXCERPTS FROM THE BHAGAVAD-GITA

In a course of meditation such as this it would be impossible to omit the very valuable themes provided by certain excerpts from *The Lord's Song* (The *Bhagavad-Gita*), being the highest expression of the spiritual Initiation, created by our Aryan, Hindu brothers.

I am drawing your attention to a few chosen verses, containing concentrated drops of truth and am omitting all the external trimmings belonging to that far distant and legendary past epoch of the Rishis and warriors of India. There are many enthusiasts of this magnificent memorial to human genius, and some even go so far as to compare the *Bhagavad-Gita* with Christ's Gospels. In rendering all due respect and admiration to the *Lord's Song*, I recognize that is possesses first-class initiatory contents, close to the realm where the Absolute Truth dwells. And many of my readers will join with me in that admiration. Therefore, let them use the following texts to the best of their ability and may the idea of the absolute prevailing of Spirit over Matter find a fertile soil in their hearts.

But the words of the Great Teacher in the Gospels, so brief, concentrated, simple in outer form and unsurpassed in wisdom and power, point to Eternity, and they give an instant impulse to those who are ripe enough to understand them, leading into the Realm, where no worm of corruption, or thieves, or doubts have any access, as He told us. In no human teachings can we find the unfathomable spiritual oceans revealed in a few simple words, which speak straight to a man's innermost core, his heart. Perhaps this is because they are not *human* teachings.

The core of the *Lord's Song* is the Truth of Man's real being. his Self. In this the words of the Lord Krishna are unsurpassed.

When reading them one seems to realize, who inspired the last Rishi of India, the Maharshi, whom we had amongst us in our own lifetime.

1. THEME : *The Self is never born, nor does It die, nor after once having been, does It go into non-being. This Self is unborn, eternal, changeless, ancient; It is never destroyed even when the body is destroyed.*

Development : This text is so clear and simple, that no special comments are necessary, and you can start to meditate on it straight away. The only point which perhaps needs some explanation would be that about the 'changeless' Self. Some may think, that Self is progressing and developing itself during the innumerable births and incarnations. This would be a great fallacy, and we should be warned about it. If we say, that man *evolves*, it never means that his Spirit-Self is progressing. A ray of the Immortal, Blissful, Perfect ONE, how could this Self participate in any changes? It is our 'envelopes', our means of cognition, and finally our CONCIOUSNESS which advances, becoming more and more aware of its eternal, immortal and perfect CORE—the Atman, Spirit, Self, no matter how we care to call IT! And therein lies the whole difference between the peaks and valleys of our awareness. Those, who are conscious of That, what they really are, are advanced souls, and those who still believe they are their different bodies (physical, astral, or mental) —belong to the as yet undeveloped beings.

Resurrection means nothing less than just the awakening of that PURE CONSCIOUSNESS, which never dies. And now you may see why Christ insisted that without that resurrection there cannot be any salvation for the sons of Man.

This verse of the *Bhagavad-Gita* produces some statements about the 'properties' of the Self, which should be well understood.

2. THEME : *Some look upon that Self with wonder, some speak about It with wonder, some hear about It with wonder and yet others, even after hearing about It, know it not.*

Development : The most real, the unique real THING which exists, our SELF, is very often unknown, even when a man hears about It and has access to teachings about It. This is because not all who have ears can hear, and not all who have eyes can see.

3. THEME: *Regarding alike pleasure and pain, gain and loss, victory and defeat, fight thou thy battle. Thus sin will not stain thee.*

Development: Knowing that you have nothing in common with the mortal body and its conditions, you should behave as Krishna teaches in this verse.

4. THEME: *To work alone thou has the right, but never to the fruits thereof. Be thou neither actuated by the fruits of action, nor be thou attached to inaction.*

Development: A striking moral law of non-attachment to the fruits of one's work! Look around, at all the great souls, Saints, Teachers, Rishis, and you will see the full realization of this rule. It is the law of spiritual life.

5. THEME: *The wise, possessed with knowledge, abandoning the fruits of their actions, become freed from the fetters of births and reach that state which is beyond all evil.*

Development: Attachment to action and its fruits is the cause of births and deaths, the source of all evil and suffering.

6. THEME: *The man of steady wisdom, having subdued all his senses, becomes fixed in the Supreme. His wisdom is well-established whose senses are under control. Thinking of sense-objects, man becomes attached thereto. From attachment arises longing and from longing anger is born.*

Development: Control of the senses is the attribute of Wisdom in man. And Wisdom means none other than the fixing of the whole of attention on the Supreme, or God. Attachments are the roots of evil emotions.

7. THEME: *There is no wisdom for the unsteady and there is no meditation for the unsteady and for the un-meditative there is no peace. How can there be any happiness for the peaceless one?*

Development: This is the most important verse for all of us, who are studying meditation. We see that in order to get the ability to meditate, the mind must be stabilized, that is, its uncontrolled activities curtailed. That is why, in the first part of this manual, you find such a strong emphasis placed on good preparation for meditation, which is CONCENTRATION. It makes the mind steady and this ability allows us to start true meditation, which is otherwise impossible without the submission of one's mind. Another cardinal statement is, that without meditation there is no peace for a man. So, we can see where lies the foundation of INNER PEACE.

Finally, without peace, there cannot be any true happiness, so, in the whole chain of steps towards happiness, the intermediary phases are: first, Concentration, then Meditation, Peace and finally, the Bliss of the Achievement, or the solution of the eternal problem of our own being.

8. THEME: *As the ocean remains calm and unaltered though the waters flow into it, similarly a self-controlled Saint remains unmoved when desires enter into him; such a Saint alone attains Peace, but not he who craves the objects of desire.*

Development: Desires are the fulcrum of every obstacle on the Path. They are without end, and their satisfying only means further enslavement by them. Desires destroy all peace in man, but their objectives are not limited by yielding to those desires, since they only grow in number and strength. That is what the meditating disciple must realize and thus find the chief enemy, who prevents him from regular meditation.

9. THEME: *A man does not attain to freedom from action by non-performance of action, nor does he attain to perfection merely by giving up action.*

Development: This is the solution to the age-old problem, which troubles many seekers: the role of activity in their lives in relation to their Liberation. The fact that we are here, in this world of action, may well mean that we have to perform a certain role in it. But, as the Great Rishi Ramana also taught, our action must be without attachment, and, as we saw in the former verses, without any expectation of the fruits of action. Only then will it not be binding for the wise man, but only like a dream, having no influence on a man's waking life.

10. THEME: *That man, who is devoted to the Self, is satisfied with Self and is content in the Self alone, for him there is nothing to do.*

Development: Spiritual life, starting when a man becomes immersed in his true Self and united with IT, sets him free from all activities. Awareness of one's SELF means the end of the school of life, spent in separate existences, in separate bodies.

Spiritual consciousness in the Self brings the final Bliss and contentment, which does not exist in any other condition.

Such is our true aim.

11. THEME: *Those who find fault with the Lord's teaching and do not follow it, such self-deluded ones, devoid of all knowledge and discrimination, know them to be ruined.*

Development: It is a well-known story, that those men without spiritualized consciousness, are very eager to find any imaginary imperfection in the most elevated and pure of teachings. This is their way of seducing themselves and others. The root of such an attitude is known to us: it is a kind of justification (false and useless as it is) for their own inactivity and laziness. Lack of the cardinal virtue, necessary for every seeker, that is, DIS-CRIMINATION is clearly visible here.

12. THEME: *The senses are said to be superior (to the body), the mind is superior to the senses, and intellect is superior to the mind; and that which is superior to the intellect is HE (Atman, Self).*

Development: Translated into contemporary occult terminology known to many of us as: astral (emotions and senses), mental (concrete mind), higher mental (world of ideas) and Spirit (Self), this verse becomes understandable for meditation. What is most important is the experience of that Atman, that is, conscious-ness above all manifestation of the mental, the mind. It is possible, if we have developed domination of our thinking principle. The blissful state beyond all thoughts, emotions and body's feelings is the FOURTH STATE, the final and the last stage of our evolution.

No reading, or study will make us closer to IT, but only incessant work, control of mind and body, through the art of concentration and the exclusion of everything, except our ultimate 'I'.

13. THEME: *He who sees inaction in action and action in inaction, he is intelligent among men; he is a man of established wisdom and a true performer of all actions.*

Development: The mysterious balance between action and inaction as seen by the outer and ignorant world, is for the wise man a fruit of his spiritual initiation. While being still in the world, he is truly 'NOT OF THIS WORLD', as Christ said. Even on the lowest level of physical work, the exclusion of the astral element in it, that is, desire and excitement (see my *Trilogy*) makes the same work much more efficient and less tiring. One who puts his 'nerves' and moods into his actions is a fool, who only exhausts himself for no profit: neither for himself, nor for the quality and quantity of performance. Such is the wisdom of action.

14. THEME: *The ignorant, the faithless and one of doubting mind perishes. There is neither this world nor the next nor any happiness for the doubting self.*

Development: The *Bhagavad-Gita* is thousands of years old, but its knowledge of the human soul, or what we now call— psychology, is readily applicable to the modern world. Ignorance and faithlessness are most evidently deadly obstacles for spiritual attainment, but these are present now in our own time, when we can see the destructive results of doubting human minds. If we look around us, we will see masses of people who 'are seeking', as they tell us, for some higher life, but their minds prevent them from any success in their endeavours. They leap from one theory to the next, from one sect to another, and from one bit of non-sense to still more disappointing conceptions. They are unable to concentrate and discriminate when true Light is before them. Finally, the end comes, and they depart for another unknown and often frightening world, without having obtained any enlightenment or certainty in their further destiny and life.

Discrimination and a doubting mind are two opposite poles and not allies! Without reasonable and enlightened discrimination we will be the victims of rogues and dark forces, and with an ever-doubting, undecided and uncontrolled mind we will simply never take any first step on our long Path, remaining indefinitely in the same place, without progressing and only wasting incarnations.

That is why Krishna says, that for such people there is no happiness, or achievement in any of the possible worlds.

This verse of the Lord's Song is a powerful warning for us and it must be accepted as such.

15. THEME: *Renunciation of action and performance of action both lead to liberation. But of the two, performance of action is* SUPERIOR *to renunciation of action.*

Development: We find an important teaching in this verse: action performed without attachment to it is, of course, more recommendable because of its greater usefulness on the Path. By this the old doubtful belief, that in order to get Liberation, one must forget the world and deny any activity in it is definitely shattered. Meditate about this until the Light comes!

16. THEME: *The omnipresent Lord partakes neither of the good nor of the evil deed of any. Wisdom is covered by ignorance, thus mortals are deluded. But those, whose ignorance is destroyed by Self-knowledge, their knowledge of the Self—like the Sun, illumines the Supreme.*

Development: Since time immemorial the relation of the omnipresent and all-penetrating Lord to the Creation has been the stone on which many otherwise enlightened men have broken their heads. It has happened because they could not discriminate in full as regards the role of the treacherous mind, which tries to set up an anthropomorphic image of the Supreme before deluded seekers. They simply do not distinguish between the OMNIPRESENCE AND ALL-PENETRATION, and the responsibility for deeds committed by the separate consciousnesses. The *Bhagavad-*

Gita deals a mortal blow to such a heresy. We must never forget this truth again!

This ignorance can be destroyed by the omnipotent sword of Self-Knowledge, or Self-Realization, when the full Light is seen, and no illusion can darken the screen of the awareness of the wise man. Why is this so? Do you remember some former meditations, when you were told about the non-attachment of the true Self to our deeds, feelings and thoughts? That the Self begins there, where all of the three veils just mentioned are fully realized, and rejected as unreal before the ultimate tribunal of Spirit-Self? If so, then you know that the Great, Infinite and Absolute SELF which we call—God, is beyond and above all actions and the law of cause and effect.

I know scores of intelligent people who, during all their lifetimes, have tried to penetrate the mystery of God with their minds, and in that way they unconsciously ascribe to the Lord, dependence upon the laws which bind us on this earth! The truth that for the Lord there are no laws, or bonds, or causality, is sometimes too hard for certain people to swallow.

This fallacy must be firmly rejected, and then our Spirit will be free of the bondage of the mortal mind.

17. THEME: *He, whose heart is unattached to external contacts of the senses, realizes the happiness that is in the Self; being united with Brahman by meditation, he attains to eternal bliss.*

Development: We already know a lot about the importance of breaking the bonds of attachment, but why is it so difficult for the majority of people, even when possessing a fine intellect? This is because they still have a subconscious fear, that if they abandon their egos, and cease to strive for earthly aims, they might become miserable and lose the status they still cherish. This is the main trouble which plagues such people. The final detachment from the egoistic, that is, materialistic life is hard, no doubt about it. But it MUST be performed, if one is to attain the true happiness! The outer conditions about which we are so anxious, are only very limited in time and space, so why stick to them so desperately and thus lose what we all would like to obtain—*true happiness*? Vedanta tells us, that the power which prevents this decisive step ahead is the power of MAYA, that world-illusion, so hard to overcome. But we know that those who did, never regret their leap ahead, but are blissful in their Attainment.

In everyone of us there is a silent Light, deep in the heart of our being, independent of anything, but enlightening everything in its vicinity. This quiet Light of the indestructible Self is all we really possess, or, much better, ALL THAT WE REALLY ARE!

No additions are necessary, for they all finally perish, and the Inner Light alone remains, uniting us with the Great Spiritual Sun of God.

18. THEME: *The Self-subjugated Rishis (Truth-Seers), whose impurities are washed off, whose doubts are destroyed, and who are engaged in doing good to all beings, attain supreme Liberation.*

Development: There is not much to add to this verse, as it is too clear to be further dissected. In it the results of the Attainment are emphasized once more. We should again note well the statement about the 'Rishis whose doubts are destroyed'. One of the surest signs of approaching Enlightenment is the absence of doubts and problems. On the other hand, if you feverishly seek 'new' theories or teachings, be sure that the enemy—mind still has you in his unholy grip. Attainment is possible, for around you are those who have done it.

19. THEME: *He who has conquered himself by the Self, he is the friend of himself; but he whose self is unconquered, his self acts as his own enemy like an external foe.*

Development: Here the Self spelt with a capital 'S' means the true Self in us, and with a small 's'—the perishable and conquerable ego-mind, which is inimical to Self-Realization. Just as a wild horse is not happy with the efforts of a tamer, directed to its subduing, so the same applies to the human mind. If I can spend all the time when I am not compelled to think by outer circumstances, without any thought in my silenced mind, this mind becomes a slave instead of the overlord, as is the case with the majority of men. And mind is a power, possessing its separate intelligence, limited, but still often greater than that of an untrained thinker. It is only natural that this power does not like to be tamed and bound.

But the binary—'I or *my mind*' must be solved to the advantage of my 'I', or I am lost. Meditation about this verse should bring you more light.

20. THEME: *A Yogi should constantly practise concentration of the heart, remaining in seclusion alone, subduing his body and mind and being free from longing and possession (sense of ownership).*

Development: Only a few explanations are needed here. The 'heart' here means man's deepest recess of awareness, in which there is always peace. Submission of the body does not mean sleeping on a bed of nails and similar nonsense, but simply resistance to the unreasonable and superfluous desires of our physical nature, such as the liking of special foods and drinks. Submission of the mind by means of concentration is already well known to you.

21. THEME: *He whose passions are quieted and mind perfectly tranquil, who has become one with Brahman, being freed from all impurities, to such a Yogi comes supreme bliss.*

Development: This is only a further definition of the former themes of meditation, so it does not need any more explanation.

22. THEME: *Those who know Me in the physical realm, in the Divine realm and in the realm of sacrifice, being steadfast in heart, they know Me even at the time of death.*

Development: It means, that we have to realize the Supreme, to think about It and to be firmly attached to IT in all conditions of life: in the body-consciousness, in feelings and thoughts. Then comes the steadfastness of the HEART, that is, of the Spirit in us. No wonder that we are then with the Lord when we finally leave our bodily form.

23. THEME: *I am the Origin of all, everything evolves from Me. Knowing this, the wise worship Me with loving ecstasy.*

Development: If we meditate constantly about this theme, realizing the great Truth contained in it, we will reach the indescribable ecstasy of inner Peace and Bliss, leading us to Samadhi. Realization, that one is always in the Lord, and that He is our surest refuge destroys all one's fears and doubts forever.

24. THEME: *Those who, fixing their minds on Me, worship Me with* PERPETUAL DEVOTION, *endowed with supreme faith, they are the best knowers of Yoga.*

Development: Here Krishna points out the supremacy of true devotion to the Lord, as the foundation of every spiritual search, here called 'Yoga'. And all those who ever practised meditation will agree, that the best part of their work is done when they raise their hearts to the Supreme.

*　　*　　*

We are now at the end of our study of meditation proper and on the threshold of the next step, which leads to the study of CONTEMPLATION. Let us not forget, that it can be successfully continued only if the material, as given in Parts III and IV has been duly worked through. At this time I recommend that you choose from these two parts of the book a certain number of meditative themes, which you like more than others and which you consider will act as a basis for Contemplation. Write them down on a separate sheet of paper and attach it to Part V. In this way you will have material, well known to you from the study of meditation, which will be easy to memorize and use for advanced purposes.

You will find that Contemplation is very different from meditation, because the whole effort of it is centred not in the mental work upon the themes, but just in the transcending of thoughts and entering into the realm beyond them.

Some students may ask if ALL the themes of meditation as given in the foregoing chapters must be worked with equally, or if some of them could be omitted.

My advice would be to work with all of them in a normal way, paying special consideration to those themes, which attract you more than others. The real *work on themes* is the meditating on them using the development as a start, while not allowing any foreign and unrelated thoughts to disturb your work. Briefly, think only about what is required, and do not deviate from the theme and its development.

Insufficiently concentrated meditations will disappoint you, as the results may be below your expectations. This is only natural, if you do not fulfil the requirements, as given in this book. Who then would be to blame?

Success cannot come other than from your own efforts, since I cannot meditate instead of you so that your consciousness will be enlarged and refined.

I hope you do not have any such ideas!

If you are a devotional type of man, start every meditation, or contemplation with a prayer, which you may take from my book—*Theurgy: The Art of Effective Worship*[1] in which you will find many texts, arranged systematically and taken from different sources and epochs, according to the effectiveness and inspiration contained in them.

[1] 1962, Allen & Unwin.

PART V

INTRODUCTION TO CONTEMPLATION

CHAPTER XXIX

Mute Meditation

THE Great Rishi Ramana, in his remarks about meditation, says, as quoted in *Maha Yoga* (that inspired book about his teachings, written by one of his few true disciples) that: *'Meditation (dhyana) is a battle; for it is the effort to keep hold of one thought to the exclusion of all else; other thoughts arise and try to sink that thought; when the latter gains strength the others are put to flight.'*

During your work on the previous parts of this book, you most certainly experienced the truth of this saying of the Sage.

The battle of meditation must be won, otherwise no results can be expected. We find one of the Maharshi's very important injunctions about the secret of mind-control in another quotation from *Maha Yoga*: *'The mind cannot be controlled by one that takes it to be something that really exists.'* In this course you have already found that as the condition of success, as given by the writer, *one must separate from one's mind, and not identify* (consciously or unconsciously) *oneself with one's mental activities.* This stage precedes the attitude, recommended by the Maharshi, which is the final solution of the great problem of spiritual life. If you separate from your mind, the next step will come easily, for common sense and some investigation will show you clearly, that this 'separated mentality' does not exist at all as such and appears only when a man calls for it and allows it to occupy his consciousness. Moreover, even the simple philosophy of life tells us, that *'Reality cannot be overcome or abolished'*. In the case of the mind, if it were real then it never could be dominated or annihilated (as the Maharshi liked to say), for reality can never be destroyed.

After the battle-like period of our meditation, we must come

317

to the next, the highest phase of it : MEDITATION WITHOUT
WORDS AND VERBALIZATION IN ONE'S MIND. We call it MUTE
MEDITATION.

Properly speaking, it is the only meditation worthy of the
name. Our problem now is how to transform our mental meditation, as was practised in the foregoing parts of this book, into
the true, MUTE one, independent of any language meditation?
Quite a formidable task, especially so as it is most difficult to
describe or convey, as is everything which is beyond speech. But
I will try to do my best. The difficulty is, that at this stage the
student must invariably be well acquainted with the previous
forms of meditation (Parts II to IV). If he is not, the access to
the highest kind of it will most certainly not be available to
him; for here I can use only language understandable to men
who are already separated from their own mentality and are
able to 'endure', 'for some time' without any thoughts in their
awareness.

If you have reached this point then read further. If not, go
back and practise the aforementioned Parts of this work until
you succeed. The following instructions are for those who have
been successful.

(1) Choose a short theme which is especially attractive for you.
I recommend foremostly : 'I AM', 'WHO AM I?' and 'AUM' (the
meaning of which must be well understood). Then come the
AXIOMS OF TRUTH, which are unsurpassed for this purpose,
followed by the Themes Nos. 1, 4, 7 and 8 of Chapter XXII,
Theme No. 12 of Chapter XXV, Themes Nos. 1, 2 and 3 from
Chapter XXVI and finally, everything which inspires you and
quells your mind (thinking), allowing you to reach some period
of inner peace, independent of the vibration of the thinking
processes.

(2) As before, meditate upon one of the chosen subjects and
after having worked with the development with special care,
face the theme and remain thus for as long as you can. Gradually
transform the words of the theme into the IDEA. What is the
practical difference between an IDEA and a THOUGHT? Are they
not very close relatives? Not at all! An idea is the highest
function of our mind, just on the border of awareness, living but
being free from mind's pollution (that is, thinking). An idea
can be clothed in a thought, but it can exist just as well with-

out any thoughts. In order to experience it, you must declare total war on any verbalizing processes in your consciousness, that is, to stop thinking in words. From this point you may find the proper way to the world of ideas, to stay and to live in it, thereby performing the MUTE MEDITATION, as required.

Technically speaking, you should hold the idea of the theme as if before your eyes, or better still, before your mind's eye, immovably and while not indulging in any thinking. Saturate your awareness with the theme, digest it, and exclude everything else. That is all that can be said in words about Mute Meditation. Under what circumstances can you be successful? Only if you realize what I am trying to convey now, with the insufficient language of human words and thoughts. Here your inner ripeness will be the best criterion.

At this point one of the dangerous obstacles will be a tendency to fall asleep, when you try to exclude all verbalization from your consciousness. It comes as a result of insufficient (or delayed) development of the brain, which may still be unable to reflect what you require from it, that is, pure facing of ideas.

The chief remedy, of course, would be an energetic and faithful performance of the previous types of meditation, as they do directly influence the development of the convolutions on the surface of your brain. There is no other means for that purpose, except for the waiting through many incarnations for that achievement. Here we strive after results while still in this life, and from this are born our difficulties. But they can be surmounted, for many have succeeded in overcoming them, so why not you?

I need hardly say, that the physical side should not be forgotten. Never sit for meditation when you are sleepy or feel that you have had an insufficient period of rest when sleeping. No doubt advanced souls—as were and are some saints and occultists of good standing—are strong enough to deprive their bodies of sleep and rest for long periods, which is inaccessible to ordinary men. Their inner strength allows them to do so. If you feel you can step after them, try it! There is no danger in it, but remember that you should be duly prepared for defeat, and not become frustrated or desperate because of it.

Finally, I will make an attempt, be it successful, or otherwise (it depends upon you and not me) to try to describe the experiences of a man, who undertakes mute meditation, after due preparation as given previously.

Be aware, that the words you will read now, are NOT an exact picture of these experiences—which are beyond all words—but something like the cross-section of a complicated piece of mechanism.

THEME : *The Truth*

Development into mute meditation :

(a) It IS. It is the only thing which really IS. All Being belongs to Truth, and without it nothing exists. (Now empty your mind for some moments—about one or two minutes—and face the TRUTH. . .)

(b) *Truth fills the whole of Manifestation, to the last galaxy and beyond it, straight into Infinity.* (Again stop thinking.)

(c) *Truth is like Space, all-penetrating, silent, all-transparent, unaffected by anything.* (Put out everything from your mind. Face the endless emptiness, filled with Truth and be glad of it. If you cannot, stop the attempt for you still have a lot of learning ahead of you before you succeed.)

(d) *Truth is Bliss: permanent, immovable, immaterial, nameless, all-penetrating Bliss.* (Live it !)

(e) *Truth is in me. No, it is I, when I raise myself to Its heights. It will not descend to me. It is I, who must go to It.* (Merge into the space-like 'substance', which is the symbol of Truth. Forget everything else, yourself included. You cannot exist APART from the Truth, only dissolve in It.)

(f) *I am dissolving my being in the Infinity of Truth. . .*

The dish has been offered to you. Did you taste it?

In the same way develop other themes into *mute meditation* substituting the theme with the idea chosen by yourself. Apply directions to them similar to those in items (a) to (f).

CHAPTER XXX

Mute Prayer

As was mentioned at the beginning of this course, there is a very close affinity between *mute* (that is, the highest) *meditation* and *mute prayer*, and the techniques are similar. By now you know a lot about the former (mute meditation) and can have detailed knowledge about the latter (mute prayer) from *Theurgy*. Hence I shall not repeat much from that book, limiting myself merely to a definition, which embraces the whole concept of prayer. It is: THE RELATION OF MAN TO HIS MAKER.

You see, prayer is not just the begging of the Supreme for deliverance from illness, or other difficult circumstances, when all human means have proved useless. We know that the great souls, who spent all of their lives in prayer (as did many saints) did not limit themselves to asking of God, but rather of offering their whole being to Him. From their lives we also know, that they prayed mostly in silence, merged in their adoration and love of the Lord. Now you can see, that the highest form of true prayer is very similar to the highest form of meditation, when both are silent, beyond words and even thoughts.

If you remember the role of clichés in man's inner (spiritual) life, the resemblance will be still more striking.

An eminent occultist tries to contact the highest possible cliché through the highest aspect of his meditation. This kind of cliché, as we know from former chapters, is beyond the three-fold limitations of time, space and planes of material existence (physical, astral and mental). This means the purely spiritual realm, in which the primordial clichés dwell, created by the Lord, and beyond time and space.

Now, does not a Saint, in his prayers, strive after the same spiritual realm in which he hopes to encounter the Supreme?

Let us still add a far-reaching statement by the Sage Ramana that: 'That one point in which all religions meet is Realization', and the identity of true spiritual meditation and prayer (both mute, of course, beyond words and thoughts) will appear clear to us. Because of all of the foregoing, you will realize that there is little possibility of giving an exact definition, or description of spiritual meditation or prayer, at least, in terms accessible to all and sundry. Certain personal experience is absolutely necessary, if we are to realize something of this sublime region of Life. Words remain only words, even if they are used to describe the super-mental states of consciousness.

Therefore I will mention some ideas which undoubtedly belong to MUTE, SPIRITUAL PRAYER.

(a) Concentration in such prayer reaches the full exclusion of all thoughts from the mind of the praying person.

(b) The passive form of concentration does not remain as such in the consciousness, but is immediately transformed into the MERGING IN ADORATION AND LOVE of the Supreme.

(c) This means that in the state of mute prayer man transcends both forms of concentration (active and passive), which are well known to us, and the apparent vacuum is filled with Spiritual Awareness, which is different from both, but having both as its supporting pillars, a condition without which this sublime state cannot be realized.

People, who have been successful in *concentration* (both forms, of course), say that their meditation then became very close to prayer, and their prayers almost identical with their mute meditation. But, they say that when practising these elated flights, there is not even the slightest thought about the means, which allowed them to achieve those flights, that is, the techniques of concentration.

Something the same as with a trained violinist, who plays directly from the notes lying before him and who does not think at all as to which finger he has to press and on which point of the instrument's neck. All transferring from the paper of his score into the living sounds as the work is performed is done as if automatically.

This idea seems to be the closest to the reality of mute prayer and meditation. Think deeply about it, until it becomes utterly clear to you, and until you see the light, showing you how you can start these experiences for yourself.

A man who has learned these experiences, necessarily possesses a firm and unshakable faith in God, and his unique aim then becomes the constant and ever-increasing deepening of that living faith. Is there a final, definite aim, after the reaching of which a man can 'rest on his laurels'? This is a hard problem, but a certain approach to its solution can be attempted.

In certain great religions and occult philosophies we find that *'if a man has reached a definite level of spiritual development* (Nirvana, the Kingdom of Heaven, Liberation, and so on) *he does not return into this world any more, as he has learned all the lessons that this earth can offer him'*. This truth is logical. But is it expressed to the last word? *Certainly not!* This attainment is great, but still relative. And this is because the earthly existence is not the peak, and final deliverance from it does not mean that there is nothing to achieve any more.

God is INFINITE, so are the possibilities of merging in Him, of admiration and of love for Him. This is certain, but WHO KNOWS what lies beyond the finished school of life in separate existences, as occurs during the planetary incarnations.

It is useless to guess, or think about it. Nevertheless, it has been said in the Scriptures that 'the eye cannot see and the ear cannot hear the bliss, prepared by the Lord for the faithful'. This was to emphasize the greatness of the 'reward'.

* * *

Of what does MUTE PRAYER consist?

If it is not any begging for earthly or other boons, then it must be *attraction* to and *admiration* and *love* for the Lord, which dominate such a prayer. And this is what we have to do: to merge, without words and thoughts in Him, through some of the aforementioned elements of mute prayer. That is all! If you can find something apart from them, equally uplifting and enlightening for you in your prayer, then do not hesitate to use it. Many are the ways in which we come to the Lord, and every soul has something peculiar to it, taking it to Him, and these individual forms of worship are as a blessed gift.

We know only a few general lines, two of which are as mentioned in this work, the path of MEDITATION and that of PRAYER. Which is better? The answer is that which is natural for you. Some must meditate just as others must pray. That is all!

CHAPTER XXXI

Contemplation as a Synthesis of Both

BOTH *meditation* and *mute prayer* have essentially the same aim, that is, MERGING IN THE SUPREME REALITY, GOD, SPIRIT, which terms are synonymous, but not one of which can really be described in words. Experiences beyond words belong to a different world, not known to anybody except those few who managed to reach and to dwell in it. Also, certain approaches can be made in speech, translating into it some of the most general lines of those transcendental experiences.

The state wherein we face the Supreme, as far as our limited awareness allows us, is called CONTEMPLATION. It is immaterial whether we reach it by meditation, or prayer, for on this level both are equal, and lead to the same Eternal Cliché of Truth. It is easy to commit a theoretical error when speaking about Contemplation without personal experience in it.

Many occultists, who have only guessed about it, while not having raised their own consciousnesses to the height of Contemplation, make little difference between it and the peaks of meditation, or prayer. And it is this by which you can recognize the compilers from the genuine knowers.

Vedantists know the difference well, for it has been very often underlined in their Scriptures, especially in Advaita Vedanta (that based on non-duality). Our Tradition agrees with our Indian brothers in full. Meditation and prayer are still *actions*, they are a degree of Attainment, they lead to that Attainment, no matter whether we call it the Kingdom of Heaven, Nirvana, Liberation, or Paradise. There is still the meditating or praying man, and the object of his efforts.

IN CONTEMPLATION, THE SUBJECT AND THE OBJECT ARE MERGED INTO ONE, AND ALL DUALITY DISAPPEARS FOR EVER. This is the difference and this must be well understood. In Contemplation the seeker confronts his final Aim, but cannot remain separated from It. So both merge. The Great Circle embraces the smaller one, as an ocean dissolves the raindrop which falls into it. These similes are almost all that can be told about Contemplation of the Highest. Because of the sublimity of the means leading to the Aim, it cannot be anything less than the Supreme. You cannot contemplate anything material or sensual. If you think so, the object is low and then what you believe to be contemplation is only a thinking process, belonging completely to the mental realm, that is, having nothing in common with Spirit. Its cliché is in the threefold limitation of time, space and thought and has no connection with the *Real Eternal Cliché* (see Chapters II, III and XVII, and so on).

If Contemplation is long and can be experienced by the will of the adept, it usually passes imperceptibly into another spiritual experience, that of true Superconsciousness, or Samadhi (see Chapters IX and X). If it is accompanied by an attribute of Power in it, it means the manifestation of the Hyperconsciousness, in the terminology we have adopted in this work. This means that I am discriminating between two apparently identical terms but, as I explained in Chapter X, there is no other way, if two different clichés had to be recognized as such.

In some other works on similar themes you may perhaps encounter conceptions about 'contemplating certain virtues', such as Love, Purity, Wisdom, Charity, and so on. But let us go deeper into their analysis. As you already know, the element of duality has been completely banned in true Contemplation, and this makes the real difference even in the highest degrees of meditation.

When you contemplate on the ONLY THING which can be *contemplated* upon (not meditated upon!), it is always the *Supreme* Itself. And in this state of Enlightenment you could not exist apart from IT. There is nothing else.

Are the *Virtues* of the same range as the *Supreme*? In the best case they are only ATTRIBUTES, which must belong to someone, even to you, if you have reached them in your heart. But the Lord is INFINITE, and beyond all attributes, if contemplated beyond the mind's realm. You cannot substitute the Infinite and Transcendental by that which is finite and definite.

So we can only meditate about Virtues, but not contemplate them in the true sense of that word.

You may ask me, what about the experience of the PRESENCE of GOD, as mentioned in one of the former chapters? All we can say is that certainly such an experience is far above any meditation, although it can come as a result of successful and spiritual meditation. Personally I think that the Presence of God may find another synonymous term, and it will be our CONTEMPLATION; for nothing less, or different will satisfy our intuition.

We have now reached the last part of this chapter, the practical methods of which are useful in order to raise one's consciousness to the peaks of Contemplation. How can it be done?

While not taking any prerogative of exclusiveness, I can point out some path on which the Aim can be reached, as experience teaches us. In order to CONTEMPLATE, you first have to develop your Meditation, or mute Prayer to the point where they transcend the realm of thoughts. This is the condition.

Then your own conception of the Supreme, without verbalizing in your mind, must take the place of the former aim of your meditation and so remain: *immovable, unchangeable* and *formless*.

The conditions are similar to those of *Samadhi*, and be sure that Contemplation, like that Superconsciousness, will not come either easily, or quickly, unless you are close to sainthood, or Realization of your true Self. But in this case you do not need any instruction, for the eternal Source of Wisdom, present in every human being, although veiled and hidden in the majority of men, will then teach you directly everything you may need on this degree of development.

On the other hand, do not fall into pessimism or scepticism, for both sublime states (sainthood or Self-Realization) are *attainable*. And on this earth, in this period, there are living men who have reached them. But they do not boast of this, nor do they write this fact on their foreheads, so that others may recognize them! They may live like other people and only those who have developed in themselves some subtle 'senses' (actually, these are rather a spiritual sensitivity, of course), may be able to recognize their advanced brothers. And they will keep silent about their incredible discovery, aware of the dangers of 'casting pearls before swine', as Christ warned us.

CHAPTER XXXII

Mystical Powers in Contemplation

WE are now confronted by an amazing truth, supported by innumerable facts from the lives of spiritually advanced men on this earth. We all know about the miracles of Christ, and those of His Saints and the martyrs. In the Eastern Initiation there is voluminous literature in the Hindu Sacred books about the powers of their Rishis and Yogis. All of these cannot be flatly rejected with an absolute 'no'. While there is always the possibility that some legends have been added to the basic facts, superphysical phenomena cannot be disregarded by those who take the trouble to investigate and verify these facts.

However, this is not the place to divert our attention from the main subject and therefore, I will pass directly to that mystical Law, which rules the energy we call 'consciousness' in us. The Great Rishi Ramana, when speaking about the miracles of Christ, clearly expressed this truth of the DYNAMIC POWER OF CONSCIOUSNESS, AS BEING THE FULCRUM OF ALL MIRACLES, that is, acts performed beyond all known physical laws. This is what you have to realize: the basis of all supernatural phenomena is the ACTIVE CONSCIOUSNESS, which operates them. Taken superficially, this is only a confirmation of the axiom that: SPIRIT RULES MATTER. But these words often become a trivial statement, which is not much believed in the turmoil of the outer world. We are liable to pass over them without really understanding their actual meaning.

What we need is an explanation and examples.

'Jesus, the man, was utterly unconscious of being a separate finite personality, when He worked His miracles and spoke His wonderful words. It was White Light, the Life, which is the Cause and Effect, acting in perfect concert. MY FATHER AND I ARE ONE.' So spoke the one, who himself had the highest spiritual experience accessible to man in his earthly life. It was the Maharshi, the last Great Indian Rishi, who rendered homage to Christ, and who was more fitted in this epoch to pronounce these great and beautiful words? He knew, and he spoke the language of true Wisdom.

In this short sentence we find everything we need, apart from our own study in the previous chapters of this work. You know a lot about the powers contained in the *Hyperconsciousness*, generated by right meditation and finalized in Contemplation, which is just the merging of the human consciousness in the 'Sea of God', as the Maharshi also told us. We heard of the power of true *Faith*, which can move mountains. But do you know WHAT that FAITH is? I presume you are ripe enough—especially if you have studied *Theurgy*—in order not to confound 'beliefs' with FAITH, which is a Power not connected with the mental theories, which form those beliefs.

I do not like to dogmatize, therefore I will not express my own innermost conviction in that matter. But if you realize that, deep in your *heart* (the mind is absolutely inadequate for this great task) what the *Hyperconsciousness* is like and what state of awareness true *Faith* is, then you may reach the same conclusion, which is the IDENTITY OF BOTH. '*Everything is possible for him who has Faith.*'

In this or another way, one is compelled to reach a final conclusion, that THE CONSCIOUSNESS, ITS STATE, IS THE REAL FACTOR RULING THE UNIVERSE. In its ultimate meaning, it is the infinite consciousness of the Creator, penetrating every atom in the illimitable Cosmos, and being the ultimate substratum of every thing and every happening. That is why, when instructing humanity, all Great Souls were so definite in insisting on the *reformation and resurrection* (from the deadly sleep in matter) of the *human soul* (that is, the consciousness in us), as being the only action which counts here and in all other worlds.

Explaining to us the relation of Christ to the *Father*, the Rishi Ramana has shown to us the Truth of Spiritual Power. It was nothing unusual for him, as Advaita Vedanta, the highest philosophical system in his own country—India, is based on just that UNITY of Spirit, which many nominal Christians have almost forgotten.

Now it may be clear to you, why all the widening and strengthening of consciousness in us also leads to acquisition of

Power. It is an *Initiation*, expressed in a few words, but those ripe enough and who have eyes to see and ears to hear, will make full use of it! Now you see, that in Contemplation, which is a powerful leap ahead for us, there are contained forces, about which ignorant people have no idea whatsoever.

We call these forces 'mystical' because, for the majority of contemporary humanity, they are mysterious, or even problematical, but for those who have approached close to them, they are a living reality.

They cannot be exhibited cheaply, or in order to impress. They belong to the sacrosanct core of the human spirit, for which all the visible and perishable world around is just 'like a shadow', to quote the words of the Maharshi.

CHAPTER XXXIII

The Possibility of Miracles

THE basic laws which rule over the happenings, which humanity calls 'miracles' have been explained in the former chapters. It remains only to clarify the matter and give examples. Everywhere, where there are powers acting beyond the limitations of the physical laws, there must be an advanced CONSCIOUSNESS acting behind them.

I have read reports about some 'miraculous' cures at Lourdes, and not from any nervous or similar disorders, which could be explained in many ways other than those of supernatural actions. There have been cases, established beyond all doubt by specialist doctors concerning malignant changes in bodily matter, visible even to the eyes of a layman, which were removed in minutes and with full recovery of the dying patient. Interested people may find details in the writings of Dr Carrel describing a miracle at Lourdes, published a few years ago in an English translation, fragments of which appeared in the popular *Reader's Digest*. My personal experience in 1949, showed that a man, who was undoubtedly suffering pathological changes in his lungs, confirmed by X-rays in the writer's country and accompanied by all the well-known symptoms of tuberculosis, after meditation and prayer at the tomb of a local Muslim Saint in Tiruvannamalai (the abode of the late Maharshi), *next day* obtained an X-ray picture of a completely clear chest which allowed him to leave India forthwith.

Everyone knows that such a disease cannot possibly disappear without any trace in twenty-four hours, together with all its outer symptoms, such as fever, pain, weakness, and so on, and never return again.

In this case it was once more a radical change in the *material structure* of the affected organs (lungs), which otherwise, in the case of a 'natural' cure by special treatment and drugs, takes many months (if not years) and, what is more important, can always be diagnosed later because of the remaining scars and calcified tubercles, visible in all subsequent X-ray examinations. In this case, twenty-four hours was sufficient to eradicate all trace of them.

It also happened that I was able to observe another 'miracle' with my own eyes, despite the fact that I was very critically minded as regards the experiment I will now describe.

During my stay in India, I occasionally visited a town, where a famous fakir exhibited his powers. This time he was walking on a bed of glowing charcoal, several feet long. The man, a conventional-looking, dark-skinned, tall Hindu, sat quietly in the lotus position as if in deep meditation and very evidently performed intense pranayama, while the coals were prepared and arranged into a bed about seven yards long. Finally, when everything was ready, he rose with his arms crossed on his chest, eyes turned upwards and stepped slowly on to the fiery bed. I observed every one of his movements intently and saw only, that his feet were firmly buried among the glowing coals every time he transferred the weight of his body from one to the other, just as in normal, very slow walking.

There was no smell of burning flesh, nor were his feet hot or damaged, when he finished that fantastic walk. I later read in London newspapers, about a similar experiment made by the same man in England, in the presence of many doctors and other people, who were strong disbelievers in such 'miracles'. No explanation was ever offered, only the plain, unvarnished facts.

For me, of course, these facts provided no 'miracle' at all. I had long since known about the power, which certain states of consciousness can exercise over material events. The fakir used a certain inner attitude, most probably connected with a high degree of concentration and performed dhyana, which allowed him to make the skin of his feet temporarily impervious to certain physical factors, in this case—intense heat.

But what I am trying to convey in his chapter is the fact that, as we read in Chapter XXXII, consciousness can decidedly affect physical matter.

For what purpose am I quoting examples of this Law and their explanations? Well, you are now on the threshold of the study of meditation, which undoubtedly is aimed at influencing, or even transforming your consciousness and to make you aware of things, which you previously did not know about. I believe, that the student should know as much as possible, and that is why I am delving into examples and their explanations in the two concluding chapters of this book.

Accordingly, an inevitable warning must be sounded. Your aim must firmly remain as the development of your awareness, which is in accordance with the law of evolution or spiritual progress. In doing so, a man fulfils the will of his *Father*, his *Maker*, and he is entitled to know it and to ask for assistance in such a virtuous undertaking.

It will be granted to him, if he does not allow himself to be blinded by the foolish desire to *obtain the powers* as the foremost aim of his efforts. If he does, he is digging a pit for himself. For it has been verily told to all of us: 'SEEK YE THEREFORE FIRST THE KINGDOM OF GOD, AND HIS JUSTICE, AND ALL THESE THINGS SHALL BE ADDED UNTO YOU.'

* * *

You already know that the real power beyond all manifestations of life in the universe is that of CONSCIOUSNESS, which can also be termed SPIRIT. It is the only creative Power, which is responsible for EXISTENCE, as we know it, and also beyond all our knowledge. Because of the difficulty (actually, close to impossibility) of defining it, attempts have been made by those who were able to contact IT more closely than others, to give IT names more accessible to the human mind and its language. Hence we find an astonishing example in the Gospel of St John, where he call IT—the VERB, or—the WORD-LOGOS. This Word has created everything, that is, the Central Cliché of the universe as a whole.

This means, in its ultimate development and as a logical consequence, that the Laws ruling the universe, and among them those few which we have been able to 'discover', belong to the same Creation, and the Power imposing them may also well act beyond, and above them. We must realize this truth beyond any doubt in our minds, for otherwise we will be unable to follow the next statements.

Therefore, to us, living in the realm of certain Laws, which we can see as firm and unchangeable, everything transcending these Laws appears to be a *miracle*.

But miracles may have not just one, but TWO explanations:

(1) They are the result of the application of some Laws of a superior kind, UNKNOWN to us in our limited world.

(2) They may be the results of a direct act of the *Creative Consciousness*, which imposed those Laws, but which is above all of its creation and Laws.

In former chapters we said enough about the role of *Consciousness* and its ruling over matter, in order not to repeat it here again. Therefore the final confirmation, that Consciousness-Spirit (I mean the ABSOLUTE CONSCIOUSNESS, not just any limited one, belonging to separate beings) is the *omnipotent factor*, will be easier for you to realize and to accept.

In trying to explain this idea, the Maharshi used the simile of the *screen* and the *pictures* appearing on it. This unchangeable SCREEN he said, is the SELF (His term for Spirit-God) and the manifestation of the world forms the pictures on IT, which do not exist apart from that screen, but the screen can exist even without them.

Another basic idea, that the *all-penetrating, omnipresent* creative Consciousness is omnipotent because of these two attributes, may also require some deep meditation in order to be realized by you. But this realization IS accessible, for many have reached it, thereby achieving peace and wisdom for ever.

Now we are close to the realization of the possibility of existence of that which we call (not too accurately)—*miracles*. *Their range depends solely upon the range of consciousness, operating behind them.* The Maharshi, in speaking about miracles and the teachings of Christ, expressed just such a similar idea, when he attributed them to Christ's unity with the Father, meaning the ultimate possible extension of consciousness and, consequently, the *ultimate in miracles*.

We cannot call Christ's actions other than miracles since they showed complete mastership over matter and its manifestations. The reviving of a decaying corpse, the transmutation of water, the transformation of a small amount of food into an enormous quantity of it, quite apart from the innumerable cures, which also required changes in the structure of living matter, all of

which belong to that supreme category of the POWER OF CON-
SCIOUSNESS, which dominates everything.

Now we come to a most interesting conclusion. A certain
gradation of miracles must exist in accordance with and propor-
tionally to the greatness of the Consciousness operating in them.
And in this we have the necessary examples in the lives and
miracles of advanced human beings even on our own earth.

Western and Eastern Saints supply enough material for
investigation, for those who are interested in this subject. It
means that, through the development of the Light of Consciousness in us, we may approach closer to both theses, mentioned in
items 1 and 2 in the middle of this chapter.

Also we find that:

(a) We may become acquainted with laws so far unknown to us.
(b) We may participate in the Consciousness-Spirit, being the
    beginning and the ruler of every thing existing.

Some people, perhaps, may retire in the face of such a statement. Well, there is no factual conviction in such a matter,
except a man's own ability to raise his consciousness beyond the
average level and operate in the realm of intuition (knowledge
without thinking).

But for those who are very 'incredulous' I would like to drop
a small hint: do you know, that all that we are performing
in our three dimensional world would be an unbroken chain of
miracles to, say, a being limited to only two dimensions? And
further, that many mathematicians and philosophers have
expressed ideas about the necessary existence of more than just
our three dimensions?

But a single application of a law, with its possibility of belonging to a 'superior dimension' would inevitably be connected with
a score of 'miracles' for us, unacquainted with, and not existing
in those dimensions. Also, for beings, living in them, our most
advanced techniques, such as space travel and atomic energy
included, would appear like clumsy inventions and conditions
of life of stone-age men.

I have given the foregoing to my readers as certain material
for independent thinking and they should find their own
solutions to it. You already know about the possibility of
influencing matter by certain operations of the human conscious-

ness, based on recent records, such as the story of the fakir, walking on glowing charcoal.

The development of our abilities of cognition, judgement and spiritual Realization depend upon our own efforts, and for that purpose a practical study of meditation is the chief means.

For those who are mathematically minded I am providing a few hints here about the possibilities connected with the existence of dimensions superior to our, as we believe, own well-known three.

We will first refer to elementary geometry. A point, which can be defined as an intersection of two (or more) lines, has no dimensions in itself, it cannot be measured, or compared with others, since all points are equally deprived of any size.

But this non-material conception contributes to the formation of our FIRST dimension: move the point, and it will trace a line, a geometric element which already has a measurable factor. *This is its length*, its only dimension.

How can we form the next dimension in the simplest way, using the first as a starting point? Only by putting another line at one end of our original one in a perpendicular direction to it, and then moving the second line along until it comes to the other end of the first. We will see that this operation has traced a new figure—a rectangular one. For the purpose of simplification in these experiments, let us always take a length considered as a '*unit*', such as an inch, a foot, and so on. Then the new figure, already having TWO dimensions (length and width) will for, a unit of area, or surface, be equal to a square inch, or a square foot, according to the linear measure used by us.

But our world extends even beyond these two dimensions and if we repeat the process of forming a new unit, we will have to add another one to our square, along and perpendicular to the side of that square and move it again in the same position until we reach the opposite side. Looking at the figure thus traced, we will see it forms a CUBE, having THREE dimensions: length, width and depth. Once more it will be a unit in its own realm, a cubic inch, foot, or some other measurement.

This third dimension terminates the world in which we believe we live in this life.

Is it the end? Apparently not: for several mathematicians and almost all occultists insist that there must be still higher dimensions, inaccessible to our senses, just as, for a two-dimensional being (if such would exist), our three-dimensional world would appear only like a cross-section of it with the basic, perfectly flat and illimitable surface (area) being the aspect of the two-dimensional world. Thus our cube will be only a square, a ball only a circle, to a two-dimensional being, and if we trace a closed line around such a being, we will enclose it as if in a prison with impenetrable walls. This is because, having no third dimension (here, like the thickness of a line) the perfectly flat creature would be in no position to separate itself from its flat world.

Now comes our crucial point. Let us seek the next dimension by using (which is only logical, since we are aware of the law about the formation of dimensions) a similar method (see Figs. 7 to 10).

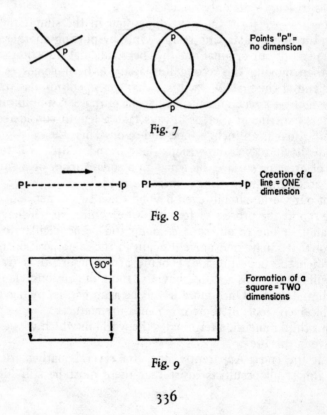

Points "P" = no dimension

Fig. 7

Creation of a line = ONE dimension

Fig. 8

Formation of a square = TWO dimensions

Fig. 9

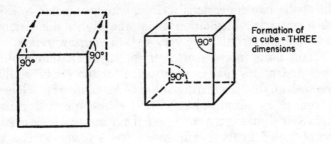

Formation of
a cube = THREE
dimensions

Schemes of dimensions

Fig. 10

Take a unit of our actual highest dimension, that is, a cube, add another, similar one to it and move this in the perpendicular direction as was done with the formation of the cube and square.

You may say that it is unthinkable! Well, but a two-dimensional being would profess exactly the same when spoken to about the cube or other three-dimensional body, refusing to believe in their existence! Yet we will disagree and remain with our 'superior' knowledge of things, holding the cube in our hands as proof.

In this way we may well live in a limited world, which is only a cross-section of a superior dimension, and so imagine that anything else is impossible.

P. D. Ouspensky, a thinker of considerable depth, tried to reconcile occult phenomena with science and proposed to explain the 'miracles' as actions deriving from superior dimensions. He believed them to extend to five or even six. We may see, that a being say, from the *fourth* dimension, would be able to play tricks on us, similar to those we might do to two-dimensional beings, as I just mentioned. Some occultists of good standing accept that there are separate dimensions for the Astral and Mental worlds, which seems to be logical. This will explain why, in occultism, the physical world is conceived of as a reflection of the Astral, which possesses a much wider extent and possibilities than the former. Mediumistic and other phenomena connected with the appearance and disappearance of solid objects, and so on, may be analogous to our removing of them from the

337

sight of the two-dimensional beings, who are unable to explain such a 'miracle'. Meditation about the higher dimensions, as given here, may contribute very well to your awareness.

Certain hints in the matter of special meditation about the higher dimensions may appear useful for those who really are interested in this fascinating subject. Alas, 'interest' alone will not suffice: a formidable ability for abstruse and clear-cut, imaginative thinking is a condition, if a reasonable hope of success is to be raised in us. I will give a well-known exercise as an example, which is very effective in spite of its apparent simplicity, which, at the same time, is a good test of the abilities of an aspirant, trying to 'peep' into the next dimension.

(1) Take a small box, say, a match-box, or something similar. Look intently *inside* it and study it, so that every detail will be firmly impressed on your mind and you can then recreate it in your imagination in full, when you are not actually looking into the box. It is not easy, I know, but no important undertaking, which is rich in results has ever been easy!

(2) When you have finished with the 'inside' of your box and can build an exact picture of it in your mind, pass to a study of its *outer* surface, exactly as you did with the '*inside*'. Check the results carefully, so that the new picture is just like the first (see No. 1), clear-cut and definite.

(3) Now comes the actual test: try to get a *simultaneous* picture in your mind of the inside and outside of your box. If you succeed, you have enriched yourself with a certain enlargement of consciousness, which leads to a realization of the possibility of higher dimensions.

This exercise may take a lot of time (weeks or months) if it is to be performed as intended. And it is quite possible that you will feel yourself completely unable to perform it. Then leave it alone, nobody can exceed his actual powers, and it is not essential.

Most probably, you would like to hear how a unit of, say, the *fourth* dimension may look in relation to its predecessor, the cube. Well, it must be built by the creation of a body, which will be simultaneously perpendicular to all the surfaces of our cube, as our former deliberations about the three known dimensions and their formation have shown us. Only a mathematically skilled mind may see such a possibility clearly.

The problem is up to you to decide and try it for yourself.

Incidentally, this 'fantastic', four-dimensional unit, derived from a cube, is often called 'THE TESSARACT'.

EPILOGUE

AFTER you have finished the reading of this book two possibilities can arise. You may not be interested in the practical use of its contents and consider it to be only a current theory for study, which finds no response in you. In such a case this Epilogue will add little to the chapters you have left behind you. But, some of my readers may find, in this manual, something for which they have been seeking, and in it they may see the path, leading to their long sought for attainment. For those I have a few words to say.

As with every study, MEDITATION requires endurance on the part of the student. It will be harder, perhaps, because this will be your own, your private study, which will give you no official, or bread-winning diplomas, like our usual degrees. Here is no sanction for unsuccessful learning, just as in worldly schools, where you may not obtain the certificates vital for your material well-being.

Apart from the undoubtedly growing interest in meditation and prayer, we also have to observe an undercurrent, an extremely harmful one directed by the forces of Evil. It takes most treacherous outer forms, and misguided intellectual deliberations are one aspect of it. It is nothing new. Long ago non-believers tried to advance the idea, that 'because of God's obvious *omniscience* and *omnipotence*, all "interfering" with both of these on the part of human beings is undesirable and even void. Nobody can teach the Supreme what It should do', and so on.

This 'logic' can convince only very shallow-thinking men, deprived any spiritual light and being close to thinking like automatons. Such a 'philosophy' tries to deprive us of our most treasured value—PRAYER, as a natural form of the relation of man to his Creator. But this theory defeats itself.

If we should not ask the Almighty about anything, as being

His children praying to their Father, then what sort of relation to Him has to be accepted? Certainly, we are unable to *order* Him to do anything, nor would any sane man accept the relation of *equality* with Him, as with our fellow men.

Only nothingness, or the absence of any relations remains and this is the obvious aim of those, who try to dissuade us from the power of prayer.

They will 'kindly' speak about the abstruse and barren 'non-personal' approach to God, for they know that it would be only a lifeless, negative attitude. And so, by putting forward an abstract and indefinite mental effort as their ultimate aim, they undermine the natural tendency of the human heart: *to adore the Supreme with love,* presenting this as being something 'primitive and unworthy'.

You know about 'mute meditation and prayer', and you most certainly can see, that such ability is not arrived at from today to tomorrow, but *is a* PEAK, *attainable only after intensive work.*

To put to all and sundry an actually unattainable aim, no matter how 'sublime' it may be, means nothing else than preventing one from any intermediary steps, which are absolutely necessary and essential for every achievement. For, when an unripe person tries to leap ahead, far beyond his possibilities, the sole result will be disappointment and frustration. Both are our deadly enemies.

And yet, when I look into the past, I find that the reverses which ensue from non-endurance in the study of meditation, do exist, although on a different level. How frustrated I would feel had I abandoned, many years ago, the study of concentration and meditation, so tedious in the beginning, which later were to play such a deciding role in the forming of my inner world.

In this endeavour we men are all alike! We may react differently to losing, or winning some materialistic business, but in the spiritual realm we cannot afford to lose. We can only delay, and this delay is a very costly business in itself.

In our last hour we will invariably remember the lost opportunities and the bitterness of this awareness may follow us into our further wanderings, in other worlds and under other conditions.

For truly, man is just his CONSCIOUSNESS, and he takes it it with him beyond what here we call—his grave.

The formation and enlightening of this consciousness is the highest thing that a man can undertake, for in this matter there is no limitation of age, sex or any outer condition. The only deciding thing is the INNER LIGHT in a man, which enlightens his paths during his incarnations. A strong will and power of endurance are the INNER CONDITIONS upon which depends success, or failure.

That is why I am putting so much emphasis on them. If you do not have them in you in any appreciable quantity, my admonition will not help you, as it will remain without any answer in you. But if you are on the point of choosing your way, and if you were interested in the thirty-three chapters you have just read, then this Epilogue may be the grain, which will tip the scale of your decision.

Perhaps, the cliché of your future Attainment was waiting until you became acquainted with the material expounded here and consequently, it is now facing you.

You already know how to act in the presence of a desired cliché. But do not forget that, if not accepted, it does not remain indefinitely! It can be lost, as well as won.

Usually, seekers are perplexed and anxious in their problems, questions, doubts, and failures, until they find the real Path and start to walk on it. They cannot walk without the assistance of that powerful walking stick, which is successful study, allowing us to dominate our mind and to take our destiny into our own hands. One of the most effective means of study will be that of meditation, if you are not devoted to Theurgy, that is, to the Path of Worship.

Then know, that success in both, means full and final delivery from all the aforementioned afflictions. Those who succeeded have no problems, uncertainty, doubts or fears: all of them being burned in the fire of Inner Wisdom, which comes when a man participates in the Great Consciousness, lifting him beyond the reach of all troubles.

This 'miracle' will not be written on your forehead, and most probably no one other than yourself will ever know about it. But what does it matter? Can someone else live your life and can you be liberated by the sole fact, that another has achieved It?

The most intimate, perennial and sublime element in a man—

his CONSCIOUSNESS-SPIRIT belongs only to the man, and it is that 'Dew-drop which finally falls into the Sea of Allness'.

The study of awareness, which has been partly expounded in the present work, is perhaps one of the most fascinating of subjects for many scientifically-minded readers. For them I would like to add the following account of my own first-hand experiences with the so-called hallucinogenic drugs, which are now much in use in practical psychiatry and psychology.

I undertook the experiment because it was, and is, my presumption, that physical means (here referring to the drugs), being material factors, can influence only the material counterpart of man, in this case his brain and nervous system, perhaps through the enzymic changes and other conditions, known better to the medical world. As the thinking processes are undoubtedly connected with the brain, it seems to be logical that they may be similarly affected by the drugs. Therefore, the possibility and justification of hallucinations in the form of visions, and so on, cannot be logically denied.

But what will happen if a human being is able to transcend the usual compulsory activity of his mind without, in the slightest, losing his awareness of life, of continuous existence as such?

Before I started my experiment with the drugs, I did not believe that they would be able to involve me in any involuntary mental processes, of which visions, and so on, are a major part. But experience alone could give the categorical answer. So, to that end, I arranged for a session with three friends, all of whom were doctors and each having had personal experience with Psilocybin and Mescalin.

The first dose of 15 mg. of Psilocybin, taken orally, was probably insufficient. Apart from tension in the ears and deformation of the faces of those present little else occurred. I was quite conscious of everything and was even able to start a game of chess on the suggestion of one of the doctors. There were no visions, nor any emotional, or mental disturbances.

However, it was the second test, to which I invited two of the doctors from the first one and a psychologist (who had had personal experience with the drug L.S.D.) to ensure full control, which proved to be successful.

Denis (one of the doctors) took all the necessary precautions, duly testing my heart, blood pressure and lungs and finally declared me completely fit to proceed. This time the dose was much stronger, being about 24 mg. The antidote, in the event that I would want to interrupt the action of the drug, was placed ready, along with a small glass of brandy just in case nausea might become unbearable, as sometimes happens with certain people. Ronald, the psychologist, said that he would like to make tests when the drug started to act. We waited and talked for about twenty minutes. Then I started to feel the effects of the drug: strong pressure in the ears, connected with the first feeling of slight nausea in the region of the solar plexus. Then the faces of those around me appeared to become about twenty years older: noses elongated, chins sharpened and there were peculiar expressions of savagery in certain moments. But this occurred only when I allowed the drug to hallucinate me. However, at any moment, an effort of will was all that was necessary to restore the outer world to its normal form. Dr Eva, who had had a similar experience, stated that she could not stop the illusions. 'But I can easily,' I told her, 'and according to what you say, my dose was larger than yours.'

By now Ronald, with his pencil in his hand was asking me to describe the room, as I saw it under the first stages of the drug. 'Nothing changed,' I answered. 'I only feel as if levitation is taking over my body, but only so far as I permit it. I can stop it whenever I wish.'

We four then sat and talked quietly, while my wife was absent preparing dinner, which was served two hours later, around 8 p.m. in the same room. Meanwhile, nausea had become more insistent and unpleasant, although by no means beyond endurance. I mentioned this to Denis and he measured my pulse and checked my pupils. 'All right!' he declared. 'But if you are very uncomfortable you can take a little brandy at any time and put an end to it.'

Another twenty minutes elapsed and I felt nothing except more nausea. 'Probably this test is also a flop,' I said to my friends. 'I think I had better take the brandy and finish the business.'

'You are probably immune to the drug,' said Ronald, 'for in my practice this is the first time that a patient has reacted (or rather not reacted) in such a way.'

'Quite possibly!' said Denis. 'Or it may be your subconscious resistance, because you can stop your mental functions at will.'

I wanted to reply and then it happened! Next moment I was as if beyond the room and beyond my own personality. Fully conscious and with eyes closed, I was aware of my body as if from a great distance, while it sat quietly on the divan, but I was in no way connected with it. I knew that everything was well with it, but its pulse was imperceptible to ME. I saw nothing, neither darkness, nor light. An overwhelming feeling of happiness, no, much more, of a great bliss embraced all my being. It was full of absolute peace, beyond time and the slightest thought, or emotion. I was merged as if in a crystal-like, immaterial substance, being, at the same time, my true awareness, I was inseparable from IT, IT was ALL! By which means did I record all of this? It was not by any thinking, it was direct knowledge, beyond any mental processes. I knew that I could speak, if required and could hear words directed to me by my friends around the table, a yard or so from me. And I made a firm decision—NOT TO FORGET THIS EXPERIENCE FOR ANY PRICE. Then I ordered my distant (but, at the same time, very close when I wished) body to speak. 'It has happened!' I said. 'I am in that State, beyond all and everything, but I am alive and aware more than ever. I cannot compare the powerful bliss of this State with anything, it is beyond all words and thoughts. Forgive me if I am speaking slowly, but I do not feel any desire to talk. It is for the purpose of the experiment that I am speaking. But I must choose every word. It is quite different to the ordinary state of consciousness.'

'We can understand you very well,' Ronald's voice said, 'do not talk if it is painful for you!'

'Painful for me?' How could anything painful touch me now? My nausea was forgotten and I knew that my body was over-flowing with well-being.

'Ask me anything that is required for your records,' I said.

'Well!' said Ronald, 'let us make an introductory test. Can you see this room and us, and if so, how do you perceive everything in it?'

I opened my eyes and said: 'Everything is normal, no visions. But, when I close my eyes again, I know that in order to remain centred in this wonderful world of Reality in which I am now, I must avoid using my physical sight. It is not necessary as I can see your faces even through closed eyelids, if I so wish. Aloofness, blissful freedom and absolute harmony, this is an infinitesimal part of my present state, which I can describe in words. It is similar to my first experience of spiritual consciousness, experienced in the summer of 1949, at the feet of an Indian Rishi—Ramana. Later, the same state was induced many times by deep meditation, based on complete concentration of the mind, by excluding every thought, but it always required stillness of the body, separation from all the senses and the impossibility of speaking, hearing, or moving. And all the time one is compelled to be watchful, in order not to be thrown back into the physical world, because of interrupted concentration. But now, it is all so simple, so effortless! I am that concentration itself, and when I do contact the abandoned world, it is only a concession, like stepping down for a while.'

'Have you a deeper feeling of knowledge of our individualities, more sympathetic, perhaps?' asked Ronald.

I looked through my closed eyelids and said: 'Rather no, for I do not see your personalities, your perishable expressions, but just that, which you really are, beyond all limitations, as I am now.' And I felt an overwhelming desire to unite all of them, as they sat around that table, in my magic orb of absolute consciousness, of that indescribable peace and bliss. Then I said slowly, with due gravity: 'Come to me here, into this state of Truth, of Eternity, be with me, as blissful as I am!'

Ronald said: 'We will try, I think that I have some idea of your present experience, as I lived through something similar, but briefly and perhaps incomplete.'

Then Denis spoke: 'I wish to be with you, it must be so wonderful!'

And I felt that my will was being fulfilled, at least, in part, for Ronald's face became so solemn, inspired, head aimed upwards, eyes closed. Denis held his head in his hands, evidently concentrating strongly and with tenseness, while Eva had a half smile on her face, silent, but evidently tuned to our magic circle. Silence followed and this silence could persist for ever: who would like to interrupt this spiritual inheritance made accessible to us? I have found the Thing, the only important one, before which everything else is only illusion and a fleeting mist. I told this to my three friends and said: 'Try to find it, it is beyond everything, when you have IT, nothing is needed any more. Everything is illusion, except that State of Truth!'

My senses seemed to become sharper. I heard the whisper between Ronald and Denis: 'I have never seen anything similar, it is so different from all my former tests and we have had more than 200 of them to date!'

'He must see the clichés,' said Denis, 'I will ask him.'

Then I heard his voice, close to my ear, so that the others could not hear. 'Can you tell me about my former incarnation? What awaits me in the future? Did Christ travel widely before His three years of ministry? Do you see the fact that some say that Christ had brothers? Did the Virgin Mary really have other children apart from Jesus?'

I knew that these questions could be answered, but were they necessary? Having lost my own personality and being absolutely free from all limitations of the individual, narrow life, how could I merge again into the world of relativity, inquiries, desires? If all of that did not exist for me, it should be that way for my friends. They would not be elevated by satisfying their curiosity.

I explained this to Denis and he reluctantly accepted my point of view. But there was something I had to tell him, for Truth compelled me to do so.

'Denis, know that Christ never left Palestine, and that the Virgin Mary had no physical relations with any man.'

'How can that be,' I heard him say.

'You wanted the truth and I have told it to you. That is all!'

By then I was aware of the smell of food in the room. It was probably the soup, which my wife had brought to the table. My body's senses registered everything, but I could not even think about eating. However, I had no objection to the others taking food. I was actually living in two worlds: this real one, full of eternal bliss, my true fatherland, my state when I will finally leave my body, and that outer world, extending beyond my closed eyelids. A slight movement, and I returned back to it. But I did not wish to. I felt that I must take this real world back into my everyday life, which still awaited me when the hours of Light were over. Yes! I would be able to do so, I would never be the same man as before!

Some formal tests followed. I answered all the questions,

slowly and willingly, but always as if from an infinite distance, as if from another galaxy, or planet. I knew that I had lost the ability to be inimical to anybody: I simply could not find such a feeling any more. Was I in God? But once more, that was a word, a limitation, no longer acceptable to me. Eternity, Truth, Love, Harmony, Peace, Bliss—if they are His attributes, then I was in Him. I did not know anything more, but If I wished I could know everything, that was certain! Only, there was nothing in me which would inquire about anything. I am—that is all, for ever!

'Have you any feeling of time?' asked Ronald. 'Tell me, how long do you think you were in that State?'

Without imagining any clock face with its hands, I said simply: 'It must have been an hour or so.'

'That is correct!' I heard his voice confirm.

Then they ate their dinner, while I remained in my new world. I felt that I was gradually 'coming back'. But, even this process was so natural and painless, that I was almost unable to perceive it. I would never be as I was before, so why worry about the 'return'?

Then I sat with open eyes, while the four people at the table ate their dessert. A chair, which had been reserved for me was empty, so I went over and sat down on it.

Together we tried to draw conclusions from my experience.

'If your state was basically similar to those you had previously, by your own efforts, then the drug was like a back-door to the same temple, giving access without toil and effort,' said Ronald wittily.

'Yes, it seems so to me,' I replied. 'But that back-door can stay open only for those, who have been in the temple before, entering through the front one by their own labour.'

'What then is the actual role of the drug?' asked Denis.

'Judging from the fact, that the majority of people who take it have no spiritual experience, but simply visions and hallucinations, which augment their own mental faculties and memories, it would seem that the drugs merely perform the functions of a magnifying glass, operating on the existing values in man. But they cannot "create", or "add" anything. There is no wisdom to be achieved by drugs, and no revelation can be produced.

'Nevertheless, in cases where the individual has been able to eliminate his mind's consciousness before the experience, as in my own case, the magnifying glass is unable to catch any "object". Instead, the drug evidently contributes to the suppression of all the lower functions in man, just as the efforts at concentration and meditation did before, and then it leaves the man facing his own imperishable counterpart, his spiritual Self. An apparent privilege is, that then we are not compelled to enter into any trance, as some yogis and occultists do, in order to experience the highest and, without losing our spiritual State, we can communicate with our environment with mutual profit. And still there remains something in us, which makes the next experiences easier, even without any drug.'

But can we recommend the use of these drugs to all and sundry? It would be the greatest mistake and nonsense, as we may see from the foregoing. Only a few, who have been able to exclude the whimsies of their minds for good beforehand, can count on true spiritual experience. For all the others, the magnifying glass of the drug will only enlarge their weaknesses and frailties. No man of common sense would enter on to such a useless and dangerous path. That is what we have to know.

THE END

BIBLIOGRAPHY

(Books to consult in conjunction with *Meditation*,
as recommended by the writer.)

ASHTAVAKRA GITA (Translated by Hari Prasad Shastri).

AUROBINDO, Sri Ghose, *Selected Thoughts*.

BHAGAVAD-GITA (Texts from Lin Yutang's *Wisdom of India*).

DHAMMAPADA (Texts from Lin Yutang's *Wisdom of India*).

MAHARSHI, Sri Ramana, Teachings (published before 1950 only).

KANT, Immanuel, *Aphorisms*.

NOLA, Alphonso M. Di, *Prayers of Man*.

PLOTINUS, *Enneads*.

SADHU, Mouni—Trilogy (*In Days of Great Peace; Concentration; Samadhi*); *Theurgy: the Art of Effective Worship; Ways to Self-Realization*.

SANKARACHARYA, Viveka-Chudamani (*The Crest Jewel of Wisdom*) (Translated by Mohini M. Chatterji).

SÉDIR, Paul, *Initiations*.

THE SERMON ON THE MOUNT, Christ's Gospels.

THOMAS A KEMPIS, *The Imitation of Christ*.

'WHO', *Maha Yoga*.

INDEX

Balance 22, 74, 112, 234, 251, 264, 265, 307
Beauty 20, 165, 225, 296
Belief 96, 129, 135, 264, 328
Bhagavad Gita 297, 302, 303, 307, 308
Bhakti 115,156
Bible 29, 256, 257, 286
Binary(ies) 21, 185, 205, 232, 311
Birth 33, 186
Black occultism *see* Occultism
Blasphemy 130
Bliss 66, 167, 169, 170, 175, 183, 234, 235, 241, 246, 269, 287, 300, 306, 309, 311, 312, 320, 346, 347, 349
Bodhisattva 54
Body 23, 31, 36, 37, 38, 44, 50, 57, 62, 63, 64, 69, 71, 74, 77, 79, 80, 81, 92, 93, 110, 112, 113, 115, 134, 135, 138, 163, 166, 178, 181, 183, 194, 197, 206, 207, 208, 211, 233, 236, 246, 249, 251, 257, 264, 266, 267, 273, 294, 307, 348
Bondage 188, 309
Brahma 259
Brahman 309, 311
Brain 12, 19, 20, 21, 23, 41, 42, 43, 47, 71, 72, 73, 113, 121, 136, 139, 140, 175, 190, 194, 249, 344
Breathing 34
Buddha 174, 175, 177, 180, 181, 182, 188, 198, 259, 295
Buddhism 28, 41, 79, 174
Bungling 38, 202

Caesar 21, 190, 192, 293
Calculus 23, 217
Caricature 104
Carrell, Dr 330
Cat 78
Catalepsy 92, 246
Catherine II 269
Catholic 28
Causation 241, 301
Cause and effect 181, 243, 287
Certainty 65, 74, 158, 174, 187, 206, 217, 265
Chain of Initiates 27
Charity 284, 295, 325
Choice 25, 38, 54, 207, 209, 210, 251
Christ 87, 93, 96, 149, 156, 175, 180,
182, 191, 198, 215, 216, 217, 223, 225, 226, 228, 230, 231, 232, 234, 236, 240, 247, 267, 268, 270, 275, 279, 290, 293, 295, 300, 301, 302, 303, 307, 326, 327, 328, 333, 348
Christian 28, 41, 116, 171, 180, 258, 274, 277, 279, 328
Christianity 156
Churches 28
Clairaudience 27, 92, 244
Clairvoyance 27, 31, 45, 48, 68, 69, 92, 132, 133, 134, 135, 244
Cliché(s) 20, 26, 27, 28, 29, 30, 31, 32, 33, 34, 35, 36, 37, 39, 40, 41, 42, 43, 45, 48, 49, 51, 52, 53, 58, 62, 68, 69, 70, 91, 95, 100, 104, 106, 110, 127, 128, 129, 130, 131, 133, 145, 146, 147, 148, 149, 150, 151, 196, 207, 208, 209, 210, 220, 230, 236, 240, 242, 247, 256, 269, 287, 297, 321, 324, 325, 332, 348
Cognition 29, 54, 64, 68, 95, 150, 199, 215, 250, 257
Commandments 25
Common sense 14, 16, 58, 80, 126, 132, 249, 255, 350
Compassion 186, 224, 225, 295
Compulsion 21
Concentration 12, 13, 15, 22, 23, 24, 25, 26, 46, 48, 51, 52, 56, 59, 60, 61, 62, 64, 72, 76, 77, 79, 91, 94, 95, 99, 101, 102, 103, 108, 109, 110, 111, 112, 118, 119, 120, 122, 125, 128, 130, 143, 146, 148, 149, 151, 154, 155, 156, 163, 164, 171, 176, 178, 185, 187, 196, 200, 201, 202, 207, 208, 216, 240, 246, 247, 248, 252, 253, 255, 257, 273, 277, 282, 286, 296, 305, 307, 311, 322, 331, 342, 347, 350
Confidence 101, 148, 217, 265
Confusion 103, 130
Conscience 24, 224, 293
Conscious 207
Consciousness 15, 19, 20, 23, 25, 26, 28, 31, 35, 37, 40, 41, 42, 43, 45, 46, 51, 52, 57, 61, 64, 65, 68, 77, 78, 79, 83, 84, 85, 87, 89, 91, 92, 93, 95, 104, 106, 107, 109, 122, 125, 126, 128, 129, 135, 140, 141, 145, 152, 167, 169, 170, 177, 178, 180, 185, 187, 190, 191, 193, 194, 196, 197, 198, 202, 204, 205,

Sect(s) 250, 253, 279
Sédir, Paul 61, 222, 252
Seer(s) 197, 198, 210
Self 35, 39, 41, 46, 53, 65, 96, 106,
    129, 143, 165, 166, 167, 168, 171,
    174, 180, 184, 185, 190, 191, 194,
    195, 196, 197, 198, 199, 201, 206,
    217, 228, 244, 246, 249, 250, 255,
    258, 265, 300, 302, 303, 306, 307,
    308, 309, 310, 326, 333, 350
Self-admiration 220
Self-indulgence 59
Self-inquiry 106
Self-pity 59
Senses 41, 77, 102, 141, 167, 184,
    304, 306, 309, 348
Sensible 197
Separateness 244
Separation 84, 169, 188, 206, 210,
    211, 317
Serenity 167
Sermon on the Mount 25, 215, 216,
    218, 219, 220, 221, 222, 223, 230,
    231, 234, 236, 263
Sex 44, 73, 75, 114, 294
Shade 232, 254, 264, 278
Siamese twins 56
Siddhis 92, 244, 245
Sight 109, 117, 122, 147, 202, 246,
    254, 273, 284, 347
Silence 33, 84, 142, 150, 158, 169,
    170, 174, 181, 184, 185, 195, 196,
    197, 204, 205, 208, 209, 210, 211,
    240, 246, 247, 248, 252, 275, 302,
    347
Sincerity 25, 186, 216, 254, 267, 275
Sine curve 22
Slavery 66, 172, 177, 188, 193, 310
Sleep 54, 57, 78, 93, 139, 157
Smoking 72, 105
Solar system 23, 49
Solitude 195, 196
Solution 19, 20, 21, 22, 40, 80, 189,
    196, 205, 211, 216, 305
Son 270
Soul(s) 168, 171, 182, 184, 186, 187,
    217, 242, 244, 248, 259, 270, 273,
    319
Source 52, 54, 65, 74, 85, 86, 88,
    102, 143, 172, 173, 183, 193, 198,
    199, 204, 205, 207, 209, 226, 227,
    240, 267, 268, 271, 299, 326
Soviet 134

Space 30, 42, 52, 95, 103, 131, 141,
    150, 169, 184, 197, 205, 207, 216,
    218, 232, 241, 249, 255, 259, 261,
    269, 270, 272, 273, 301, 320
Speech 135, 147, 150, 196, 197, 211,
Spirit 15, 21, 23, 27, 30, 39, 41, 55,
    104, 105, 113, 150, 154, 186, 187,
    188, 192, 197, 198, 199, 200, 207,
    208, 210, 211, 216, 217, 219, 220,
    224, 225, 238, 245, 247, 248, 249,
    252, 259, 260, 261, 265, 266, 269,
    270, 275, 278, 286, 298, 299, 300,
    302, 303, 306, 309, 311, 324, 327,
    328, 329, 332, 334, 344
Spiritism 115, 116
Spiritual 80, 93, 100, 113, 116, 150,
    155, 171, 173, 174, 180, 185, 190,
    191, 192, 208, 216, 217, 229, 247,
    249, 250, 252, 254, 257, 258, 265,
    268, 274, 276, 283, 294, 304, 306,
    322, 323, 347
Spirituality *see* Spiritual
Stability 208
Steadiness 22, 25, 172
Stillness 94, 257, 258
Strain 109
Strength 172
Subconscious 20, 83, 85, 95, 207
Subject 15, 21, 30, 48, 50, 68, 69, 70,
    102, 104, 122, 139, 155, 207, 251,
    259, 263, 270, 273
Substance 23, 256, 298
Success 15, 22, 75, 87, 106, 118, 122,
    124, 147, 148, 177, 202, 282, 283,
    313, 317
Suffering 21, 33, 40, 57, 143, 166,
    167, 168, 178, 180, 187, 193, 221,
    234, 238, 241, 249, 265, 268, 272,
    275, 278, 283, 285, 287, 289, 290,
    293
Suggestion 46, 68, 127, 139
Superconciousness 88, 89, 91, 92,
    93, 228, 246, 297, 325, 326
Superhuman 210, 222, 240
Supermental 119
Supernatural 39, 327, 330
Superphysical 57, 327
Supreme, The 58, 85, 96, 112, 146
    154, 185, 191, 196, 227, 228, 241,
    243, 252, 253, 254, 255, 256, 259,
    260, 261, 262, 263, 264, 265, 266,
    270, 271, 274, 277, 278, 294, 304,
    308, 311, 312, 321, 322, 324, 342

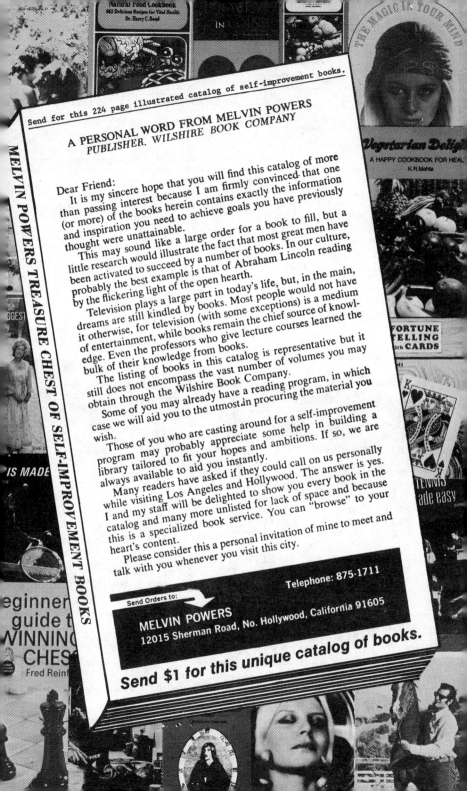

Melvin Powers
SELF-IMPROVEMENT
LIBRARY

ASTROLOGY

ASTROLOGY: A FASCINATING HISTORY *P. Naylor*	2.00
ASTROLOGY: HOW TO CHART YOUR HOROSCOPE *Max Heindel*	2.00
ASTROLOGY: YOUR PERSONAL SUN-SIGN GUIDE *Beatrice Ryder*	2.00
ASTROLOGY FOR EVERYDAY LIVING *Janet Harris*	2.00
ASTROLOGY GUIDE TO GOOD HEALTH *Alexandra Kayhle*	2.00
ASTROLOGY MADE EASY *Astarte*	2.00
ASTROLOGY MADE PRACTICAL *Alexandra Kayhle*	2.00
ASTROLOGY, ROMANCE, YOU AND THE STARS *Anthony Norvell*	2.00
MY WORLD OF ASTROLOGY *Sydney Omarr*	3.00
THOUGHT DIAL *Sydney Omarr*	2.00
ZODIAC REVEALED *Rupert Gleadow*	2.00

BRIDGE & POKER

BRIDGE BIDDING MADE EASY *Edwin Kantar*	5.00
BRIDGE CONVENTIONS *Edwin Kantar*	4.00
HOW TO IMPROVE YOUR BRIDGE *Alfred Sheinwold*	2.00
HOW TO WIN AT POKER *Terence Reese & Anthony T. Watkins*	2.00

BUSINESS, STUDY & REFERENCE

CONVERSATION MADE EASY *Elliot Russell*	2.00
EXAM SECRET *Dennis B. Jackson*	2.00
HOW TO BE A COMEDIAN FOR FUN & PROFIT *King & Laufer*	2.00
HOW TO DEVELOP A BETTER SPEAKING VOICE *M. Hellier*	2.00
HOW TO MAKE A FORTUNE IN REAL ESTATE *Albert Winnikoff*	3.00
HOW TO MAKE MONEY IN REAL ESTATE *Stanley L. McMichael*	2.00
INCREASE YOUR LEARNING POWER *Geoffrey A. Dudley*	2.00
MAGIC OF NUMBERS *Robert Tocquet*	2.00
PRACTICAL GUIDE TO BETTER CONCENTRATION *Melvin Powers*	2.00
PRACTICAL GUIDE TO PUBLIC SPEAKING *Maurice Forley*	2.00
7 DAYS TO FASTER READING *William S. Schaill*	2.00
STUDENT'S GUIDE TO BETTER GRADES *J. A. Rickard*	2.00
STUDENT'S GUIDE TO EFFICIENT STUDY *D. E. James*	1.00
TEST YOURSELF — Find Your Hidden Talent *Jack Shafer*	2.00
YOUR WILL & WHAT TO DO ABOUT IT *Attorney Samuel G. Kling*	2.00

CHESS & CHECKERS

BEGINNER'S GUIDE TO WINNING CHESS *Fred Reinfeld*	2.00
BETTER CHESS — How to Play *Fred Reinfeld*	2.00
CHECKERS MADE EASY *Tom Wiswell*	2.00
CHESS IN TEN EASY LESSONS *Larry Evans*	2.00
CHESS MADE EASY *Milton L. Hanauer*	2.00
CHESS MASTERY — A New Approach *Fred Reinfeld*	2.00
CHESS PROBLEMS FOR BEGINNERS *edited by Fred Reinfeld*	2.00
CHESS SECRETS REVEALED *Fred Reinfeld*	2.00
CHESS STRATEGY — An Expert's Guide *Fred Reinfeld*	2.00
CHESS TACTICS FOR BEGINNERS *edited by Fred Reinfeld*	2.00
CHESS THEORY & PRACTICE *Morry & Mitchell*	2.00
HOW TO WIN AT CHECKERS *Fred Reinfeld*	2.00
1001 BRILLIANT WAYS TO CHECKMATE *Fred Reinfeld*	2.00

Melvin Powers
SELF-IMPROVEMENT
LIBRARY

_____1001 WINNING CHESS SACRIFICES & COMBINATIONS *Fred Reinfeld* 2.00

COOKERY & HERBS

_____CULPEPER'S HERBAL REMEDIES *Dr. Nicholas Culpeper* 2.00
_____FAST GOURMET COOKBOOK *Poppy Cannon* 2.50
_____HEALING POWER OF HERBS *May Bethel* 2.00
_____HERB HANDBOOK *Dawn MacLeod* 2.00
_____HERBS FOR COOKING AND HEALING *Dr. Donald Law* 2.00
_____HERBS FOR HEALTH How to Grow & Use Them *Louise Evans Doole* 2.00
_____HOME GARDEN COOKBOOK Delicious Natural Food Recipes *Ken Kraft* 3.00
_____NATURAL FOOD COOKBOOK *Dr. Harry C. Bond* 2.00
_____NATURE'S MEDICINES *Richard Lucas* 2.00
_____VEGETABLE GARDENING FOR BEGINNERS *Hugh Wiberg* 2.00
_____VEGETABLES FOR TODAY'S GARDENS *R. Milton Carleton* 2.00
_____VEGETARIAN COOKERY *Janet Walker* 2.00
_____VEGETARIAN COOKING MADE EASY & DELECTABLE *Veronica Vezza* 2.00
_____VEGETARIAN DELIGHTS — A Happy Cookbook for Health *K. R. Mehta* 2.00
_____VEGETARIAN GOURMET COOKBOOK *Joyce McKinnel* 2.00

HEALTH

_____DR. LINDNER'S SPECIAL WEIGHT CONTROL METHOD 1.00
_____GAYLORD HAUSER'S NEW GUIDE TO INTELLIGENT REDUCING 3.00
_____HELP YOURSELF TO BETTER SIGHT *Margaret Darst Corbett* 2.00
_____HOW TO IMPROVE YOUR VISION *Dr. Robert A. Kraskin* 2.00
_____HOW TO SLEEP WITHOUT PILLS *Dr. David F. Tracy* 1.00
_____HOW YOU CAN STOP SMOKING PERMANENTLY *Ernest Caldwell* 2.00
_____LSD — THE AGE OF MIND *Bernard Roseman* 2.00
_____MIND OVER PLATTER *Peter G. Lindner, M.D.* 2.00
_____NEW CARBOHYDRATE DIET COUNTER *Patti Lopez-Pereira* 1.00
_____PEYOTE STORY *Bernard Roseman* 2.00
_____PSYCHEDELIC ECSTASY *William Marshall & Gilbert W. Taylor* 2.00
_____YOU CAN LEARN TO RELAX *Dr. Samuel Gutwirth* 2.00

HOBBIES

_____BLACKSTONE'S SECRETS OF MAGIC *Harry Blackstone* 2.00
_____COIN COLLECTING FOR BEGINNERS *Burton Hobson & Fred Reinfeld* 2.00
_____400 FASCINATING MAGIC TRICKS YOU CAN DO *Howard Thurston* 2.00
_____GOULD'S GOLD & SILVER GUIDE TO COINS *Maurice Gould* 2.00
_____HARMONICA PLAYING FOR FUN & PROFIT *Hal Leighton* 2.00
_____HOW I TURN JUNK INTO FUN AND PROFIT *Sari* 3.00
_____JUGGLING MADE EASY *Rudolf Dittrich* 1.00
_____MAGIC MADE EASY *Byron Wels* 2.00
_____SEW SIMPLY, SEW RIGHT *Mini Rhea & F. Leighton* 2.00
_____STAMP COLLECTING FOR BEGINNERS *Burton Hobson* 2.00
_____STAMP COLLECTING FOR FUN & PROFIT *Frank Cetin* 1.00

HORSE PLAYERS' WINNING GUIDES

_____BETTING HORSES TO WIN *Les Conklin* 2.00
_____HOW TO PICK WINNING HORSES *Bob McKnight* 2.00
_____HOW TO WIN AT THE RACES *Sam (The Genius) Lewin* 2.00

Melvin Powers
SELF-IMPROVEMENT
LIBRARY

Melvin Powers
SELF-IMPROVEMENT
LIBRARY

_____ENCYCLOPEDIA OF MODERN SEX & LOVE TECHNIQUES *Macandrew* 2.00
_____GUIDE TO SUCCESSFUL MARRIAGE *Drs. Albert Ellis & Robert Harper* 3.00
_____HOW TO RAISE AN EMOTIONALLY HEALTHY, HAPPY CHILD, *A. Ellis* 2.00
_____IMPOTENCE & FRIGIDITY *Edwin W. Hirsch, M.D.* 2.00
_____NEW APPROACHES TO SEX IN MARRIAGE *John E. Eichenlaub, M.D.* 2.00
_____·PSYCHOSOMATIC GYNECOLOGY *William S. Kroger, M.D.* 10.00
_____SEX WITHOUT GUILT *Albert Ellis, Ph.D.* 2.00
_____SEXUALLY ADEQUATE FEMALE *Frank S. Caprio, M.D.* 2.00
_____SEXUALLY ADEQUATE MALE *Frank S. Caprio, M.D.* 2.00
_____YOUR FIRST YEAR OF MARRIAGE *Dr. Tom McGinnis* 2.00

OCCULT

_____BOOK OF TALISMANS, AMULETS & ZODIACAL GEMS *William Pavitt* 3.00
_____CONCENTRATION—A Guide to Mental Mastery *Mouni Sadhu* 2.00
_____DREAMS & OMENS REVEALED *Fred Gettings* 2.00
_____EXTRASENSORY PERCEPTION *Simeon Edmunds* 2.00
_____FORTUNE TELLING WITH CARDS *P. Foli* 2.00
_____HANDWRITING ANALYSIS MADE EASY *John Marley* 2.00
_____HANDWRITING TELLS *Nadya Olyanova* 3.00
_____HOW TO UNDERSTAND YOUR DREAMS *Geoffrey A. Dudley* 2.00
_____ILLUSTRATED YOGA *William Zorn* 2.00
_____IN DAYS OF GREAT PEACE *Mouni Sadhu* 2.00
_____MAGICIAN — His training and work *W. E. Butler* 2.00
_____MEDITATION *Mouni Sadhu* 3.00
_____MENTAL TELEPATHY EXPLAINED *Hereward Carrington* .50
_____MODERN NUMEROLOGY *Morris C. Goodman* 2.00
_____NUMEROLOGY—ITS FACTS AND SECRETS *Ariel Yvon Taylor* 2.00
_____PALMISTRY MADE EASY *Fred Gettings* 2.00
_____PALMISTRY MADE PRACTICAL *Elizabeth Daniels Squire* 2.00
_____PALMISTRY SECRETS REVEALED *Henry Frith* 2.00
_____PRACTICAL YOGA *Ernest Wood* 2.00
_____PROPHECY IN OUR TIME *Martin Ebon* 2.50
_____PSYCHOLOGY OF HANDWRITING *Nadya Olyanova* 2.00
_____SEEING INTO THE FUTURE *Harvey Day* 2.00
_____SEX & HUMAN BEHAVIOR BY THE NUMBERS *Alexandra Kayhle* 2.00
_____SUPERSTITION — Are you superstitious? *Eric Maple* 2.00
_____TAROT *Mouni Sadhu* 4.00
_____TAROT OF THE BOHEMIANS *Papus* 3.00
_____TEST YOUR ESP *Martin Ebon* 2.00
_____WAYS TO SELF-REALIZATION *Mouni Sadhu* 2.00
_____WITCHCRAFT, MAGIC & OCCULTISM—A Fascinating History *W. B. Crow* 3.00
_____WITCHCRAFT — THE SIXTH SENSE *Justine Glass* 2.00
_____WORLD OF PSYCHIC RESEARCH *Hereward Carrington* 2.00
_____YOU CAN ANALYZE HANDWRITING *Robert Holder* 2.00

SELF-HELP & INSPIRATIONAL

_____ACT YOUR WAY TO SUCCESSFUL LIVING *Neil & Margaret Rau* 2.00
_____CYBERNETICS WITHIN US *Y. Saparina* 3.00
_____DOCTOR PSYCHO-CYBERNETICS *Maxwell Maltz, M.D.* 3.00

_____ DYNAMIC THINKING _Melvin Powers_		1.00
_____ GREATEST POWER IN THE UNIVERSE _U. S. Andersen_		4.00
_____ GROW RICH WHILE YOU SLEEP _Ben Sweetland_		2.00
_____ GROWTH THROUGH REASON _Albert Ellis, Ph.D._		3.00
_____ GUIDE TO DEVELOPING YOUR POTENTIAL _Herbert A. Otto, Ph.D._		3.00
_____ GUIDE TO HAPPINESS _Dr. Maxwell S. Cagan_		2.00
_____ GUIDE TO LIVING IN BALANCE _Frank S. Caprio, M.D._		2.00
_____ GUIDE TO RATIONAL LIVING _Albert Ellis, Ph.D. & R. Harper, Ph.D._		2.00
_____ HELPING YOURSELF WITH APPLIED PSYCHOLOGY _R. Henderson_		2.00
_____ HELPING YOURSELF WITH PSYCHIATRY _Frank S. Caprio, M.D._		2.00
_____ HOW TO ATTRACT GOOD LUCK _A. H. Z. Carr_		2.00
_____ HOW TO CONTROL YOUR DESTINY _Norvell_		2.00
_____ HOW TO DEVELOP A WINNING PERSONALITY _Martin Panzer_		2.00
_____ HOW TO DEVELOP AN EXCEPTIONAL MEMORY _Young & Gibson_		3.00
_____ HOW TO OVERCOME YOUR FEARS _M. P. Leahy, M.D._		2.00
_____ HOW YOU CAN HAVE CONFIDENCE AND POWER _Les Giblin_		2.00
_____ I WILL _Ben Sweetland_		2.00
_____ LEFT-HANDED PEOPLE _Michael Barsley_		3.00
_____ MAGIC IN YOUR MIND _U. S. Andersen_		2.00
_____ MAGIC OF THINKING BIG _Dr. David J. Schwartz_		2.00
_____ MAGIC POWER OF YOUR MIND _Walter M. Germain_		2.00
_____ MASTER KEYS TO SUCCESS, POPULARITY & PRESTIGE _C. W. Bailey_		2.00
_____ MENTAL POWER THRU SLEEP SUGGESTION _Melvin Powers_		1.00
_____ ORIENTAL SECRETS OF GRACEFUL LIVING _Boye De Mente_		1.00
_____ PSYCHO-CYBERNETICS _Maxwell Maltz, M.D._		2.00
_____ SECRET OF SECRETS _U. S. Andersen_		3.00
_____ SELF-CONFIDENCE THROUGH SELF-ANALYSIS _E. Oakley_		1.00
_____ STUTTERING AND WHAT YOU CAN DO ABOUT IT _W. Johnson, Ph.D._		2.00
_____ SUCCESS-CYBERNETICS _U. S. Andersen_		2.00
_____ 10 DAYS TO A GREAT NEW LIFE _William E. Edwards_		2.00
_____ THINK AND GROW RICH _Napoleon Hill_		2.00
_____ THREE MAGIC WORDS _U. S. Andersen_		3.00
_____ TREASURY OF THE ART OF LIVING _edited by Rabbi S. Greenberg_		2.00
_____ YOU ARE NOT THE TARGET _Laura Huxley_		3.00
_____ YOUR SUBCONSCIOUS POWER _Charles M. Simmons_		2.00
_____ YOUR THOUGHTS CAN CHANGE YOUR LIFE _Donald Curtis_		2.00

SPORTS

_____ ARCHERY — An Expert's Guide _Don Stamp_		2.00
_____ BICYCLING FOR FUN AND GOOD HEALTH _Kenneth E. Luther_		2.00
_____ COMPLETE GUIDE TO FISHING _Vlad Evanoff_		2.00
_____ HOW TO BEAT BETTER TENNIS PLAYERS _Loring Fiske_		3.00
_____ HOW TO WIN AT POCKET BILLIARDS _Edward D. Knuchell_		2.00
_____ HOW TO WIN AT THE RACES _Sam (The Genius) Lewin_		2.00
_____ MOTORCYCLING FOR BEGINNERS _I. G. Edmonds_		2.00
_____ PRACTICAL BOATING _W. S. Kals_		3.00
_____ PSYCH YOURSELF TO BETTER TENNIS _Dr. Walter A. Luszki_		2.00
_____ SECRET OF BOWLING STRIKES _Dawson Taylor_		2.00
_____ SECRET OF PERFECT PUTTING _Horton Smith & Dawson Taylor_		2.00
_____ SECRET WHY FISH BITE _James Westman_		2.00
_____ SKIER'S POCKET BOOK _Otti Wiedman_ (4¼″ x 6″)		2.50
_____ TABLE TENNIS MADE EASY _Johnny Leach_		2.00
_____ TENNIS FOR BEGINNERS _Dr. H. A. Murray_		2.00
_____ TENNIS MADE EASY _Joel Brecheen_		2.00

WILSHIRE MINIATURE LIBRARY (4¼″ x 6″ in full color)

_____ BUTTERFLIES		2.50
_____ INTRODUCTION TO MINERALS		2.50
_____ LIPIZZANERS & THE SPANISH RIDING SCHOOL		2.50
_____ PRECIOUS STONES AND PEARLS		2.50
_____ SKIER'S POCKET BOOK		2.50

NOTES